# The OUTDOOR WORLD of GRAEME DINGLE

Other books by Graeme Dingle

*Two Against the Alps*
*Wall of Shadows*
*The Seven Year Adventure*
*First Across the Roof of the World* (with Peter Hillary)

# The OUTDOOR WORLD of GRAEME DINGLE

## Graeme Dingle

REED

Front cover: Dingle ascending "Ego Trip" (grade 18), Whanganui Bay.
Lake Taupo is visible below. *Bob Carter*

Illustrations by Trevor Plaisted and Murray McKeich

First published 1983

A. H. & A. W. REED LTD
68–74 Kingsford-Smith Street, Wellington 3
also
7 Kirk Street, Auckland 2
85 Thackeray Street, Christchurch 2

ISBN 0 589 01389 0

Typesetting by Quickset Ltd., Christchurch
Printed by Warren Printing Co., Ltd., Hong Kong

To Ed Hillary
for all he has shown and given,
both to me and New Zealand.

*If you have health, a great craving for adventure,
at least a moderate fortune and can set your heart
on a definite objective, which old travellers do
not think impractical, then travel by all means.*

Francis Galton, *Art of Travel*, 1872

# Acknowledgements

I wish to extend my thanks to my Mum and Dad, Anne and Bert Dingle, for their love and encouragement; to Enid Bond, my favourite teacher, for her care and good teaching; to Hutt Valley High School for driving me to the freedom of the hills; to the south face of St David's Dome (Hicks) for good climbs; to Doug Wilson for proofreading and advice which saved me from libel; to Wendy Gallie for typing the manuscript; to Janene McDermott, my editor; and to my many friends found through the mountains and at the Outdoor Pursuits Centre.

I would also like to thank Mike Gill and Stu Allan for their advice, and I wish to acknowledge the help and advice given to me by the late Graham McCallum. Colin Abbott provided appreciated assistance with the illustrations, and Peters (Ed.) *Mountaineering — The Freedom of the Hills* (The Mountaineers) proved an invaluable reference for some of the pictures especially drawn for this book. I am also grateful to Ian Mardell of the Alpine Centre, Wellington, and to the Scout Outdoor Centre and Living Simply, Wellington, for supplying equipment for illustration.

My thanks go to the following for permission to quote from various sources: Kaye and Ward Ltd. (*Between Heaven and Earth*, Gaston Rebuffat); A.H. & A.W. Reed Ltd. (*Bushcraft*, the New Zealand Mountain Safety Council), (*The Mountains of New Zealand*, Rob Hewitt and Mavis Davidson); Sierra Club Books (*Climbing Ice*, Yvon Chouinard); and K. G. Ogilvie, Major Hugh Charles Oakley-Browne, Dr Ieuen Jones and Colin Abbott for use of various unpublished papers.

Finally, I wish to thank Hallmark International for a job that allows me to climb.

G.D.

# Contents

# CONTENTS *continued*

# Introduction

THE art of living in the Earth's wild places has largely become forgotten, but today most people desire more than a secure job and to be housed in a comfortable box. As a result there has been a tremendous resurgence in adventure activities over the last few years.

So people are learning the art of survival in the wilds, but not this time as a way of life — instead outdoor activities are seen as a way to make life more full, and modern communication and technology should enable adventurers to learn the necessary techniques less painfully than was the case with their forefathers. Because there is much common ground among the various outdoor arts it is possible for the modern man or woman to be a city-dwelling business person, a Sherpa, an Eskimo, a jungle Indian and an ancient mariner all rolled into one (if he or she is exceptionally adventurous). Some of this common ground I have mentioned in the first incident described in this book under the heading "Nearly a disaster". The lessons learnt here can overlap into all the other areas of outdoor pursuits — the bush, the rivers, the sea, the mountains, the rocks and the air. The techniques may be different in each case, but the basis of the activities (one's mental attitude) remains much the same.

My philosophy of education comes through in the presentation of this book. Many traditional textbooks are a waste of paper in our modern world — would-be learners need to relate to experience. All learning must be done by comparison so I have endeavoured to relate true incidents from which the reader can draw conclusions.

Experienced outdoor people may prefer a certain technique or piece of equipment, but some of their choices have not been included here. My objective has been to compile a manual of my ideas and recommendations, and if information on various techniques or equipment does not appear it is because I do not wish to recommend them. Thus this effort is not intended to be the final word or the complete manual on the outdoors, but a collection of good, solid grounding material for outdoor adventurers.

Throughout the book I have related a series of true incidents, each followed by a brief summary of lessons to be learnt from these experiences. Usually the incidents themselves were reasonably controlled and well executed, but in the first story many members of the party escaped death by a hair's breadth. I have therefore analysed this incident more carefully than the others — the lessons to be learned here on planning, leadership and execution are vitally important to all aspects of outdoor pursuits.

New Zealand is synonymous with the outdoors — we have blue skies, green forests, clear oceans, snow-capped mountains and healthy people. Above everything else we must strive to preserve these. With the current upsurge in the number of youngsters becoming involved in outdoor pursuits through their schools, one of my personal dreams is being fulfilled, and the future for the New Zealand outdoor scene and, as a result, New Zealand, is bright.

Whether you are teaching outdoor pursuits, trying to make one of these activities a way of life or simply filling in weekends, I hope you find the outdoors as fulfilling and stimulating as I do.

I ask your forgiveness for my cynicisms and reactionism. My humour is of an odd brand, but as we say in the outdoor pursuits trade, "You get that!"

Good reading.

GRAEME DINGLE

The Dingle kids, *circa* 1947. Back right to left — Brian, Anne, John. That's me in the front.

My Sanson School class when I was aged nine. I am on the extreme right in the front row. My brother John is seventh from the left, second row.

2

# 1

# The first 30 years

*I must not demonstrate my anthropoidal tendencies by swinging in herbage surrounding this institution.* Lines written 200 times at high school

IT TOOK 13 years for my lust for mountains and adventure to reveal itself. I knew I was searching for something, and when I discovered the hills I knew with a tremendous feeling of finality that I had found part of what I was looking for. My real education was about to begin — as much as I hated school, I'm prepared to concede that it may have led or forced me to my discovery of the hills.

I was born in Gisborne, realm of the Ngati Porou, youngest son of a South Australian battler called Bert and a lovely New Zealand lady of Irish descent called Anne. When my parents began work on the Dingle family the country was struggling out of the Great Depression, and my father had been out of work for four years. I screamed my grubby way into their lives at the end of November 1945 and soon became the scrawniest of the fold.

My schooling was pretty haphazard and never very happy. It reached a zenith at intermediate school where I fell in love with my teacher. This facilitated my learning wonderfully, but following intermediate I was admitted into an academically oriented high school where the subjects did little for my development. I took a professional course — Latin, French, general science, mathematics, and so on, but very little of the book bashing rubbed off. However, I could muddle through because of my good memory. My main attributes were aggression, an almost embarrassingly spindly body and an artistic streak.

The seemingly pompous headmaster told my worrying parents, "Graeme must understand that his education is not complete with only one subject."

That subject was art, but I argued vigorously that I had another subject — the hills. A particularly arrogant prefect was probably nearer the mark as far as my eventual career went when he made me write 200 times the lines reproduced at the head of this chapter....

A particularly arrogant prefect was probably nearer the mark as far as my eventual career went . . . .

3

I was thoroughly hopeless at army cadet training and, at almost every session, I would faint through having to stand in one spot for more than a few moments.

My proofs of attainment after 12 years of schooling were three pieces of light cardboard: School Certificate, Endorsed School Certificate and Fine Arts Prelim.

Work gave me more time and the facilities to get into the hills. It even offered some outlet for my adventurous nature, much to the horror of my employers. There were many awful events that occurred as a result of my "anthropoidal tendencies", but the following deserves relating.

I worked as a display artist at a city department store which had recently opened a new furniture section — their pride and joy. The managing director was to inspect the new area one morning and, before his arrival, the display manager, Len Goldspink, and yours truly were required to make a final check of various displays amidst exotic potted plants and other decorations. I was darting between expensive suites, titivating this and tidying up that when I happened to glance up and notice that hanging from the false ceiling was a fluorescent tube held only by the pins at one end. There was no great urgency, but youthful exuberance and a natural flair for acting without thinking saw me springing to the rescue. I climbed up on to a bannister and reached out to grasp part of the false ceiling with one hand. It was out of reach, and my romantic mind saw the only solution as a daring swing. So, with the grace of an orang-utang in full flight, I swung out towards the tube, grasping it in my free hand as I went.

From below I could hear a very concerned Len Goldspink shouting "No!" Just as I triumphantly grasped the fluorescent tube I perceived a terrible groaning noise within the ceiling above, and my highly developed sense of survival told me that I should drop to the floor and run for my life. This I did just in the nick of time, because a moment later a huge section of false ceiling, complete with live wires

Me on Ruapehu in 1967. This photograph was taken moments before the fall which put paid to my plans for the rest of the year. *John Rundle*

and fluorescent tubes, came crashing down from the roof, squashing a rather valuable suite and leaving one display manager turning various strange colours while ladies shepherded their squealing children from the store.

I was not exactly sacked, but life became more difficult for me and it wasn't very long before I left the job to begin a signwriting apprenticeship.

Life in the hills at that stage seemed to be safer, and I went ahead planning adventures with fantastic enthusiasm.

By 1962 I was giving the Tararua tops and valleys a hard time and, in 1963, I had my first taste of the high peaks of the Southern Alps. In the seasons of 1966 and '67 I did my first new routes in the Southern Alps, first with Jill

Tremain and then with George Harris, Murray Jones, Peter Gough and John Andrews.

But 1967 was my year of commitment. During the winter I would do a traverse of the Southern Alps from one end to the other. This would immediately be followed by an Antarctic expedition, then a Peruvian expedition, then climbs in the European Alps — and my ultimate objective was the Himalayas. Early in the winter I was solo climbing an ice wall near the top of Ruapehu when I fell, landing back first across a lump of ice and hurting myself quite badly. Instead of the trip through the Southern Alps I spent three months in plaster, and then I wasn't fit enough to go to the Antarctic.

Suddenly my world caved in and I began to question my ideals. Was my dream to climb mountains everywhere, no matter how hard, the dream of a madman? Would I not be better to settle down, like the others in my family, to a marriage and children and an eight-to-five job? I decided to ask my mother, and in a most loving way she told me the following intriguing story.

"When I was expecting you, I had very strange restless feelings and I used to pester your father to take me to the top of Kaiti Hill near Gisborne to look out over the sea. Any hill would have done, but it was usually Kaiti Hill that we went up. When you were finally born the restless feeling left me completely and, although I've been frightened that it would happen, I always really believed that you would be a mountaineer."

The story fascinated me intensely, then and now, and whether it was relevant or not I decided never again to question my need for mountains and adventure.

The following year I went to the Andes ... a few tremendous ascents of big peaks, a trip down the Amazon on a balsa raft and then off to Britain to learn to climb rocks (that is, to learn to climb them properly). During the summer of 1969 I went out to the European Alps with Murray Jones and together we had the most mind-boggling season. It was generally believed that New Zealanders weren't very

During 1968 Murray Jones and I climbed all six classic north faces in Europe. Here Murray completes the last few metres to the summit of the notorious Eigerwand.

good technicians and, although competent enough mountaineers and perhaps strong at high altitudes, they didn't stand much chance of getting up the most technical climbs.

Murray and I set out to prove this incorrect. Despite claims that "Walter Mitty had nothing on us" we were determined to climb all the classic north faces of the European Alps and more. By the end of the season we had chalked up at least a dozen grade-6 routes, amongst them the superb Bonatti Pillar, the north face of the Matterhorn, north face of the Eiger, north face of Piz Badile, north face of the Lavaredo, north face of the Grandes Jorasses and north face of the Dru. From Europe I went back to Britain to another job in an outdoor education centre and then drove out to the Himalayas to join one of Ed Hillary's expeditions. Finally, after a sojourn of about three years, I returned to New Zealand.

Above: Ian Jowett on the north face of Jannu in the eastern Himalayas. *Graeme Dingle*

Left: Roger Bates on Yerupaja in the Peruvian Andes. *Lloyd Gallagher*

The year 1970 saw sparks flying on the New Zealand mountaineering scene, and most of the last, great unclimbed faces saw their first ascents — such faces as the Caroline Face of Mount Cook, the Whymper Face of Elie de Beaumont, the south face of St David's Dome and so on. It seemed that suddenly New Zealand mountaineers were as good as their modern counterparts overseas; for the moment the small-island-isolation complex that hobbles New Zealand seemed to be dissolving, at least in the world of mountaineering.

For 1971 I planned a trip to test myself as an all-round mountaineer — the first traverse of the Southern Alps from one end to the other. During the winter months — July, August, September and part of October — Jill Tremain and I had our great mountaineering experience. It wasn't as if the trip was technically very difficult, but it was physically and mentally taxing and an all-round test of mountaineering skill. Above all, it was extremely pleasant spending 100 days in the alps with a good friend. This was perhaps my most memorable mountain trip so far, possibly because it was a sort of mountaineering cocktail, a trip that allowed us to sample all the important ingredients of mountaineering — great mountains, bush-clad hillsides, rivers, skiing, climbing, tramping, isolation, individual achievement, comradeship, danger and satisfaction at having completed a self-set task.

Strangely, it is perhaps because of the traverse that I eventually managed to achieve one of my ambitions: to set up an outdoor training centre so the outdoors could be better enjoyed by young and old alike and which would offer an aid to a society that I thought was going wrong.

The centre became easier to establish because of the tremendous publicity the traverse received. I became recognised as an expert on outdoor training, which was only superficially true, but I wasn't going to tell everyone that and I took full advantage of the situation to achieve my goal. To cut a long story short, the Outdoor Pursuits Centre of New Zealand (OPC) opened its doors to the first course at the beginning of 1973 and is now a thriving centre with an annual intake of nearly 3,000 students.

My future is very bright. I do an overseas expedition at least once a year, have become technical advisor to an enthusiastic and go-ahead outdoor-equipment manufacturer, Hallmark International, and will continue to be intensely interested in outdoor education and young people. I have no intention of slackening off my activity as far as personal adventure goes — on the contrary, the next 10 years look like being my most active yet.

Now for a diversion.

## The Bludger from the Scrub

(the censored version)

*As night was slowly falling, over valley, peak and scrub,*
*From a hut in the Tararua came the chief guide of the club,*
*And his yodel clear and mellow floated out upon the breeze,*
*And a dozen tramps in shorts and boots fell down onto their knees.*

*And the chief guide jerked his finger at a stranger on a stump,*
*Whom he qualified politely with words like skier, bum and chump,*
*And he made this introduction, "It's that fellow from the scrub,*
*(Bleep) me, he wants to join us, be a member of the club."*

*And the stranger made his reply to the chief guide of the club,*
*Saying "(Bleep) you indeed, I'm the bludger from the scrub.*
*I've skied down every mountain from old Ruie to Mount Cook,*
*I've climbed the rocks of David's Dome and climbed them at first look."*

Said the chief guide to the bludger, "Would you
   climb down Bowen Falls?
Would you solo climb Mount Tasman, do it with
   no rope at all?
Would you live for climbing mountains, knock
   off proper work for good?"
Said the bludger, "My silver-plated colonial
   bloody oath I would."

So they looked upon each other with an animal
   respect,
And the bludger broke a stick of wood and
   scratched his hairy neck.
"Would you care to have a cuppa?" said the chief
   guide of the club.
"I'll have the whole damn billy," said the bludger
   from the scrub.

So the trampers all took council saying, "(Bleep)
   me but he's game,
We'll make him our star bludger, he'll live up
   to his name."
So they took him to their club house, that
   bludger from the scrub,
And they looked upon his presence as an asset
   to the club.

But they soon found out that bludger was more
   than they could stand,
So the chief guide of the club thus addressed his
   merry band,
Saying, "Listen here you (bleepers), looks like
   we've caught a tartar,
At every kind of bludging, this bludger is a
   starter.

"Whenever there's a stew to eat he eats three
   times his share,
And whenever there's hard work to do he's never
   ever there.
He'll never bludge off other clubs, it's only us
   who're suckers,
So why should we put up with him, the lousy
   bleeding (bleep)er?"

So in the Tararuas the members of the club,
Planned a dark and dirty ambush for the bludger
   from the scrub,
But on the slopes of Hector the bludger made
   his stand,
A nasty grin upon his face, an ice axe in each
   hand.

They came upon him in a rush, but one by one
   they fell,
With crunch of bone, unearthly moan and agon-
   ising yell.
Till finally came the chief guide spitting teeth
   and streaming blood,
His nose all cut and broken, his face bedaubed
   with mud.

"You low polluted (bleep)er," snarled the chief
   guide of the club,
"Get back to where your kind belong, that's
   somewhere up the scrub.
May great heaps of misfortune one day rain
   down on you,
May some great rockfall catch you and batter
   your body blue.

"May the itching piles torment you, may corns
   grow on your feet,
May frostbite worse than hell let loose rot off
   your horrid meat.
May the pain of windy spasms through your
   bowels dart,
May you (bleep) your ragged shorts each time
   you try to fart.

"May you take a swig of dog's (bleep) mistaking
   it for beer,
May the next club you impose on throw you out
   upon your ear,
And when you're down and out and a total
   bloody wreck.
May you slip down through your own (bleep)hole
   and break your bleeding neck."

(With apologies to Henry Lawson)

# 2
# Nearly a disaster

*We the undersigned, forming an expedition about to explore the interior of . . ., under Mr A., consent to place ourselves (horses and equipment) entirely and unreservedly under his orders for the above purpose, from the date hereof until our return to . . . or, on failure in this respect, to abide all consequences that may result. We fully recognise Mr B. as second and Mr C. as third in command; and the right of succession to the command and entire charge of the party in the order thus stated.*

*We severally undertake to use our best endeavours to promote the harmony of the party and the success of the expedition.*

*In witness whereof we sign our names.*

Nineteenth century expedition contract.
Francis Galton, *Art of Travel*, 1872

IN THIS episode names have been changed to protect the guilty.

The epic began with an everyday sort of phone call. "Hello, Outdoor Pursuits Centre," I said automatically.

"Hold the line, please. Captain Plank calling," replied a dolly bird voice — probably fat with curlers, I thought!

"Hello, Captain Plank here. Major Dorcan has recommended that I phone you people. I am running a course for 18 of my cadets. We will be snow caving for a week in the crater of Ruapehu and I want them to finish the outing with an ascent of the highest peak."

Just supervision, I concluded, after agreeing to do the job. On the surface it didn't sound like a difficult task; in fact, it sounded as if it was going to be quite a holiday — a helicopter ride to the top of Ruapehu, good army tucker, lots of sunny climbing and that sort of thing, but something told me it wasn't going to be as easy as it seemed. I decided I had better take another experienced instructor. My wife, Roie, was very keen, particularly because the helicopter would deposit her with her skis right at the entrance to the snow cave. "I'll ski down all the stuff they climb up," she enthused.

The officers' mess was warm after the chill air of the early winter morning. Outside it was frosty and dead still. The mountains rose sparkling white into the steely sky. A wisp of smoke arched out of Ngauruhoe and descended abruptly into the Oturere Valley, while Ruapehu's broad top nurtured a small battalion of perfectly sinister cigar-shaped clouds.

"The weather doesn't look so good, Captain Plank. It will probably be short and vicious," I volunteered between mouthfuls of delicious bacon and eggs. "No wonder you lot get fat," was my next thought. "At least it will probably keep you warm on the mountain."

After breakfast we drove to the helipad where the troops crouched expectantly by their packs, ice axes at the ready, unrecognisable in

"Two were cradling bowls of eggs in front of them; one carried a 20-kg jerry can of petrol in his left hand."

woolly hats, snow goggles and jungle green.

"Hi lads."

"Graeme, this is our helicopter pilot, Richard Byrd." Ha, ha — what a name for a helicopter pilot — Dickie Bird!

"Gidday, can you tell me where you want to dig your snow cave?" said the smart-looking character in the flying suit.

"Yes, I don't want to be too close to the crater. The mountain has been murmuring a little lately. The best place will be directly under the summit of Te Heu Heu — to the east."

"Okay let's go."

The first load included Roie and myself, three officers and a couple of cadets. The other cadets would follow in two further loads.

The jet engine burst into life, and slowly the big blades began to turn faster and faster until, thrashing the air wildly, they lifted the green beast into the air and we were flying off towards the mountains. The flying kerosene can was soon bucking through the air over the tussock and climbing steadily towards the mountain top.

"Pretty turbulent up there," pointed the pilot.

We whoop-whooped and shuddered our way to just over the top of Te Heu Heu and, for a short time, hovered there above the snowy summit. The pilot's voice sounded edgy through my headphones.

"We can't land. I'll drop down the north side to about 2,000 m."

We landed on a small rocky flat and sat about chatting while the chopper went off for the rest of the troops. Above us the mountain rose symmetrically for nearly 1,000 m; below the land spread out toward the Desert Road — golden tussock and dark-green patches of bush contrasted with the snow around us. A cold wind forced us to shelter behind rocks.

By mid morning we were all gathered — 11 cadets, three officers, Roie and me — and the epic began. By the way of an introduction I explained the principles of snow caves. Then we sat about again for a little while waiting for someone to give the order to move out. Nobody did, so after a short time I announced as low key as possible, "Okay, let's go." The troops immediately picked up their gear and tramped off up the hill. "Hang on a minute," I cried. Two were cradling bowls of eggs in

Ruapehu from Waihohonu hut. Te Heu Heu is the highest point in this picture. The first snow caves were where the lines bisect. The cliff I nearly fell over can be seen as a dark horizontal line, just below the position of the caves.

front of them; one carried a 20-kg jerry can of petrol in his left hand. I clapped one hand to my brow. "Oh God, I thought these guys had some experience!"

I sat down on a rock and waited for the troops to work out what was wrong.

"Great stuff!" cried Captain Plank. "This is the way they learn."

The troops followed my example and sat down. We waited for a directive, and once again I soon got tired of waiting. I guessed they had forgotten how to act without being commanded.

"Okay, distribute the eggs and unpack that pack," I shouted in my best army voice.

"Now, put the jerry can in that pack. Okay, this time . . . ."

Sapper Jones shouldered the pack of petrol and we were off again. For a group of guys who were supposed to have done a snowcraft course they looked most awkward indeed, walking like badly co-ordinated ducks with their trenching tools slapping against their thighs as they waddled.

The ridge we were ascending narrowed a little and the snow became firmer. I decided to conduct a little personal test to see if the troops knew how to stop themselves if they did slip (and other associated skills required for mountain climbing). I walked close to the edge of a 10-m slope which ended in a gentle run out into a narrow gully. I thumped my boots into the snow as I walked. The troops followed, looking most awkward, and, like Rangi who was in the lead, they walked as if the soles of their boots had special adhering abilities. Instead of following my example and thumping his boots into the steps I had already made, Rangi tried to place his sole flat against the angle. It wasn't long before one foot shot out from under him and he was bundled off down the slope into the gully. Like well-bred lemmings the others followed, one by one over the side, tumbling harmlessly into the gully.

"Okay, lesson number two," I shouted, and proceeded to demonstrate kicking up the slope, across the slope, down the slope and self-arresting with an ice axe.

When we eventually set off again I was much happier, but the weather was deteriorating quickly and after about 150 m I felt it was time to dig our snow cave.

"I think we will dig in here."

But Captain Plank had another idea and wanted to push on nearer the top. Stupidly, I let my judgment be swayed. Ironically, Morgan, who had failed his Coopers test (the standard forces fitness test) because he couldn't do enough press-ups, was the fittest of the group and shared the step plugging with me. The rest plodded grimly on, usually well behind.

At about 2,500 m we marched into the teeth of the storm and reeled under the blast of an ice-laden southerly wind. It was blowing about 70 knots. This time I asserted myself with conviction.

"We *will* go back down!"

So off we went, the troops slipping, sliding and sprawling, with their digging tools falling from their holsters and sliding off ahead. Roie, like a good mother hen, scurried about collecting them up, no doubt with the intention of keeping the tools to use in her garden.

By the time we reached a possible place to dig the snow caves the full force of the storm was on us. The drifting snow obliterated everything below knee level and the troops looked as if they had just emerged from Stalingrad — their army green was already white and frozen stiff.

I marked out four cave sites on a fairly steep slope and explained as best I could over the screaming wind what was needed for a comfortable night (ha ha!). I could have said, "Let's start with some proper alpine equipment — jungle gear doesn't seem to be much of a hit in a violent arctic storm at 2,000 m above sea level."

"Right, dig," commanded Captain Plank. Smith and Rangi looked particularly miserable and stood stiffly, more like wooden soldiers, than the real thing.

"I said bloody well dig," screamed the captain above the wind.

Smith and Rangi began to dig, but the party morale was not aided any by the captain's regular abuse. The outing had already turned into a miserable freezing hell for most of the cadets, who now began to look more like kids than men (in fact, that is what they really were). They squeezed and grovelled and dug their way into the hillside to make their meagre shelters, and they shivered in their jungle gear. By dark, four adequate shelters had been completed.

After dinner I went visiting, but was not very encouraged with what I found. The troops were now most definitely reduced to a miserable group of shivering little boys. Some had squeezed together into a single sleeping bag; others didn't have the strength to get anything together to eat for dinner. I returned to the "Officers' Mess" and suggested that, to aid morale, Captain Plank should take a brew to the troops. However, this idea did not appeal. I delivered the brew and, as I did so, suggested to the lads, or almost pleaded with them, that they keep the cave entrances clear during the night. The storm was now so vigorous that all the entrances were drifting over about every 15 minutes. About 7 p.m. Sergeant Hura set up the radio, a 14-kg monster with 900 channels. There was only one problem — the wrong aerial had been packed!

The night was spent grabbing what sleep we could between clearing cave entrances. By morning all the lads were really worn, and I was worried. I judged that the storm could last a few days at the very best, or over a week at the worst. In their jungle gear the troops probably wouldn't last at all. Once again it was necessary for me to assert myself. We would descend to Waihohonu hut and continue the course from the level at which it should have been started.

Outside, the weather appeared to be giving us a chance and, for a change, the wind had dropped and visibility had increased. Everyone put on extra storm gear and packed, but the stuff was heavier than ever (if that's possible for army gear) and seemed much bigger when frozen. Many wet sleeping bags and other bits of essential equipment were strapped on the outside of the small army packs. When we were ready to go the 20-kg jerry can remained half buried in the snow. I asked the obvious question. "Who is going to carry this?"

They were really a dead-beat looking lot.

My question was met with morose stares, as if I had just said, "Mary had a little lamb." I was about to add the awkward can to my own gear when Morgan stepped forward and lifted it on to the top of his pack — he was now carrying about 40 kg which, for an unfit "Cooper's test failure", seemed a pretty reasonable effort to me.

Finally we set off, raggedly descending a broad gully. For a while all went well, but then the wind came up again and visibility dropped to about 5 m. I was soon staring blindly. My only reference was the compass clutched near my face. I had a mildly gripped feeling in the pit of my stomach, but felt that things were still in control — just. As long as I could keep them moving we would get down. The worry that nagged at my mind was that we would be stopped by a cirque of cliffs, which I was sure was somewhere below us.

The wind shrieked over the ridges and buffeted us viciously even in our relatively sheltered gully. It coated our hair and clothes with ice. I stopped to take a look at the party and

talk to Roie. They were a really dead-beat-looking lot. Roie and I went about hitching up their pants, pulling on their gloves, which hung like dead things off the end of their arms, and turning their balaclavas so the hole in front co-incided with their eyes and not their ears. I shouted over the wind into Roie's ear, "What do you think, Roie?"

"I think we should head further west. I'm sure there are cliffs from here around to Tukino," was her sobering reply.

I took Roie's advice and we crossed a ridge and gained the shelter of another gully. Here I rather uncertainly led my pathetic charges. I was feeling my way very slowly when suddenly I felt that something was very wrong. I leapt backwards — it most certainly was! I had walked out on to the edge of a very big and fragile snow cornice which overhung the cliff. On my hands and knees I went out as far as I dared. That old hollow feeling in my groin made me feel sick as I peered desperately through the mist and driving snow. The cliff plunged 100 m to the valley floor and I could not see the end of it to the east or to the west. I felt trapped, and it didn't help to look back at the staggering, ice-encrusted troops.

After a few moments to collect my wits, I climbed quickly up a relatively steep slope to the west, plugging great big steps as I went. The horror of the situation was feeding tremendous strength to my muscles. From the top I watched those at the front of the party begin up and then slide pathetically back down again. They just didn't seem to have the strength to get up. I glissaded back to the gully and plodded off upwards again, leading them like mindless sheep until an easy escape presented itself on the right. We climbed on to a broad ridge and stumbled along it, leaning at a wild angle against the wind. I hated it. The wind was like an insane monster trying to stop us from getting down to safety — I figured some blasts must have been near 100 knots. We hadn't gone far along this ridge when a scream from Roie made me stop. She approached, eyes narrowed, brow lined with concern. "We can't go on like this, Graeme. Rangi is on his last legs."

I took a look at poor Rangi, and had to agree that he didn't have more than 30 minutes of consciousness left if we kept this up. From beneath ice-encrusted eyebrows his eyes looked out with a glazed, lifeless stare. His arms hung by his sides like those of a rag doll. Christ, what was I to do? I looked round desperately at the mad, white world for somewhere to hide — the ridge was almost flat where we were and offered no refuge at all. I looked again at the iced-up almost human forms, their wild eyes peering through balaclava holes, sleeping bags frozen stiff and covered with ice atop their packs. I knew I was trapped, and I knew that if anyone died the blame would be put squarely on my shoulders, despite the fact that I was supposed to be only an advisor.

In a moment I made my decision. It was only 200 m back to the shelter of the gully, but that was too far. That 200 m could mean the difference between life and death for some of these poor wretches. We had to dig in where we were. It was so frustrating knowing that only 500 m

down the mountain was a safe, sheltered valley; and 500 m up the mountain there were four relatively warm snow caves. "Why me, Lord?"

I took the officers aside and shouted at them, almost accusingly. "We are going to dig in here. I suggest that we get them all in a line digging a trench. Once they're all out of the wind we'll dig into the slope. We want one chamber, just big enough to hold everyone snuggled together. Once the cave is started, Roie and I are going to leave you and go out for help. I want you to put the worst of them in the middle of the cave and I want you to light the primuses and not let them go out until I get back. Do you understand?"

They nodded their consent and we began digging the trench. In a surprisingly short time everyone was out of the main force of the wind and digging reasonably steadily, but without enthusiasm. Roie and I then left the group. In some ways I felt as if I was deserting in the face of danger, but it would have been absolutely foolhardy just to sit in that spot and wait for someone to die. We had to do something.

I said a silent prayer that we would be able to find the place and the hapless troops again — alive.

Roie and I soon disappeared into the blizzard and began fighting our way down a ridge where large rocks covered with ice poked through the snow. This gave me some hope that it wouldn't be too difficult to find the snow cave site again, as long as the rocks and the cave didn't drift over. We literally fought our way down to the top of the cliffs and, on a couple of occasions at least, were picked up and bowled wildly in the opposite direction to that in which we wanted to go.

It wasn't long before we had picked a way down through the cliffs and were descending fairly quickly. We came out on a long snow slope, descended this and then continued down a gentle gully to the top of a second cirque. We descended this on the left-hand side and then traversed back into the top of a broad valley. It was an impressive place with cliffs lining both sides and the cirque bordering the top.

We had come down in the only possible place. I only hoped we could get down the valley and that our passage wouldn't be blocked by an unclimbable waterfall or gorge. What a relief it was to be out of the mad gale!

Now we began to move very fast, the urgency of the situation lending a spring to our strides. After about three hours of hard going we reached Ohinepango Stream. We virtually swam across these freezing waters and reached the Waihohonu track. Down this sloppy path we tramped quickly, glad to be out of the snow and feeling relatively warm.

We had almost reached the Desert Road and had decided to stop a car to take us to head-quarters when suddenly we heard a tremendous noise — was it several powerful engines? We stopped and looked at each other. A moment later around the corner came what looked to us like three tanks. In fact, they were only Armoured Personnel Carriers (APCs), but they looked very big! We held up our hands as a stop signal. To our amazement they stopped, and we spoke, or at leasted shouted, to the man who protruded from the first turret, looking for all the world like Rommel, desert goggles and all. "Can you turn that bloody engine off?" I shouted up rather arrogantly. The engine spluttered to a stop.

"There are some of your blokes up the hill and they're in a pretty bad way."

I had scarcely finished when the Rommel-like character said, "Yes we know. We're going to get them."

"You what?" Then I thought about it for a moment and said, "Well what can these things do, anyway? I mean how steep can they go up?"

"Oor — they can go up about 30 degrees," said Rommel.

I found myself almost being swayed, but then realised that if we weren't careful we would have another 20 people stranded together with three APCs. Suddenly, I was quite convinced that this wasn't the way to help the guys in the snow cave. Fortunately I managed to convince Rommel of this and so the APCs turned around, picked us up and clattered off down

the Desert Road. After several kilometres we were transferred to a Land-Rover which took us back to base where we found the place in quite a flap.

I was curious to find out how they had learned of the party's predicament. Apparently Major Flunkin became worried about his troops after their disappearance of two days and sent out a Land-Rover with radio equipment to try to locate them. The Land-Rover was proceeding along the Desert Road when the occupants heard the people in the snow cave desperately trying to call up without their aerial. It was a weak signal, but enough, and they immediately set up a good radio station at the top of the Tukino ski road, about 4 km in a straight line from the cave. The outing now became known as Operation Frigid Flash!

At the camp we went straight to the control room and almost immediately I said my piece. I had rehearsed it so well that the words almost fell out on top of each other: "I think the only way we are going to save these guys is to get a very good civilian helicopter pilot, and I know a man, Otto Gram, who I'm sure will do the job. We can ask him to fly up the valley that Roie and I descended. I will go with him, and we will stand by at the base of the cirque below the snow cave. As soon as there is a lull in the weather we could shoot up to the snow cave and fetch out the worst. I really don't believe there are any pilots in the forces who are good enough to do this job."

This was really putting my head in the noose, but one thought about the poor devils up in that white hell and I knew I was right. The brass weren't happy at all about bringing in civilian help and, after a little thought, the controller made a deal with me.

"We are in control of the situation at the moment because we have almost continuous radio contact with the snow cave, and they say that Rangi has improved slightly and there is no immediate danger. I suggest that the Iriquois that is coming from Whenuapai tomorrow with some Singaporean colonels on board should be diverted to the rescue, and that a ground party go in at first light in support."

I reluctantly agreed.

It was late when we got to bed. We were up again at 3.30 a.m., and I was surprised to find my feet were swollen and I had some difficulty getting them into my boots. I peered out at the wild night through the rain-lashed window and wondered how the guys in the snow cave were.

Once again we ate a delicious breakfast (enjoyable even at that hour) and then piled into a bus to meet the APCs parked in the scrub near the Waihohonu Track. We crowded into the tin boxes with a jolly bunch of Special Air Service (SAS) men and headed off across the Tongariro National Park, sending hebes and tussocks flying in all directions and leaving a swath behind us. Down steep banks, into little gullies, across them and up the other side — on we went. In the leading APC, Rommel still had his head stuck out of the turret and I protested to him, "Bloody hell, what do the Tongariro National Park people think of you driving your tanks across their land like this?"

"Oor, they don't mind," he said "as long as we're on rescues."

"I'd like to hear you tell that one to a park ranger!"

After about an hour of ducking in and out of gullies we reached the valley Roie and I had walked down, and we turned up this towards the mountain. The weather was as violent as ever and I wondered how much longer the storm was going to last. The tracked vehicles only made a few hundred metres up the valley before they could go no further. We were about 3,000 m in a straight line from the snow cave and 1,000 m lower.

Out we got into the cold, blustery morning and prepared to set off on foot up to the snow cave.

"Where are the radios?" I asked innocently.

"Radios?" somebody said. "We didn't bring any radios. We thought we'd get all the way there in the APCs."

"Oh dear, what about tents?" I asked, keeping my patience.

"Oh, we haven't got any tents either," came the reply.

I decided to ask Roie to stay with the APCs and, if the "chopper" came, to ask if we could have some portable radios and a couple of tents.

The ground party set off, totalling about 12 fit men — or, at least, several were very fit and the rest dogged. We made surprisingly quick time up the valley, and, after about two hours, we reached the base of the cliffs. The party divided itself naturally into two — the fit group and the dogged group. I asked the slower group to stay where they were and dig a snow cave there at the bottom of the cirque to shelter the cadets if we could get them down from above.

We sat at the foot of the cliffs for a short time fuelling up. I contemplated the blank cliff stretching 100 m above us in a series of large overhangs — the cliff I had nearly fallen over the day before. God, it seemed like a long time ago! After a short time, one of the keener blokes who had been peering rather quizzically up the cliff questioned, "How the hell are we going to get up there?"

For me, even with the right equipment, the cliff would have been extremely difficult to ascend, if not impossible, but I decided to have him on and replied, "Oh well, I suppose we'll go up that crack there, swing out over that first overhang, climb that steep wall, swing out over that other big overhang and then go straight up to the top."

His reply was, "Bloody hell, you'll have to give me a hand."

I almost cracked up!

We set off again, under the cirque and across to a steep snow slope on the right — the snow slope that Roie and I had descended. Up this I kicked steps, noting as I went that the slope was now very dangerous because of the tremendous build-up of wind-carried snow; it was quite likely to avalanche. However, there was no real alternative, and, like so many times before, I closed my mind and plodded on up the slope, very conscious that I was the only one with an ice axe.

We reached the gentle gully without mishap, but here we were hit by the full force of the gale and could scarcely make progress against it. The ice-laden wind made me feel as though I was in a giant white sand-blaster. I was the only one who could see where I was going because I was the only one with proper goggles. The others had to stretch out a hand to touch the person in front. We battled on, bent double into the gale, in a straggling Indian file.

This was painful progress, but although it seemed to go on forever, we were probably only about 300 m up the gully before we turned off to the left and began climbing yet another dangerous, avalanche-prone snow slope. We were about half-way up this slope when suddenly there was a dull exploding noise. With a "crump" and a slight shudder, the slope settled several centimetres — it seemed like several metres to my heart! I was the only one of the group who knew what had really happened.

Somebody shouted out, "What was that?"

I didn't go into detail. "Don't worry, just get up to those rocks above."

Everyone set off up to the rocks with renewed vigour. It was with great relief that we finally arrived on the rocky ground above the snow slope, and, after a short rest, we continued on steadily. About this time we heard yet another noise rising above the shrieking of the wind. It was a sort of spasmodic whoop, whoop, and we stopped to listen, concern lining our faces. Terry spoke first. "Christ, that's the chopper. I reckon there's going to be a double disaster."

It seemed amazing to us that the chopper could even fly in these winds, which must have been gusting 80 or 90 knots. With visibility down to only 30 m or so, at least where we were, I was worried — particularly because I was sure that Roie would be in that chopper. The noise of the machine came closer, then went away again and then came back only to remain constant for some time. Curiously, the chopper seemed to remain in one position. This was difficult for us to understand. Although we

hoped the chopper would get to the cave, hope wasn't going to do the people in the cave very much good. We continued on, up through the rocks until the ridge began to narrow and flatten at the same time. I knew we were within 100 m of the snow cave and began to look around very carefully for signs.

We proceeded for about 50 m, peering all around into the mist, although looking less enthusiastically in the direction from which the wind was coming.

Before long we saw an unbelievable apparition emerge from the mist about 20 m away. It appeared to be an ice-covered rock, but then it waved an arm and shouted out and we recognised it as Captain Plank. He'd done well to survive — those fatty breakfasts had obviously done their stuff!

We went quickly down to the snow cave which had a long and deep trench for an entrance with drifted snow piled up high on each side. Three or four exceedingly iced-up cadets were standing in the trench digging. They were very glad to see us, and I to see them. In fact, I was so glad to see them alive that I had to go off into the mist for a short time for a quiet weep. They were all in remarkably good condition so we decided to get them down as quickly as possible. The noise of the chopper had now died completely and all that was left was the shrieking of the now less-violent gale. As if to concede to our impending victory, the elements began to calm down.

We arranged the cadets in Indian file with plenty of SAS men between them. Then we marched them off down the ridge, down the steep slopes, down the gentle gully and down around the bottom cliff. I managed to find a safer alternative to the first dangerous slope and we soon reached the snow cave that the SAS men had dug.

It was a great relief to be virtually safe, and the morale of the cadets rose accordingly. We had a short break at the snow cave and then began down the valley. After a short time the chopper came back up the valley and began ferrying people out to the Desert Road. The

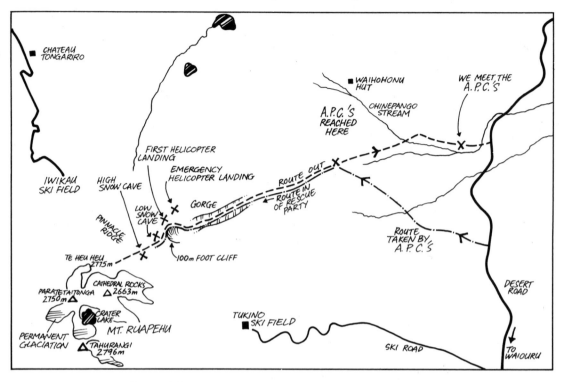

Route followed by cadets on Ruapehu training course.

epic was over.

I learned that the pilot of the chopper was one of the best. Having seen the conditions that he flew in, I had no doubt that this was true. Roie reinforced the fact, telling me how he had flown up the valley and then up on to the ridge, battling into the gale and keeping his horizon by the rocks that were sticking out of the snow. But when he came to a blank field of snow and had no horizon he put it down on the ridge and just sat there waiting for better visibility. They waited with the motor going for over an hour until the chopper got very low on fuel. After a warning to Roie to hold on to her seat, the pilot gently raised the chopper into the air. For a moment the gale took over and the chopper shot backwards, but then he brought it under control, banked wildly and dropped into the valley below before flying out for more fuel.

Back at base there was some praise for our efforts and some recrimination for getting into

the situation at all. Overall, the experience had been a valuable one. I hoped it would lead to the purchase of equipment more suited to alpine conditions than the existing jungle equipment. After all, Waiouru itself at 1,000 m above sea level is hardly tropical!

After a night in the VIP suite we awoke to a snow-covered world and went to visit the cadets in hospital where they were being treated for exposure and injuries to the feet caused by the cold. Some of them had painfully swollen feet, but they were in tremendous spirits and looked very happy for their experience. At least for once in their careers the spotlight was focused on them and they felt important.

We went up to speak to Rangi and asked him how he was. "Man, I reckon those Maoris got a good deal when they swapped that mountain for a couple of axes and a box of nails!"

# Summary of Ruapehu summit trip

Looking back, my major mistake in this exercise was not taking charge at the very beginning, despite the basis on which I was hired. In such a situation the instructor must be the overall leader and take responsibility. Both in the services and the teaching profession the legal situation is, regardless of the instructor's position, that the officer or teacher has the responsibility for the party's welfare. However, I believe the moral responsibility rests with the instructor — provided, of course, that he or she has the necessary experience. Fortunately, the Accident Compensation Scheme in New Zealand, unlike most other countries, takes away the worry of court action in the event of a mishap.

Disregarding my major mistake above, I will analyse this nightmarish trip chronologically.

▲ When planning a trip on land, sea or air, mental pictures of fine, sunny weather can be hazardous as one can be influenced to leave out important bad-weather gear. A good rule is to plan for the very worst and to accept fine, sunny weather as a bonus if it occurs. Of course, had the cadets been properly equipped we would not have been forced to leave the shelter of our snow caves. Responsibility for this omission must go to the highest level of administration.

▲ Weather signs are very important when planning to fly into an area, particularly if the area is unknown. In this case, because of the bad weather we were forced to land in an area unknown to any of us and therefore an emergency exit from the site was made more difficult. The weather signs that morning quite obviously heralded violent weather; the lenticular clouds (known to mountaineers as hog's backs) that present over Ruapehu are a very obvious sign of imminent bad weather. They can be particularly misleading because it may well seem perfectly fine at low levels. The weather signs should have influenced us to change our plans on the ground rather than wait until we were forced to change them in the air.

▲ Another major mistake was that nobody seemed to have checked the cadets' equipment. I later read a questionnaire to the cadets which read, "Did you read *Safety in the Mountains* as ordered? Did you dubbin your boots as ordered?" and so on. Service-type leadership might work when it is necessary to send men into battle, but much of it has minimal application in outdoor pursuits. An exception to this occurs sometimes during the utmost emergency when life is endangered.

▲ It was probably a mistake on my part to allow the party to be flown into an area that neither Roie nor I knew well. This would have been more acceptable had we possessed an accurate map of the area (the map we did possess was not sufficiently detailed).

▲ The group had no time to gel as a unit before being thrown into a difficult situation, so morale was low and this caused the cadets to deteriorate more quickly than they would have done otherwise. The situation was not embellished by Captain Plank's abusive orders to the cadets. If the cadets had had more respect for their leader, morale may have been better.

▲ Learning by experience is extremely valuable, but this technique should be very carefully administered. In an outdoor pursuits situation the learning experience could be not only dangerous but also a negative experience, driving the candidate away from the activity.

▲ My test of the cadets' competence on snow was creditable. It broke the monotony, and, apart from teaching the cadets necessary techniques, made me more aware of their capabilities.

▲ Motivation combined with fitness is more important in general mountaineering than the brute strength that is required to do press-ups, chin-ups and even short runs.

▲ The service equipment, mainly designed for jungle use, was totally inadequate in alpine conditions.

▲ A gradual build-up to the mountain and alpine conditions by walking in would have allowed us all to get to know each other. There would have been a gradual transition from low ground to an alpine situation, which would have made conditions higher up more acceptable psychologically.

▲ Three very obvious factors led to the final collapse of the cadets on the second day. During the evening and the following morning they had eaten insufficient food for their energy requirements, so their strength was sapped by the trials of the first day and the first night. It was further sapped the following day. Finally, deteriorating morale and increasing despair brought on by the uncertain situation made them perfect candidates for hypothermia.

▲ One of our saving graces was the adequate construction of snow caves on the first night. To keep the maximum number of people working, I arranged at least two entrances into each snow cave with two people working in each entrance. This allowed work for 16 people. Compared to igloos, fewer people can work on snow caves because of their constricted entrances.

▲ One of the major causes of the problems that followed the first night was failure to bring the radio aerial. While radios can be dangerous if relied on too heavily, this particularly powerful set would certainly have made contact had the correct aerial been taken.

▲ Whether we should have left the caves at all and tried to get to a lower altitude is a highly debatable point. In retrospect, I probably should have made sure that everybody had plenty of food inside them, and then waited for a more definite lull in the weather.

▲ Another moot point is whether I stopped soon enough on the descent. Exposure is not like a heart attack; it doesn't strike suddenly. It comes on very gradually from the time the victim first feels cold to the time he or she collapses and dies. This may take as little as 30 minutes, or it may take 24 hours or more, depending on the physical and mental reserves of the victim. These factors can only be assessed by a very perceptive leader. I believe, in this case, that I pushed the cadets as far as possible — perhaps a few minutes more would have lead to disaster.

▲ Did I do the right thing in leaving the group to go for help? I believe I did, because the people I left behind were quite capable of providing the party with shelter and warmth, while there was some doubt whether they had the ability to get out safely and, once out, to get back to the cave with help.

▲ I am convinced that I did the right thing in turning back the APCs, as another 20 untrained men on the hill may have led to the biggest alpine disaster of all time.

▲ Once radio contact was established with the snow cave, all credit must go to those who maintained this through the night and the next day.

▲ I believe civilian help should have been sought if only to provide properly equipped men on the mountain. Fear of embarrassment is a poor response when lives are in jeopardy.

▲ A potentially crucial error was the failure by the rescue party to take portable radio equipment.

▲ Finally, credit must go to the officers who remained in the snow cave with the cadets. Despite the atrocious conditions and continual digging that was required to keep the cave entrance clear, the cadets were in reasonable condition when the rescue party reached them.

# Leadership and communication

*Leadership is like motherhood — but with some other motha's kids!*   Author

Unlike other important aspects of outdoor training, leadership is difficult to illustrate visually. It is a much-neglected and misunderstood aspect of outdoor training, and readers will therefore find this section more detailed than others. The following draws heavily on information noted by Colin Abbott, Major Hugh Oakley-Brown and K. G. Ogilvie.

Party leadership is the steering of a group to reach a desired goal. The goal may be imposed by authority (a military objective), self imposed (a mountain summit) or imposed by necessity (an emergency).

A successful leader for all occasions would be a very rare person indeed, but there are some overlapping traits that every successful leader will have — one is the ability to communicate well with the majority of the group. It is interesting to note that of seven lists of required qualities for "leaders", including those of the United States Marine Corps, the United States Army, the R.A.F. College and the Canadian R.M.C., not one includes communication. In fact, not oné of the required qualities is common to each list!

I may therefore be pardoned for concluding that a military leader need not communicate with his personnel. However, I know this to be incorrect. The commander must transmit the message clearly and be sure that the listener understands the message, even if he or she does not agree with it. It seems to me that the automatic "Yes, sir" reply does not guarantee understanding. This is communication of a very doubtful quality. In an outdoor-pursuits situ-

Try to set up a sense of co-operation in the group.

Leadership from the front — unless care is taken the tail end of the group will suffer.

ation I believe the two-way communication link between leader and member(s) is crucial for good leadership. The link is complex to analyse, but several aspects are perhaps obvious.

1. The spoken word should be clear and the meaning mutually understood.
2. Close contact with members is important.
3. Try not to shout or be abusive; soft speaking and gentle actions often convey confidence.
4. Look at the person with whom you wish to communicate (take off dark glasses if you are wearing them).

There are many other tools and attributes that a good leader can use to advantage, most of which will also help win confidence and aid leadership:

a. The leader's good faith and care for each member should be apparent.
b. The goal should be understood by all.
c. The leader should demonstrate enthusiasm for the task in hand.
d. The leader should show an efficiency for dealing with problems — dithering does not instil confidence.
e. Try to set up a sense of co-operation in the group.

Other leadership qualities are unselfishness, loyalty to the group, decisiveness, physical stamina and endurance and sympathy for individual problems within the group.

Now that we have moulded our leader there are several ways the required qualities may be used. I have already laboured the military approach: it is authoritarian and obedience is expected. The leadership is often from a position outside the group. When leadership is from within the group it can be from three main positions: the front, the rear and the middle.

**Leadership from the front** A force pulling the group along. Unless care is taken the tail end may suffer. If leaders of this type are highly skilled and competent they may be so far removed from the level of skill in their party that they are unaware of, or unsympathetic to, the difficulties their party may be experiencing. Being at the front, this type of leader will tend to take all the decisions all the time. The group will not be involved in the experience as much as they could be. They will probably tag along blindly without any real idea of what is happening. However, this style of leadership may become necessary in an emergency, but care

Leadership from the rear — the leader may
lose control of the front of the group.

should be taken to ensure that somebody strong
stays at the back.

**Leadership from the rear** A force pushing the
group from the back. The danger here is that
the pushy ones in the group may find their way
to the front, and, out of concern for the weaker
ones in the rear, the leader may lose control
of the front. This technique can be effective if
the leader can keep the party together and
functioning at the desired speed.

**Leadership from the middle** This is symbolic of
the modern sociological concept of leadership.
This leader will generally make decisions by the
consensus method and will try to keep all the
party involved in the decision-making pro-
cesses. The leader can also watch all areas of
the party effectively, and will be seen by the
group to be a part of the party. This is the most
desirable system of leadership.

The good leader will understand how the
decision-making process works and will usually
use the decision-by-consensus method. Consensus implies that all points have been discussed, all members of the group have had a

chance to express their views and everyone
agrees that it is probably a good decision. Even
those who would have preferred a different outcome choose to accept the decision. To achieve
consensus, the more confident group members
have an obligation to check with the silent
members.

## Other decision-making processes

**Majority rule** The democratic way: a method
of decision making which is superficially tidy,
but which may leave the minority feeling unhappy about the decision, uninvolved and
uncommitted.

**Hand clasping** A clique or sub-group makes the
decision, perhaps in opposition to others or ig-
noring the opinion of others.

**Self-authorised decision** One person assumes
the authority to make the decision. In some
situations this can be helpful, but it drains
group members of initiative if it becomes a pat-
tern.

**Decision by authority** The group agrees that the leader decides, and the decision is accepted.

**Decision by default** No decision is made. This, very often, is in itself a decision. The need to make a decision may not be recognised, or the opportunity to make a decision is wasted.

Often a group of friends on an outing in the hills will have no acknowledged leader. Decisions will be of the consensus type, and this can be perfectly satisfactory and even desirable. However, the club leader, school teacher or instructor of a less experienced group is in a more difficult situation. The leader will have to find a balance between what is dangerous and exciting, or safe and dull. The problem, therefore, is to find the balance between excitement, pleasure, interest, spontaneity, enjoyment and freedom on the one hand, and on the other too much discipline leading to regimentation and monotony, or the sterile rigidity that comes from over-planning and over-preparation. The leader should always try to be aware of whether the balance is being tipped in one direction or another through his or her own arrogance or anxious lack of confidence, or through sound judgments or optimistic inexperience.

The leader must know when it is permissible to prevent the considerations of safety from intruding too strongly on the party to the point where the party cannot achieve the experience it set out to find. The leader must also know when it is necessary for such considerations to be paramount. If the safety factors can be controlled so they form a discreet background framework of good practice, working for, rather than against, feelings of excitement, interest, curiosity, exploration, adventure, achievement and general enjoyment of the hills, the leader is on the right lines.

Often, through ignorance, the apparently safe is dangerous and the apparently dangerous is safe. Rock climbing is a good example of an apparently dangerous activity which can be, and statistically is, a very safe activity — even

for the inexperienced, as long as they are properly led. Canoeing on a lake, on the other hand, can look very safe — until a strong wind blows up and drives everyone to the middle. The experience of the leader is the key.

It is immoral for the inexperienced to conduct uninitiated groups into outdoor pursuits. Through pressure, particularly in schools, this is happening in frightening proportions.

Some leaders have tickets to prove that they are leaders — these are most suspect (ticket collectors belong on buses). There is a good trend in New Zealand outdoor circles to discourage the setting up of "leadership qualifications". At the forefront of this trend is the New Zealand Outdoor Training Advisory Board (OTAB), a widely representative group of outdoor people and educationalists.

This is not to say that courses in leadership and associated skills should be discouraged. On the contrary, there is a great need for these, but the trend is to encourage a programme of progressive and onward training rather than an end-of-line qualification which can be used by a weak headmaster as a measure of competence and can become a scapegoat when so-called qualified leaders have mishaps (as they most certainly will from time to time).

An important aspect of the six-week teachers' course that we have developed at the Outdoor Pursuits Centre is to oppose the bureaucrats' requests for certification as an end-product of the course and instead to encourage a system of personal evaluation. This is designed to ensure that each teacher doing the course faces up to his or her own true ability and does not hide inability behind a piece of paper that states qualification. This is partly a conscience system, but it is very difficult for the individual not to face up to inabilities during this six-week course. Course members are then encouraged to develop their weak areas and/or to avoid conducting others into activities in which they themselves are not competent.

# Exposure and hypothermia

There is probably more information given out on exposure (to cold) and hypothermia (the lowering of body temperature) than any other aspect of tramping and mountaineering. ("This person is dying of exposure — such a stupid way to die!" and so on.) In fact, there is so much publicity about it that many youngsters manage to develop the symptoms before they even have the problem.

Of course, trampers and mountaineers are not the only people who get cold — this is common to motorcyclists, swimmers, divers, hang

---

It is possible to be comfortable in the most unpleasant weather with the right equipment. In bad weather the most important parts to cover are the head and trunk. Next in importance are the thighs. (See also pages 43 and 44.)

Parka features should include a generous hood which will give protection to the head and face; arms large enough to allow free movement; and storm-proofed cuffs. The parka should be a generous length — down to mid-thigh. Other useful features are a two-way zip and dome or velcro closure up the front, large pockets and double shoulders

Under the waterproof outer long underclothes of thin wool or polypropelene should be worn against the skin. Over this wear a thicker layer of woollen or nylon-pile garments

To date there is no fabric made that will keep an active person totally dry. *P.V.C.* is totally waterproof, but it is stiff and will make an active wearer wet from condensation. The waterproof and breathable fabrics such as *Klimate* or *Goretex* don't perform in all conditions and they are expensive. However, if the seams are properly sealed, garments made of these fabrics are the best available. *Z Kote, oiled japara* and *dry proofed japaras* are reasonably priced and are adequate for most trampers' needs, as are *well-proofed heavyweight nylons*

Woollen or nylon-pile balaclava covering the lower back of the head, the temples and the mouth

Mitts of wool or nylon pile are warmer than fingered gloves

Overtrousers should allow free movement of the legs and should have side zips to allow the garment to be put on over boots (see also comments on fabrics, opposite)

Knee-length or ankle gaiters can be useful for keeping debris out of boots

Leather work boots are the traditional tramping footwear, but lighter walking boots are more comfortable and make walking easier

glider pilots, skiers, canoeists and so on. However, in the mountains conditions are usually more severe and artificial warmth is harder to come by. It would be interesting to know how many motorcycle accidents, for example, could be attributed to loss of control or slow reactions through exposure and hypothermia.

Hypothermia is the killer, and it is usually brought on by exposure to bad weather (or cold water), most often the combination of rain, wind and cold. However it needn't be very cold; in fact, most exposure cases happen at temperatures around 10°C (50°F). The danger is increased tremendously if conditions are wet, and even more if it is windy.

As the body temperature drops the following happens:

1. Cooled blood travels to the brain, slowing mental faculties. This causes symptoms such as loss of co-ordination, irrational actions, memory lapses, incoherence and drowsiness.
2. Circulation to the extremities is slowed or stopped by the constriction of blood vessels, leading to numb hands and feet and sometimes frostbite. Many people think the best outdoor cure for frostbite is alcohol, but it is very dangerous to give alcohol to an exposure victim. Shivering and slurred speech are probably bad symptoms to emphasise in recognising hypothermia as these occur also in people who are cold, not just those suffering from hypothermia. Slurred speech can be caused simply by having cold facial muscles. The important symptoms to watch for are those indicated at 1.

If you are uncertain whether one of the party is suffering from hypothermia your safest course it to take remedial action immediately anyway.

Hypothermia occurs when more heat is being taken away from the body (usually by external conditions) than the body can generate by the oxidisation of foods. The potential for hypothermia is increased if a person is physically run down, has had sleepless nights and has had no food immediately prior to the exposure to cold

conditions. Probably the most potent cause of hypothermia is physical exhaustion.

Normally it is possible to halt or reverse the problem by taking the following action:
1. Stop the burning of energy. Stop movement.
2. Put on more clothing, particularly around the head (base of skull and temples are important) or replace wet clothing with dry. This should be done in shelter.
3. Get into shelter, away from wind or rain.
4. Take in or administer easily digestible foods

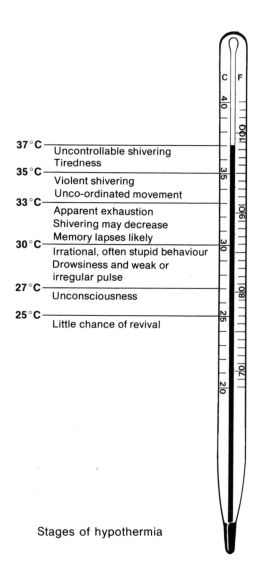

| | |
|---|---|
| **37°C** | Uncontrollable shivering |
| | Tiredness |
| **35°C** | Violent shivering |
| | Unco-ordinated movement |
| **33°C** | Apparent exhaustion |
| | Shivering may decrease |
| | Memory lapses likely |
| **30°C** | Irrational, often stupid behaviour |
| | Drowsiness and weak or |
| | irregular pulse |
| **27°C** | Unconsciousness |
| **25°C** | Little chance of revival |

Stages of hypothermia

(sugars, carbohydrates such as bread and so on).

5. If the victim is semi-conscious try to keep him awake and administer warm, sweet drinks.

Once the victim is in shelter and in dry clothes, I suspect that the benefits of the much-recommended application of external heat by putting another body in the same sleeping bag are more psychological than physical. However, the importance of psychological factors should not be overlooked. Until the body can process more energy, the most important thing that can be done is a stabilisation of the condition. What must not be done is the administration of alcohol which will cause the naturally constricted blood vessels to expand and the blood to be cooled further as it passes through extra cold flesh.

Here is an interesting experiment that can be done, particularly to show youngsters the effects of wind, rain and so on, and the value of putting on clothing to prevent hypothermia.

1. Line up four test tubes.
2. Put a thermometer in each one.
3. Put a cotton shirt on one, a woolly shirt on another, dress another with a nylon wind jacket over wool and leave the other naked.
4. Now fill the tubes with water of blood temperature.
5. After five minutes recheck and note the temperatures. If the temperatures are taken at evenly spaced times you can draw a graph for each tube. The experiment can be developed further to show the effect of rain and wind by spraying the outside of the tubes with cold water, blowing on them and so on.

# Frostbite

Frostbite is the freezing of tissues through exposure of that tissue to extreme cold. It can be classified into two main types — superficial and deep — and it is usually difficult to differentiate by looking at the affected part. A calculated guess based on the factors leading up to the condition may be the best way to decide, although it will usually make little difference to your treatment of the problem.

Deep frostbite is often associated with a generally run-down body condition, say on a long Himalayan climb. The body may have cut off circulation to the extremities to maintain the more important core temperature. Superficial frostbite will often occur as a result of a relatively brief exposure to very cold conditions — say taking off your gloves in a cold wind to do up your boot laces. Ears and nose may be affected as well as toes and fingers.

The affected tissue will be greyish-white and may begin to blister and turn purplish-black after several hours.

**Prevention**

1. The risk of frostbite is increased if the body is run down.
2. Wet socks and boots also increase the risk.
3. If your extremities are painfully cold, stop and warm them up on your own or someone else's body, or in warm water.
4. If feet are cold, loosen your boots. If you are wearing more than one pair of socks it is likely that by removing some socks you will increase the flow of blood to your feet and increase warmth.
5. Be wary of tight bands around wrists or lower legs which may inhibit circulation.
6. Putting on more clothes will sometimes warm hands and feet.

**Treatment**

1. The first thing to decide is whether the injury should be treated or not. Certainly, if the injury is to the feet, treatment should not be given until the patient is in a safe shelter—at

least a camp or hut. Once thawed there will be no possibility of the patient walking further. If the camp or hut is isolated it may sometimes be worth walking out before the frostbitten part thaws. However, this could result in some tissue damage.

2. Do not rub or beat the affected area.
3. Despite some medical advice to the contrary, I believe that alcohol administered internally will be of some value in restoring circulation. (Be quite certain, though, that the patient shows no sign of hypothermia and that con-

tinued shelter is assured.)

4. Soak the affected area in warm water (about blood temperature).
5. Sterile conditions are very important—if you are isolated with no chance of medical aid for several days, administer antibiotics.
6. Don't burst blisters or cut away any flesh.
7. Areas affected by cold may swell quite badly without actually being frostbitten. Usually this condition will go away if left for a day or so.

# Snow shelters

Deciding which type of shelter to build will depend on the terrain, snow conditions and available snow.

*Igloos* are best:

1. When the snow is windblown and crunchy. However, beware. The snow which makes the best igloos is also the snow which makes the best wind-slab avalanches. If the slope is over 20 degrees check for this danger (see the section on avalanches on page 115).
2. When the terrain is relatively level.
3. When the tools you have are snow saws, machetes, flat spades, large knives (30 cm blade minimum) or similar.
4. When you want to get all the group working.

*Snow caves* are best:

1. When you are in steep country — a slope of over 30 degrees is best.
2. When temperatures are relatively warm and you intend a long stay.
3. When you have shovels.

*Snow heap igloos* are best:

1. When the snow won't cut into blocks.
2. When the terrain is relatively flat.

If you have nothing but ice axes as tools and need a snow shelter, your preferences should remain the same, but a cave would probably be the easiest to build with these tools, although it may take longer.

**Constructing an igloo**

1. Check to see if there are any Eskimos in the area.
2. Choose a quarry site and begin cutting blocks about 60 cm×30 cm×50 cm (the size is not too important and will depend very much on the quality of snow).
3. Choose an igloo site near the quarry.
4. Scribe a circle, usually about 2 m diameter (with a rope and ice axe). The wider the circle the more difficult the construction will be.
5. Level the area inside the scribed line. Some people use this as block material, but I have generally found this is a hassle.
6. Lay the blocks on the outside of the scribed circle, bevelling the inside top edge and the ends. By doing this you can achieve the kind of arch that makes many bridges strong and eggs uncrushable (with the thumb and forefinger placed top and bottom of the egg).
7. As each succeeding layer of blocks is placed the structure should angle more to the centre, until at about head height a final block is placed over the remaining hole. The igloo should now be strong enough to hold the weight of a person standing on top.
8. Construct a covered trench and tunnel up into the igloo. Pack any holes inside and out, smooth the inside, make cubby holes for gear and, finally, poke an ice axe through the roof for ventilation.

**Building an igloo**

A is the most important Eskimo. He should use a large knife, machete or even a mess tin or similar for shaping the blocks.

B can use a plastic sheet or parka as a sledge to move the blocks.

C is the quarry manager and should use a snow saw or machete to cut the blocks. A small panel saw will do.

---

Note: keep clumsy idiots busy in the quarry or making a brew as stumblers have broken many potentially wonderful igloos.

**Constructing a snow cave**

1. Select the steepest slope in the area and check that it is safe from avalanche by taking a layer sample. (That is, cut out a section of the slope to allow examination of the snow layers. See the section on slab avalanches on page 115). The steeper the slope, the shorter the tunnel must be and the easier it will be to dispose of your diggings. The cave will also be stronger and will last longer on a steep slope.

2. Dig one or two parallel tunnels (depending on tools and urgency). The ends of the tunnels at floor level should be a minimum of 2 m below the surface, so that when you dig up, a minimum of 30 cm is left between the outside slope and the dome of the cave.

3. Dig upward from the end of the tunnels and then expand into a chamber, the base of which should not be lower than the top of the tunnel.

4. Make the chamber as big as necessary, disposing of the final snow by filling one of the unneeded entrance tunnels.

5. Smooth off the ceiling so drops of water don't accumulate on the ends of lumps and bumps.

6. Poke an ice axe through the roof for ventilation.

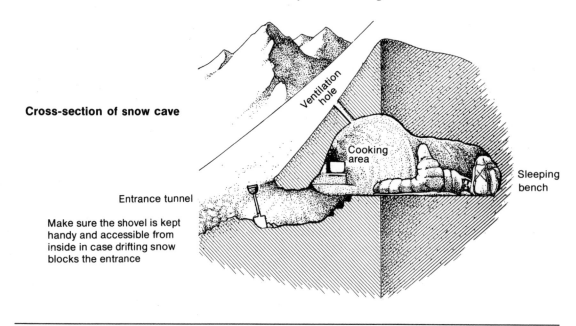

**Cross-section of snow cave**

Ventilation hole

Cooking area

Sleeping bench

Entrance tunnel

Make sure the shovel is kept handy and accessible from inside in case drifting snow blocks the entrance

**Constructing a snow heap igloo**

1. Pile up a dome-shaped heap of snow approximately 3 m in diameter and 2 m high. Compact this heap a little, but not too much, as you go.
2. Hollow out the heap, leaving walls of about half a metre thick.
3. From inside the dome, dig down into the floor and into the slope if necessary.
4. Smooth the ceiling and poke an ice axe through for ventilation.
5. Fashion an entrance tunnel.

Note: it is of crucial importance that an eye is kept on the weather while you are warmly ensconced, as a storm or wind may block the entrance and/or ventilation hole. Bad weather can not usually be heard once inside one of these shelters; but in some ways bad weather will be your friend as it will usually make the construction stronger — that is, of course, unless it is heavy rain which will wash your dome away!

# Fitness for outdoor pursuits

Mental fitness is probably more important than physical fitness if one needs to make the choice. However, the top performer needs mental preparedness as well as top physical fitness. If one's body is weighed down by thoughts of danger and problems ahead, all the physical fitness and strength in the world won't help. Commitment to the project in hand is crucial, and the more difficult the problem the greater degree of commitment required. Of course, the reverse is also true — if the mind is willing and the flesh is weak the budding outdoor enthusiast will have little success. The truth is that most people "psych-out" before they have drawn on all their physical strength.

It is generally acknowledged that the best training for outdoor pursuits is outdoor pursuits, but to be a top performer you will probably need a more diverse programme — particularly as most climbers won't be fortunate enough to live near a good cliff, canoeists near a suitable river, and so on. Many will have to make the most of their city environment to keep fit during the week in preparation for their weekends and holidays away.

Any good athletics-training programme will be suitable, with emphasis on the performer's activity and on the area of the body most important to the activity. In both canoeing and rock climbing this applies particularly to the hands and arms. In mountaineering the legs are probably more important than the arms. However, before beginning work on these specific areas you should first take care of the motor — the heart and circulation, the lungs and breathing.

Fitness can be broken down as follows in order of priority:

## The head

This involves psychological preparedness, which amounts to total acceptance of the effort, potential pain and danger involved, and a knowledge of how far you can push yourself, physically and mentally.

## The heart and lungs

Both of these can be regarded as pumps:

1. The lungs to suck in air, so that necessary gases (mainly oxygen) may be transferred to the bloodstream, and unnecessary gases (mainly carbon dioxide) may be taken out and expelled. The oxygen uptake depends on:
   a. lung capacity.
   b. efficiency of the gas transfer (to the blood) mechanism.
   c. the amount of oxygen-carrying agents in the blood.
2. The heart to pump blood to the brain and muscles, to deliver oxygen and blood sugar and to take away wastes.

## The circulation

In a fit person the blood flow will be freer than in an unfit person and there will be more channels.

## Muscle tone

In a fit person the muscle will be bigger, more dense and will have more blood capillaries than in an unfit person.

Running as a medium to general motor fitness should be done with caution, particularly on roads and hard pavements as tremendous jarring of spine, joints and muscles can occur. For example, when I attempted the arduous Himalayan climb, the North face of Jannu, I was extremely fit from a running point of view. However, I could not perform at my best on the mountain because I had damaged my spine running on roads.

It is likely that for heart and lung training, cycling is as beneficial and less dangerous than running (as long as one can keep away from the undersides of large trucks and fast cars — I'm sure this is more jarring than running!). Swimming is also very good for this core development, particularly if you are a habitual sinker like me — I have to keep moving to stay on the surface. Some people practise yoga, with apparent success, as an aid to mental and physical fitness.

It should also be remembered that people can become stale by regular pursuit of a particular activity. I often find a rest is the best training of all.

# The weather

*It rained and rained and rained*
*The average fall was well maintained;*
*And when the tracks were simple bogs*
*It started raining cats and dogs.*
*After a draft of half an hour*
*We had a most refreshing shower;*
*And then most curious thing of all*
*A gentle rain began to fall.*
*Next day but one was fairly dry*
*Save for one deluge from the sky*
*Which wetted the party to the skin*
*And then at last — the rain set in.*

Anon, *Westland Country. A centennial album,* 1977

Weather is one of the outdoor enthusiast's prime concerns. It has always seemed curious to me that minor atmospheric disturbances should be so crucial to us, but they always are. In fact, one of the major parts of our preparation for outdoor pursuits is to combat the effects of bad weather.

Most of our bad weather comes from the South Tasman Sea, and cloud out to sea on the western side is a pretty sure sign of imminent bad weather. This weather is usually very wet west of the ranges and dry and hot out to the east. Westerlies usually clear only from the south. Our very cold weather comes from the south (Antarctic) and often results in snow to low levels. However, light, southerly winds will often bring fine weather.

In some ways it is rather sad that our main mountain chains are the first obstacles the westerlies strike; thus, much of the year is spent under cloud. However, we can be grateful that if it weren't for this there would be less snow and ice and associated glaciation in our mountains, our rivers would have less water in them,

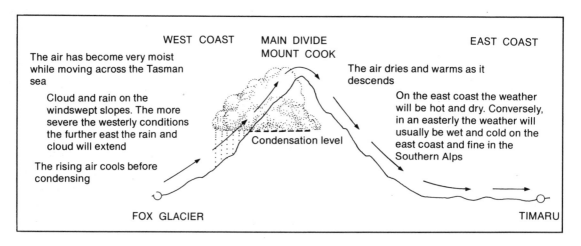

WEST COAST

The air has become very moist while moving across the Tasman sea

Cloud and rain on the windswept slopes. The more severe the westerly conditions the further east the rain and cloud will extend

The rising air cools before condensing

MAIN DIVIDE
MOUNT COOK

Condensation level

EAST COAST

The air dries and warms as it descends

On the east coast the weather will be hot and dry. Conversely, in an easterly the weather will usually be wet and cold on the east coast and fine in the Southern Alps

FOX GLACIER

TIMARU

A cross-section of the South Island of New Zealand showing the Föhn effect of the westerly wind passing over the Southern Alps. This happens in many areas of New Zealand, but is most marked through the South Island from Fiordland to North Canterbury.

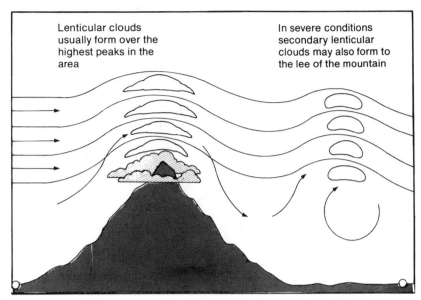

Lenticular clouds usually form over the highest peaks in the area

In severe conditions secondary lenticular clouds may also form to the lee of the mountain

Lenticular clouds or "hog's backs". These may form without any wind direction. The initial cigar shape of the cloud may develop into a denser layer or wave.

and so on. One of the reasons New Zealand is so well endowed with natural facilities for outdoor pursuits is the fact that our weather is so unruly.

## Clouds

It seems that in New Zealand, at least, very limited information can be drawn from clouds — certainly much less than is generally believed. I believe the reason for this is the fast-moving systems in this part of the world. At best, clouds can be used to indicate weather for a few hours following the observation.

There are three types of clouds: those composed entirely of water droplets; those composed entirely of ice crystals; and those which are a mixture of water droplets and ice crystals.

Derivation of cloud types from Latin:

*Stratus*: layer    *Cirrus*: fibre
*Nimbus*: umbrella    *Cumulus*: heap
*Altus*: high    *Fractus*: broken

Hence stratus, cirrostratus, nimbostratus, altostratus, cumulus, cirrus, cumulonimbus, fractocumulus, fractostratus, stratocumulus, cirrocumulus, altocumulus.

In my experience the amateur forecaster in New Zealand need recognise only a few of these.

### Lenticular clouds (hog's backs)

It is generally felt by mountaineers that these are less ominous than was once thought, and certainly this seems to be the case in my short career. However, I am rather inclined to think that it takes more than it once did to send me scurrying for the hut. These clouds are of the altocumulus type, and usually form either individually or in sinister little groups over the highest peak in the area. I have seen the weather deteriorate in one hour after the first sighting of such a cloud; but, on the other hand, I have seen it remain ominous looking for days on end and then become perfectly fine. The best advice I can offer is to continue your expedition until more definite bad-weather signs occur, such as a greater build-up of cloud.

But be wary — they do give a warning of deteriorating conditions.

### Cumulus

Round, *white* cumulus low on the horizon *plus*

Cumulus — moist clouds.

Cirrus or mares' tails — high altitude "ice clouds".

cold, clear conditions usually indicate fine weather. Tall, heavy cumulus build-ups, on the other hand, usually mean localised bad weather, often with electrical activity and heavy rain.

### Cirrus

This is caused by strong winds at altitude and sometimes does precede strong winds at lower altitude. However, the only concrete information that can be derived from cirrus is the wind direction at altitude, which may be of value in determining the nature of the system over the area. Cirrus will almost always indicate bad weather if the cloud cover increases significantly.

A lowering of any cloud layer generally indicates bad weather.

### Weather maps and systems

The most helpful thing in forecasting weather is a description of the situation or a look at a weather map.

Remember the directions of wind flow associated with high- and low-pressure systems. Anticyclones (high-pressure systems) revolve anticlockwise. Cyclones (low-pressure systems) resolve clockwise. These directions are the opposite in the Northern Hemisphere — God only knows what happens at the Equator!

The use of a barometer with a weather map will tell you roughly whether a particular system is moving on to or away from your area.

A weather map, similar to those found in most daily newspapers.

Likely weather conditions can be deduced from the weather map. In the weather situation shown a ridge of high pressure over the North Island would be accompanied by light winds (except near Cook Strait) and fine weather. Over the South Island and through Cook Strait strong or gale-force northwesterlies could be expected (isobars close together indicate strong winds). Rain in Fiordland and the southern ranges would spread northwards up the West Coast and on to the divide as the cold front moved eastwards over the country. The cold front would be accompanied by a change to cooler westerlies and possibly thunderstorms in the ranges. Showery conditions would continue on and west of the divide. East of the ranges, hot, dry weather ahead of the cold front would give way to cooler conditions, with the weather remaining dry, but some showers could spread to the eastern foothills.

Bad weather around the tropical cyclone would be very localised and would not affect New Zealand until the storm came very close, if indeed it did.

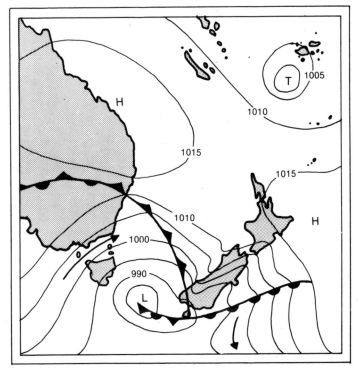

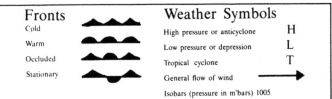

| Fronts | |
| --- | --- |
| Cold | |
| Warm | |
| Occluded | |
| Stationary | |

| Weather Symbols | |
| --- | --- |
| High pressure or anticyclone | H |
| Low pressure or depression | L |
| Tropical cyclone | T |
| General flow of wind | → |
| Isobars (pressure in m'bars) 1005 | |

# Safety

It has always seemed a great irony to me that when you are young you need gear for safety, but can't afford it. When old and experienced you can afford the gear but don't need it because safety then comes mostly from knowledge stored in your head.

# 3

# The bush, the scrub, the tussock (and the pain)

*Tramping is carrying as much as you can, as far as you can, as quickly as you can — and then coming back again. (Who said we had an energy crisis?)*

Author

AT 13 years of age I was a pale-faced and spindly, weak little boy (a bit like I am 20 years later, but now I'm more cunning!) — the kind they throw sand at on the beach. But I knew from my first outing in the bush that this was my scene. Here I could compete with anyone — well, it's nice to dream anyway. The first trip of any significance was a memorable one which I did with a much older and wiser 14-year-old, Robert Selwyn, a keen scout. It began at Eastbourne and went via Butterfly Creek to the Wainuiomata Valley Road then over the "gutbuster" and into the Catchpole.

At high school I met Ian Jowett, who was already a keen tramper and was much fitter and stronger than me, but together we were soon doing lots of good trips in the Rimutaka and Tararua Ranges. We didn't do any courses and never read any technical books. Tramping was a simple enough business that everyone, it seemed, wanted to make complex. We learned by experience and never got into any trouble — that is, except once when we forgot whether the red needle or the white needle on our old compass pointed north, took a guess and went opposite to the desired direction. I often wonder how close we came to getting into serious trouble, as I remember hearing with alarm about exposure after I'd been tramping a few years, and realised that I had had it several times. (No-one had noticed though, because I tended to act irrationally, slur my words and stumble at the best of times!) The Mountain Safety Council could probably make a tremendous "don'ts" film about our early activities.

One of my major problems in those early days was that when I became extremely tired my knees would try to bend backwards, particularly when going down steep slopes. I sobbed my way to the valley after several vigorous trips on the tops with Ian. It was a fantastic revelation when I discovered after a few years of tramping that I could actually keep up with Ian instead of bumbling and sobbing my way along in the rear. The day I made that discovery I really rubbed it in and made him suffer.

Clubs were not our scene, as large groups in the hills and the often restrictive leadership gave us both a pain in the bum. We did, however, join the Hutt Valley Tramping Club and got a great deal of pleasure and knowledge from membership. Later I even dutifully did a spell as chief guide.

I liked fast trips best and often these were solo. Although I preferred company, to achieve a particular trip I often had to go alone.

One such trip I had dreamed of for years. In the early 1960s the fittest Tararua trampers were trying a trip which became known and spoken about in hushed tones as a "Schormanns-Kaitoke" or "S.K.". The challenge was to do it in a weekend — that is, from Friday evening until Sunday evening.

The competition was quite hot, especially between clubs, and, finally, in 1963, it was done by John Tristram and Peter Daniels. John was known as "split-pin" because his legs appeared to go almost right up to his neck, and Peter Daniels was an extremely strong and formidable character. The journey required its suitors to climb and descend a total of about 14,000 m and battle sub-alpine scrub, tangled bush, jagged ridges, biting cold or parching heat — the usual Tararua cocktail. It could be seen as the ultimate in masochism. My attempts to do it in less than 24 hours began in 1964 with an athletic Dutchman, Phil van Dusschoten, who had been an Olympic canoeist, but the weather always beat us. We managed twice to do the trip in a weekend, but never seemed to have the combination of fine weather, fitness, enthusiasm and whatever else such a trip requires.

I was approaching my 20th birthday and was doing quite a lot of running when I decided, as an interlude, to see how close I could get to the four-minute mile — a kind of preparation for the effort ahead. I decided that all it required was tenacity and a little ability.

One evening I went down to the track and, after a short warm-up, burst into my first lap which I completed in just over a minute. I completed the second lap in the same time and was

With Roy Jowett (left), about to go into the Tararuas from Kaitoke, *circa* 1959. *M. Jowett*

Me at Hells Gate on one of my first tramps in the Tararuas. Note the horrible round pack, designed for maximum pain and minimum gear. *Ian Jowett*

Me dwarfed by my pack beside the Ohau River (Tararuas) on early tramp. *Ian Jowett*

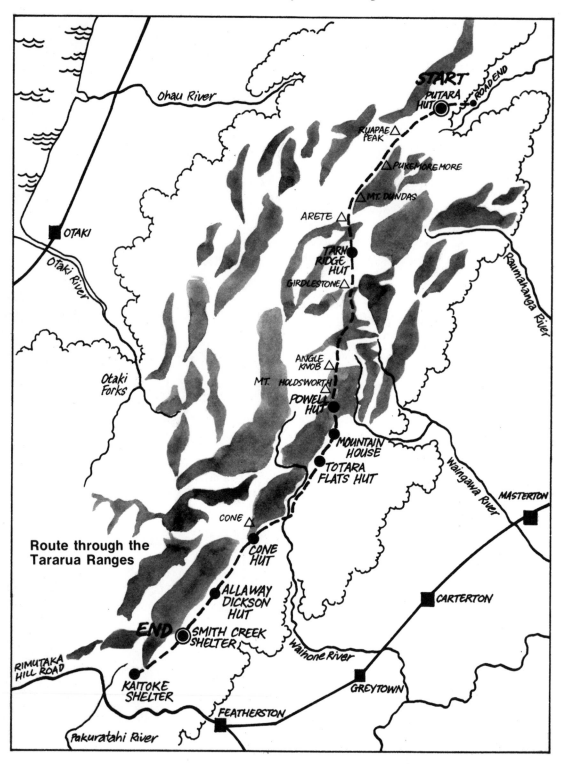

Route through the
Tararua Ranges

trying to put the pressure on in my third lap when suddenly I fell to the ground with a violent pain in my head. I picked myself up and staggered home. After a few days the pain was still present, so reluctantly I went to the doctor and told him my tale of woe. "You foolish boy. You appear to have burst a blood vessel in your head!" He gave me some pills and told me not to do anything vigorous for several weeks.

Two weeks later — in fact the eve of my 20th birthday — I journeyed up to Eketahuna on the railcar with a few of my club mates. Jan Hardwick (later Jan Heine) and Bod Hendry were to try a weekend S.K., while Ian's brother, Roy, thought he might try to tag along with me on my 24-hour effort.

The route I planned to take along the Holdsworth Ridge was slightly less demanding than the main range route, involving a mere 12,000 odd metres up and down over a distance of about 80 km — if it's possible to calculate kilometres in that kind of rough country.

We all climbed up through the bush to the first hut, Putara. It was 11 p.m. by the time I put my head down and began to doze. A short three hours later I was up again and attempting to force down a tin of cold "sausage snack" and a couple of raw eggs. I had no cooking facilities, but otherwise a fairly healthy pack containing plenty of food, a sleeping bag and storm gear.

It was 3.30 a.m. when we left the hut and set off into the mist and tangled leatherwood. It remained very misty and cool as we climbed over the first few little peaks, and I was beginning to think that this would be just another weekend S.K. But suddenly, and miraculously, at East Peak we broke through into a clear, fresh day. It was one of the most memorable dawns I had ever seen. The sky glowed orange in the east, turning to crimson the tussock and rock that seemed to stretch to infinity ahead. The rugged tops thrust up above a seething layer of cloud, like an immense carpet only a 100 m or so below us. The massive shapes of Egmont and Ruapehu were clearly visible.

With a fine day now assured, I fared the others well and loped off with Roy hard on my heels. An hour later he fell down groaning and clutching his side, so I left him to be gathered up by Jan and Bob and continued alone. It was a tremendous sensation loping across the tussock tops and over the peaks. By 8 a.m. I was on top of the peak called Arete; an hour later I reached Tarn Ridge Hut and by 10 a.m. I was on top of Girdlestone. I muttered to myself, "I'm coming to get you Holdsworth", but the peak at the other end of the range looked an age away.

By mid-day I was feeling very tired and began to have hallucinations — in one place I saw a bear dashing around the hillside, and it even growled at me. It was time to stop and get some food into my empty stomach. I sat by a tarn and crammed nuts, raisins and salami into my mouth, even though I wasn't feeling hungry, and in my bowl I mixed up a thick mixture of the new wonder food, "Complan" — it tasted terrible! I decided to have a short holiday, and a moment later dozed off, awakening with a terrible fright probably after only 10 seconds' sleep. I crawled over to the tarn, dunked my head in it and continued along the ridge like a robot.

Early in the afternoon I began up the slopes of the final peak on the journey (Mount Holdsworth), strangely feeling as if I was accompanied by an old but unseen friend. I now felt that the trip was virtually in the bag, even though I still had what normally would have been a big weekend trip ahead of me.

At Powell Hut a middled-aged-looking bloke asked me, "Where have you come from today?"

"Schormanns," I grinned. Everyone in the hut looked at me as if I had said, "Take your pants down," and I heard someone mumble, "Impossible!"

It was a pleasure to canter down through the cool bush after the parched tops, and I was soon wandering down the flats of the Waiohine River feeling at peace with the world — but it was a kind of drunken peace, I must admit.

Darkness was a psychologically bad time. My old friend had now apparently deserted me. As I left the river flats and climbed up towards

Mike Tegg in the upper Tauherenikau Valley (southern Tararua Range). *Graeme Dingle*

Ross Hislop (behind) and Graeme Lythgoe on the central Tararua tops. *Graeme Dingle*

Cone Saddle I began to feel very, very tired, the gloominess of the bush adding to my load; my steady upward movement was often halted by tangled windfalls, through which I would sometimes have to crawl. In a weak moment I decided to stop at Cone Hut on the other side of the Saddle, in the Tauherenikau Valley.

It was tremendous to see the old hut. It was just on dark when I pushed open the rickety door and stood dazed and annoyed to see the hut filled with friends from a rival club. I couldn't possibly admit fatigue in front of them, so after a very short break and muttering a few obscenities I stumbled back into the dark bush.

I became depressed thinking about the distance I still had to go — a distance that only a few years before had taken me a full day.

I had now been going continuously for 16 hours, my feet were swollen and bruised and I was beginning to wish I had worn a cricket box (the constant jogging had worn some skin off the end of my most sensitive organ).

The track in the bush was difficult to follow, so I crashed off toward the river, crossed it and found better going down the river flats. In one place I saw a patch of white in a clump of beech trees and headed towards it dopily by way of a landmark in the darkness. When I was about 4 m away from the patch it suddenly materialised into the backside of a large stag. He spun around and we both ran in opposite directions.

Despite the dark and my stumbling, I must have been moving fairly quickly because I did that day trip of three years before in only two-and-a-half hours.

At Smiths Creek, an hour from Kaitoke, my club mates had given up hope of my arrival, and were now mostly dozing by a dying fire. I drank a celebration pint of beer and happily collapsed into my sleeping bag. It was the greatest 20th birthday I could imagine.

Strangely, the Tararua Ranges then lost much of their challenge for me, but not their charm. They are most beautiful and a great facility for Wellingtonians. Maybe in my old age I will return to appreciate them properly.

---

## Summary of Tararua Range traverse

*A solo traverse of the Tararua Range from Putara Hut to Smiths Creek on 30 November 1965. Total time — 18 hours 30 minutes.*

A trip of this nature raises the complex question of responsiblity, and whether people have the right to take risks. I believe they do, but if risk is involved they have no right to expect rescue.

In this case I did act in a very calculating manner that I believe deserves the label "responsible". I knew the route intimately. I knew my own strength, I carried sufficient equipment to ensure my survival in most emergency situations and, above all, other people understood my intentions.

---

# Tramping in New Zealand

Tramping is by far the most popular of the outdoor pursuits that I have chosen to discuss. I suppose the reasons are that it is comparatively cheap and easy to get involved with and, on the surface, the required level of skill is low. Despite this, tramping is a great basis on which to build for almost any other outdoor pursuit. It shares the common ground of fitness, understanding the land, navigation, first aid (including rescue breathing, cardiac massage and treatment of hypothermia), camping skills and so on.

There are vast tramping areas in New Zealand ranging from the most straightforward walk in the Tongariro National Park to the horrors of Fiordland. Dozens of very well-established clubs cater for the needs of club-orientated people. In *The Mountains of New Zealand* Rod Hewitt and Mavis Davidson sum up the tramping creature pretty well: "The competent New Zealand tramper is a highly qualified outdoor person, with a hardiness and discipline gained from years of bivouacing in wet forest and navigating in misty conditions, contending with all types of flooded rivers, strenuous pass hopping between alpine valleys and participating in search and rescue work with the added hazard of snow in winter. Such a tramper is apt to shudder at being referred to as a 'hiker', for in this country the word 'hiker' refers only to the hitchhiker who roams the road and thumbs a ride from passing motorists.

"Many of the best alpine climbers in New Zealand have graduated progressively from tramping to climbing and still maintain allegiance to their earlier activities of the lower moutain ranges. In addition to all the physical skills required, the New Zealand mountaineer must be capable of organising long mountain trips, with food and equipment weights calculated to the last ounce."

Each weekend of the year hundreds (perhaps thousands) of New Zealanders take to the hills, sometimes tramping in club groups, sometimes as individuals. Some go like stink from Friday

## The well-dressed fine-weather tramper

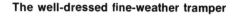

A light scarf or headband tied around your head will keep sweat and hair out of your eyes and will make a useful sling in an emergency

Many trampers wear a sleeveless woollen bush singlet on their upper body when the weather is fine. A woollen shirt or jersey would be put on over the top as the weather determines. However, there are specially made synthetic garments (for example, nylon pile and polypropylene) which are as warm but lighter and quicker drying than wool. Cotton is virtually useless as an insulating garment when wet

A Hallmark Phoenix internal-frame pack with detachable side pockets (see also the section on packs on page 44)

Full-weight leather boots with moulded rubber soles are usually worn. Sometimes tricounis are fitted to the insteps to give extra traction on wet rocks and logs. However, lighter European or American walking boots (Bullers) and even road shoes are becoming more popular (particularly among hunters), and plastic boots are now also available. Your choice should depend on the severity of the planned undertaking and on individual comfort. All footwear should *always* be well worn before your first major outing. Uncomfortable boots can be crippling

Most trampers wear light athletic shorts until the weather demands more cover

Woollen socks are the most popular, but some good synthetic socks which are easier to wash and dry are now available

Putties or gaiters stop debris entering boots and also help stop socks slipping down into the boots

to Sunday evening with great packs on their backs (usually these people are Tararua-demented demons), rushing over peaks and bumps, fording rivers, swimming sunless gorges and battling sub-alpine scrub to return to the city, scratched and muscle sore, but prepared to face another week in the circus. At Christmas many of these people head for the Southern Alps, humping their 40-kg packs up long river valleys, over high passes and so on.

The modern tramper's lot is a little easier than that of the "Pascoe era"; those stalwarts suffered from the lack of both modern transportation and equipment. Today, airdrops help save trampers' backs (but many trampers who can't find their airdrops go hungry!) and modern equipment makes life generally less spartan.

**A tramper in storm gear**
(See also page 25.)

Woollen or pile balaclava

Parka

Woollen mitts

Underneath weatherproof outer clothing wear wool or nylon-pile clothing

Overtrousers

Firm footwear with good traction is very important in bad weather

## Tramping equipment

*When your tramping clothes are dirty, stand them in the corner of the hut. When they fall over, they'll be clean again.*

Adaptation of quote by John Pascoe

One of the beauties of tramping if funds are low is the cheapness of getting involved. Of course, it is great to have all the best gear, but it is possible to equip oneself for very little.

Instead of buying a schoolbag to take to school why not use a frameless pack? It's more practical anyway; it leaves one's hands free for cycling and scrapping. Otherwise use a sugarbag with straps (pikau bag) which will be okay for loads under 15 kg. Instead of a conventional raincoat, why not buy a tramping parka?

## Pack packing

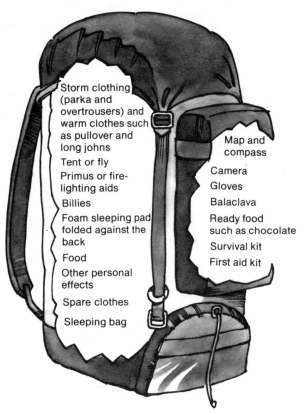

Storm clothing (parka and overtrousers) and warm clothes such as pullover and long johns

Tent or fly

Primus or fire-lighting aids

Billies

Foam sleeping pad folded against the back

Food

Other personal effects

Spare clothes

Sleeping bag

Map and compass

Camera

Gloves

Balaclava

Ready food such as chocolate

Survival kit

First aid kit

The pack illustrated is a "Magnum", a large-volume (approx. 90 litres) external frame pack for general-purpose outdoor pursuits. Whatever pack you use, the rules for packing will be similar. If you anticipate river crossings or very wet weather, pack everything in strong plastic bags. Put the most urgently needed equipment in the most accessible places (e.g. storm clothing at the top). If this is done properly, anything needed on the tramp such as snacks, map and compass or first aid kit, will be available without the need to unpack. If you stop to camp in the rain, the equipment to make shelter should be near the top so you can leave clothes and sleeping bag in your pack while the tent or fly is pitched.

Get a pair of longjohns from the local Salvation Army store and instead of boots use sandshoes. A good compass will cost little and save hours. Every household has woollen pullovers and hats, and the only remaining problem is a · sleeping bag. If you can't get a second-hand one, an adequate synthetic bag will cost much less than the average weekly wage.

If you can't earn or bludge that maybe there's no hope for you!

## Packs

There are many varieties of packs on the market. The two main dilemmas for trampers when purchasing are whether to buy one with synthetic (nylon) or natural fibre (canvas) fabrics and an internal or external frame. Most modern-thinking trampers will agree that the best choice will be an internal-framed model, like the Phoenix pack illustrated with the fine-weather tramper.

There will also be much argument about waterproofing and external pockets. The best way to ensure total waterproofing is to stow equipment in polythene bags inside the pack. The facility to be able to remove side pockets is invaluable when travelling in thick forest or when rock climbing. When forest travel is contemplated, experienced trampers will agree that the pack should not project above the shoulders.

The illustrations on page 45 show the internal-frame, external-frame and closed-cell foam-support systems. Frameless packs are usually used by climbers, trampers and hunters for outings of one or two days' duration when minimal gear is carried.

## Shelter

*Emergency type*: The desecration of bush areas to build makeshift shelters should be vigorously discouraged except in an emergency. If the skill is to be taught, dead material should be used.

The tussock tops are the worst places for emergencies in bad weather as it is so difficult to find or make shelter. Higher up, snow or boulders will often afford shelter, and at lower altitudes the bush offers welcome refuge.

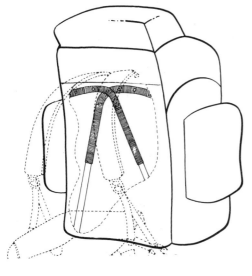

*Internal-frame pack* — this has some advantages over that using an external frame. There are no exposed horns to catch on outcrops or trees while climbing or in the bush. The load is positioned as closely as possible to the back to minimise drag on the shoulders. It could be argued that this will cause the back to sweat, but it will not prove a significant disadvantage. The frame can be easily shaped to suit most back shapes and sizes.

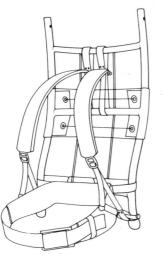

The traditional *external-frame system* is very popular. These packs are favoured for their load-carrying ability. The hiload packstyle (e.g. Hallmark Exodus) can be extended well above shoulder height to enable you to carry large loads with more comfort in open country. The semi-hiload packs (Magnum and Kodiak) are very versatile and are recommended for trans-alpine mountaineering and general backpacking in either open country or sparsely wooded areas. The shoulder-height frame styles (Everest, Featherweight, Everest Standard, Panda, Pelican, Zappa and Nomad) are the best choice for backpacking in densely wooded areas. One of the real advantages of the external frame is that the bag can be removed to allow the carriage of wood, meat and so on, on the frame.

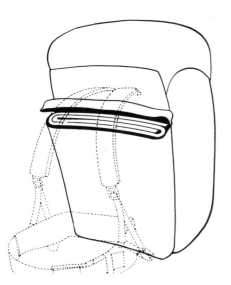

*Closed-cell foam-support system* — there are no breakable metal parts, and the closed-cell foam backpad doubles as a sleeping mat and a support system. Closed-cell foam is a rotproof, flexible synthetic which is very resilient and has excellent insulative qualitites. It does not absorb moisture and therefore gives the pack inbuilt flotation. When used as part of a pack support system it moulds to the shape of your back. The support pad provides protection from carelessly packed items and ensures maximum comfort.

The best emergency shelter in the tussock is a large waterproof nylon or plastic bag. If you have neither the best you can hope to do is to build a barrier against the wind from rocks and tussock. If at all possible, descend into the bush.

*Boulders*: In glacial areas wonderful homes can usually be found under gigantic rocks. This is also possible in the bush. However, it may be necessary to move out or share with the local inhabitants — keas, thar, chamois and so on.

*Flies*: The fly is probably the most effective and comfortable shelter for most bush camps (but, as the Australian said, "You need a lot of them on you to keep the rain off!"). They are light to carry, airy and accommodate more people

### Emergency shelter

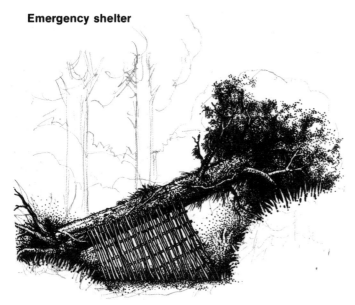

The frame for an emergency shelter against a fallen tree. The shelter should serve two main functions:
1. Keeping off wind.
2. Keeping off rain. In this function the trunk of the fallen tree wil play an important role. Therefore, the broader it is the better.

A framework of sticks should be built leaning into the wind or the anticipated windward side. This should then be thatched *thickly* with whatever foliage is available in the area. Dampness from the ground will be a problem, so foliage should be heaped in the sleeping place. Immediately in front of this a fire should be lit, preferably against a log or rock wall, which will tend to throw the heat into the shelter.

### Fly shelter

The best and strongest guying system is loops of strong tape sewn into the seams at the corners and centres with guy lines attached. The correct number of guys is related to the fly size. A 3m² fly should have eight lines (six along the edges and two at the ends)

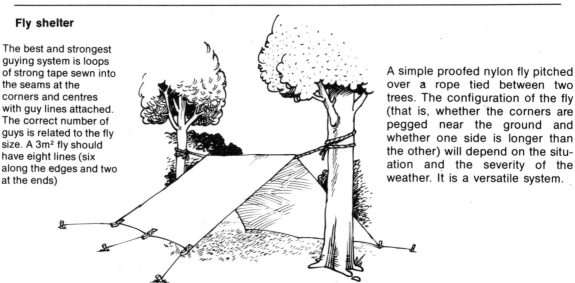

A simple proofed nylon fly pitched over a rope tied between two trees. The configuration of the fly (that is, whether the corners are pegged near the ground and whether one side is longer than the other) will depend on the situation and the severity of the weather. It is a versatile system.

in relation to their weight than tents. Their only disadvantage is that driving rain may penetrate the ends, but in the bush this will rarely be a problem. Flies can be purchased relatively cheaply, or they can be made from proofed nylon.

*Tents*: Tents are expensive items (probably the most expensive single item for trampers) so it is best to choose a good one. If you adopt the principle that in the bush flies are best, then you will generally use a tent only on the tops and in alpine situations. Therefore choose a good alpine-quality tent. All tents should be seam sealed. This is doubly important on single-skin tents. Seam sealents such as Super Sealer are available from most outdoor retail stores.

The *Free Spirit* tent. Capacity, two to three persons; weight, approximately 4 kg. This kind of design is good as an all-purpose tent for low-level and alpine conditions. It is rugged, and the bell ends make cooking and storage of equipment easy. *Bob Carter*

The *Free Spirit* tent with bell ends removed. This reduces the weight of the tent for trips where the bell ends are not required. Entrances at both ends make access easy.
1. The ruggedness of the tent is due to an aluminium-tube "A" frame at each end.
2. Insect screens at the entrances are essential in many areas.
3. The tension is kept consistent on the fly by the provision of shock cord as guy lines.

The inner tent is made of breathable nylon to allow condensation to escape, but the fly is highly waterproof to keep out the rain. The tent and the fly can be used independently, but they provide the best level of comfort when used together.

Although the shape is not the most convenient for roominess, it does shed water or snow easily. Once the bell ends are zipped in place the tent is highly weatherproof and there is a minimum of guy lines to trip clumsy people or animals. The main disadvantage of such a tent is the weight.

A single-skin (*Vagabond*) tent. Capacity, two to three persons; weight, 2.4 kg.

This is the traditonal tent shape. The single waterproof skin means that condensation is a problem, but the cost is minimal. Similar tents, such as the Nimbus, are available with a fly and breathable inner which completely reduce condensation. *Bob Carter*

A lightweight alpine tent (*Klimatent*) with sleeve entrance seen here providing an open vestibute. Capacity, two persons; weight, 1.5 kg.

This is a highly specialised alpine tent. It is made from a single skin of the ultra-modern fabric, Klimate, which allows it to breathe in most conditions but still be waterproof. This type of fabric (Klimate or Goretex) is manufactured by bonding a rubbery membrane to nylon fabric. The membrane contains millions of tiny pores which allow water vapour and gas to pass through, but droplets of water such as rain will not penetrate. It should be remembered, however, that it does not function to perfection in all conditions as the pores can be blocked by freezing or even by water itself.

To date this is the only satisfactory method devised of making the lightest tents.

While spacious and good from an aerodynamics point of view, the shape prevents snow falling off easily and is therefore a drawback in heavy snow conditions — unless the snow is cleared it will crush the tent.

The poles are made of highly flexible hollow fibreglass or tubular aircraft alloy. The sleeve entrance allows maximum protection for access in storm conditions. *Bob Carter*

The *Chrysalis*, a more general-purpose version of the Klimatent. Capacity, two persons; weight, approximately 1.5 kg.

The porch can be fixed down to weatherproof the zip entrance. On the latest model the porch has been superceded by a weatherproof vestibule.

The *dome tent* is probably the roomiest capacity for weight of all the tent configurations. It is also extremely convenient to live in. Although many such tents are made of single-skin Klimate or Goretex, the many seams make seam leakage a potential problem. A two-to three-person dome tent weighs 3–4 kg.

## Bush types and trees

Our hill and mountain lands can be divided roughly into two vegetation areas: rain forest and tussock grassland. The variety of trees in any area depends mainly on weather factors, but also on the ground on which the forest grows — factors such as soil type and drainage being important. In wet (often western) areas below 900 m, podocarp, rimu, totara, matai and miro trees are common. In some areas these have combined with black beech. The sub-alpine forest is usually red or silver beech in the North Island and mountain beech in the South. Often a scrubby belt of leatherwood, turpentine wood and scrubby beech exists between the sub-alpine forest and the tussock tops. The tussock tops usually begin at about 1,000–1,300 m above sea level, depending on the harshness of the climate.

An understanding of the forest and alpine vegetation will be repaid to you in comfort, particularly when it comes to lighting a fire in bad weather.

## Fire lighting

The art of fire lighting has become much less skilled with the advent of fire starters (wonderful little things they are). A couple of cubes carried for each day in the bush will prove of great value. Some people carry bits of candle, and others strips of rubber, as fire-starting aids. Neither is as good as "Little Lucy's" or similar, but the candle is better than rubber as it concentrates its heat rather than spreading it.

An ideal camping scene. Everyone is busy contributing to communal comfort. The fire has been built on a flat stone away from the damp ground. The girl has arranged a shelter over it to keep the rain off until the fire becomes strong enough to survive by itself. Dead wood only is being collected. A few lengths of malleable wire carried in the pack make superb billy hooks.

In wet weather it is crucial to use the correct fuel, but please use it with care as it is very easy to desecrate an area of bush if several parties camp in the same place. It is worth pointing out to youngsters that even dead wood has its value in nature's cycle — so use any wood sparingly. Many parties these days carry primuses as a mark of care for the forest.

A light axe can also be a great aid, but once again fewer people are carrying these because of the need for conservation. If an axe is to be used, a half-axe head and handle is the best combination for general tramping use.

### Stages of lighting a fire in wet weather

1. Gather a lot of small, dry material. In wet weather kindling can often be found under wind-fallen trees and banks. Sub-alpine scrub is often good burning material, even when green and wet.

   The main trees to avoid are kaikawaka (a mountain cedar that looks like totara with lots of branches), rewarewa (honeysuckle) and konini (fuschia). Sub-alpine beeches are also sometimes difficult to light, particularly when wet.

   Dead standing wood will be found to be the best. Many living trees also have dead branches and twigs which are useful.

   It is best to camp where good wood is plentiful, but if you are forced to camp in an unsuitable area you may have to forage outside that area or even descend to a lower altitude to find suitable wood.
2. If the ground is wet or damp, build your fire on a flat piece of wood or on a large, flat stone — wet ground really retards a struggling fire.
3. Place the fire-starting aid on the dry spot and build a heap of small material over it. During heavy rain it may be necessary to put up a temporary shelter to protect the fire in its early stages.
4. As the fire catches, put on large pieces of wood. Wood with sharp edges will catch more easily than that with round edges.

It is a good idea to keep a stock of fire-lighting material under shelter at night, in case the weather is wet in the morning.

## Stoves for the outdoors

There are many types and they are generally expensive items of equipment. The three illustrated form a good cross-section of what is available.

Gas Stove (Bluet) — a light and convenient stove to use, but the fuel is expensive and the stove is not as quick at boiling water as the others illustrated.

White spirit primus — cheap to run and very popular.

M.S.R. (a touch of the space age) — this is relatively light but initially expensive and it can be temperamental if clean fuel is not used. It requires careful maintenance. The M.S.R. burns petrol or kerosene and, when running well, is very efficient.

# Navigation

## Navigation by sense

It is most important that people venturing into the wilds develop a sense for the land — this becomes a sense of direction when you relate the locality of the particular area to the main land mass. There are many nebulous traits which give people a feeling for direction: the wind blowing on the side of the face; the direction in which the predominant wind has bent trees; the side of the trees on which moss grows; the rising and setting point as well as the angle of the sun; and so on. While the sense of direction may appear a mystical ability, it is really only a result of keen observation.

I had been tramping 10 years before I learned to use a compass properly, and yet I had already been on expeditions to the great ranges of the world. While instructing on British courses fellow instructors were horrified at my lack of expertise with map and compass, but while they stumbled around in mist with their noses buried in map and compass I would be using senses developed over a long period. One of the main reasons for my development of these senses was the lack of accurate maps of the New Zealand back country. As a result, accurate compass work was just about impossible for us Kiwi trampers.

There is a hackneyed old rule that if you get lost follow water because it must run to the sea. (In fact, these days it usually runs to a power station!) This idea is often more trouble than it is worth because in a geographically young country, like New Zealand, streams inevitably go through difficult gorges. There is no hard and fast rule, but in most steep areas, if you have the choice between reasonable going on

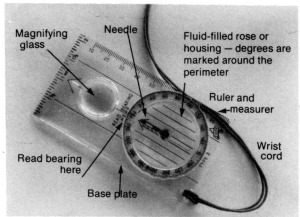

A Silva compass — the easiest compass for general hill use and orienteering. The prismatic compass as used by the armed forces is more accurate, but it is not as convenient for general use.

ridges and dropping into a stream, the ridges will often be better. It is obviously best not only to develop this natural sense if possible but also to learn the skills of map and compass work.

## Navigation by map and compass

Unfortunately, the needle of the magnetic compass does not point at the North Pole. It points at a magnetic field which is roughly in the Hudson Bay area, which, to complicate matters further, seems to be continually on the move. However, the movement is so slight that it can be disregarded for the purposes of normal bush and mountain navigation.

So our compass needle points at Hudson Bay, while the tops of our maps are aligned with the North Pole. This magnetic variation is countered by swinging the map 20 degrees to the left of magnetic North.

## PART OF A STANDARD TOPOGRAPHICAL MAP

The lines drawn across the map are grid lines which have no relationship to latitude and longitude, which is also marked (top left, 39°00'00" latitude; 175°30'00" longitude). These maps are provided with a chart of reference symbols and scale a reliability diagram (giving survey details), conversion tables and details of grid references. Before using a map, make sure you familiarise yourself with them.

Scale: This map has an imperial scale. New maps are generally scaled in metrics (i.e. centimetres to the kilometre), with each grid square representing an area 1,000×1,000m. *Lands and Survey Department*

*Railways*

| | |
|---|---|
| Double or multiple track | |
| Single track | |
| Road over railway | |
| Railway over road | |
| Level crossing | |
| Station | |
| Tunnel | |
| Cutting | |
| Embankment | |
| Bush tramway | |

*Roads*

The representation on this map of a road or track does not necessarily indicate a public right of way

| | |
|---|---|
| Three lanes or more wide | |
| Sealed | |
| Metalled | |
| Unmetalled | |
| Unfenced | |
| Tracks: | |
| Vehicle | |
| Foot | |

*State Highways:*

| | |
|---|---|
| National | metalled / sealed |
| Provincial | metalled / sealed |

*Bridges*

| | |
|---|---|
| Two lanes | |
| One lane | |
| Concrete | C |
| Wooden | W |
| Steel | St |
| Suspension | S |
| Footbridge | f |
| Ford | F |

*Electric Power Lines*

Transmission lines: (over 11,000 volts)
Pylons; actual positions
Poles; conventional spacing

Distribution lines:
(11,000 volts and under)

---

### Grid references

A grid reference states your position on a map. If you were at the point marked X (Papakai) on the map illustrated, your position would be on grid line 09 (vertical line) and halfway between 93 and 94 (horizontal lines). The grid reference for this position is 090 935. This is a six-figure grid reference. If you were at the point to the east of Papakai marked ●, your position would be 105 935. Each main grid square is divided (in your mind) into 10 mini-squares. The position marked ✹ (see enlarged inset) is grid reference 12.2/93.8 or 122 938.

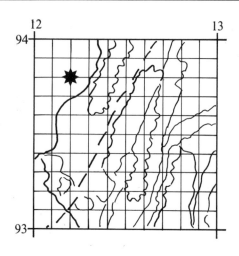

52

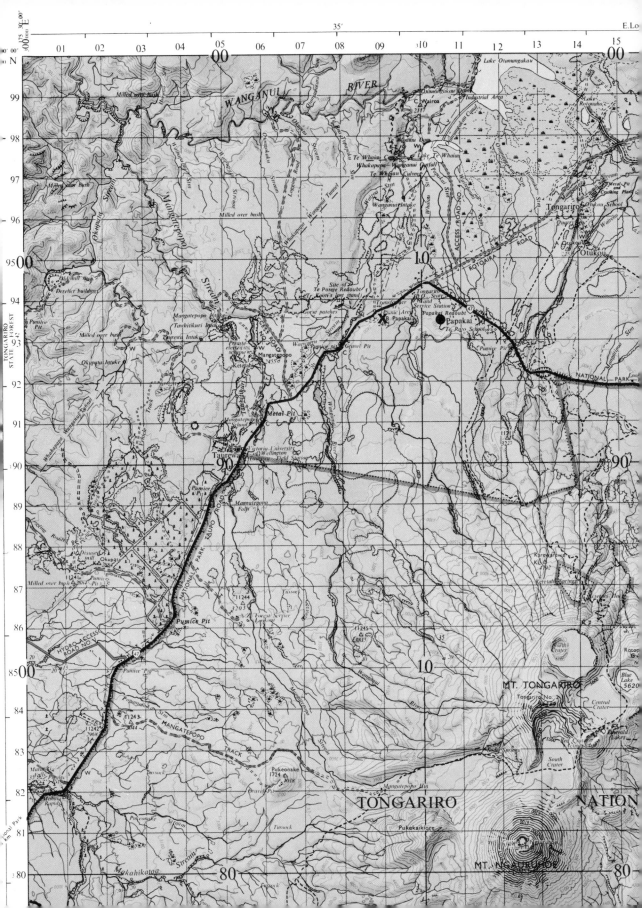

## Map bearings

If the weather is misty, if it is dark or if you are in thick bush with no vision in the direction of travel you should try to steer by using your map and compass as follows:

### Exercise A

1. Put your compass on the map with the edge of the base plate along the proposed line of travel.
2. Rotate the compass rose (housing) so the parallel lines marked on it are parallel with the grid lines on your map.
3. Read the bearing.
4. Subtract 20 degrees from the bearing you have just read.

For example, I wish to travel from the summit of Ngauruhoe to the summit of Tongariro

in "white-out" conditions (that is, limited visibility when mist makes the sky and ground seem to merge in a single mass). The bearing to follow, arrived at by following the above instructions, is 343 degrees. (See illustration.)

This technique is best because it can be done without unfolding or putting down the map; however it can also be confusing for students and you may have more success teaching the skill by orientating the map properly first as follows:

### Exercise B

1. Orientate the map by placing the compass on it — the edge of the base plate should be parallel with the grid lines on the map, and the rose should be zeroed.
2. Rotate the map until the red needle points at 20 degrees. (Now the land around you is in roughly the same position as shown on the map.)
3. Put the edge of the compass along the proposed line of travel.
4. Turn the rose until the needle points at N (360 degrees).
5. Read the bearing on the compass.

This is a longer process and is potentially less accurate.

## Taking a bearing on a land feature

You could do this if you were steering blindly and suddenly had a brief view of your objective (for example a clearing in mist or bush).

### Exercise C

1. Aim the compass at the object you wish to reach.
2. Turn the rose until the needle points at N (360 degrees).
3. Read the bearing.

This, of course, is a magnetic bearing.

## Walking on a bearing

It is virtually impossible to walk in a straight line toward an unseen objective, even on flat ground, unless one aims at intermediate objects in line with the eventual objective. The following example applies in the bush:

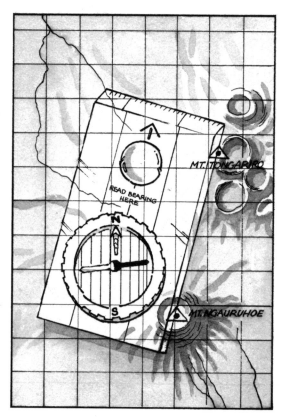

Working out the bearing from one point (Mount Ngauruhoe) and another (Mount Tongariro).

Taking a bearing on a land feature.

*Exercise D*

1. Having worked out the bearing, rotate the compass until the needle points at N (360 degrees).
2. Sight along the compass (edge of base plate is best) and note a tree on that line at the furthest point of vision.
3. Walk to the tree and repeat the exercise.

On a snow plateau in the mist it may be necessary to send one of the party out on a line directed by the navigator until the navigator begins to lose sight of the marker person. Then the navigator should walk to the marker person and repeat the process.

**Finding your position**
*Exercise E*
Cross bearings

1. Positively identify at least two points in the distance—three if possible. It is best if these features are spread through at least 180 degrees.

2. Take a bearing on each point in turn and transfer each bearing to the orientated map. (See Exercise B for orientation of map.) The bearing will be transferred to the map by:
   a. Placing the corner of the compass on the identified point (on the map) and rotating the compass until the needle points at N (360 degrees).
   b. Drawing a line along the edge of the compass from each identified point.
3. Where the lines intercept is your approximate position. This will usually be inside a small triangle.

**Other navigational aids**
The Maori people must have been great navigators to travel the oceans as accurately as they did without modern aids. Today we seem to have lost such abilities and I have yet to hear of anyone successfully using the stars or various oft-recommended techniques to navigate by in the bush when lost. However, I do have a friend whose boat was rolled over by a big wave south of Tahiti and, in the subsequent struggle to survive, he lost all navigational aids. He had a skimpy knowledge of celestial navigation and managed to steer (after several weeks) to Samoa. A study of the stars, while not often useful in outdoor pursuits, can, however, prove very interesting.

# Rates of progress

The difference in tramping rates in the hills between a slow person and a quick person is phenomenal, but there are some very general rules that may help you anticipate progress.

The old army rule that a man can walk at 6 km/h has no application in the bush, as even on a good track it is extremely difficult to walk at this speed. The British hillwalkers use a system of assessing speed called Naismith's Rule, but this is also generally inaccurate in New Zealand bush. A rough guide for anticipating progress in our bush country is as follows:

*Relatively level ground:*
1. Good track — speed up to 5 km/h.

2. Untracked but open bush — speed up to 3 km/h.
3. Thick, tangled bush — speed 600–1,000 m/h.

*Ascent*: Approximately 300 m/h.

*Descent*: Approximately 600 m/h.

Using these rates the described trip along the Tararua Ranges would have taken 45 to 50 hours instead of the 18.5 hours it took me. (There's no end to differences in rates between trampers of various levels of fitness and determination!)

## Food

There are many factors to consider in selecting food for a trip into the outdoors, but it is most important that you choose food you like and are used to. Also select food which is compatible with the rest of the party's supply. It should have good nutritional value and be light in weight. Food requiring cooking should be kept to a minimum because:

a. the conservation of fuel, whether it is carried by you or not, is important.
b. the time involved in meals will be less, thus early starts will be easier, late finishes less trying and quick meals during the day more convenient.

A medium day's tramp will burn about 4,000 calories. (During the trip along the length of the Tararuas I burned about 13,500 calories.) Carbohydrates such as sweets, sugars and bread are easily converted to energy, and therefore a large proportion of food carried should be of this type. Fats are more difficult to convert, but they are very high in calories and such goodies as salami and fatty bacon are well worthwhile. A high protein content (meat, eggs, cheese and so on) is desirable, but only really important on long trips, say over one week. Protein is the body builder, so long journeys with little protein intake will result in some body deterioration.

It is possible to live and work hard on as little as 0.5 kg of well-selected food per day. For example, 1 kg of fat can be converted by the body into 9,000 calories. On the other hand, about 1 kg of carbohydrate or protein can be converted into about 4,000 calories.

Select unprocessed food if possible — wholemeal bread, brown rice and so on. It will probably be harder to get and kids might say things like, "Ooh, this bread's got wheat in it," but your body will soon prove to you the worth of good buying. Good, solid, wholemeal bread also has the advantage of not breaking up in your pack.

During my early tramping days millet became a fad as good-value food for the hills. A friend of mine heard about this and went to buy some. He chose a hardware store with a very good salesman.

"Hi, I'd like 2 lbs of millet."

"Oh, millet. Hmmm. . . . We don't have millet but we do have bird seed — you know, it's more or less the same stuff."

"Oh well, yeah, I suppose so."

"That'll be 3s 6d. Have a good weekend!"

The bird seed didn't taste any better cooked!

The tramper's diet, especially on long trips, should not differ markedly from a normal home diet. People have different likes and dislikes and will pack their food kit accordingly (rendering even the best recommended food lists superfluous). However, I have made the following suggestions to make the task a little easier. Remember that this is the *minimum* amount required per day.

*Breakfasts*: 85 g bacon (fatty) fried quickly and eaten on 85 g bread, and a brew to wash it down. A good alternative is to make a little more stew than necessary the night before, as leftovers will make a quick breakfast. Some people like muesli, which is a quick and worthwhile food (see muesli recipe).

*Lunch and snacks*: three or four Tawhitikuri biscuits, 60 g salami, 85 g bread, 30 g butter, 30 g honey or jam. Wash it all down with a brew.

*Dinner*: 60 g bacon, 100 g mince meat (or

dehydrated or tinned meat), 30 g peas or onions. (In fact, I've never been able to see the value of peas in the hills, but I guess they give a little taste and touch of normality.) Stew it all up and, of course, wash it down with a brew.

*Puddings*: 60 g instant pudding or custard, dried apples or apricots.

*OPC Scroggin*: As well, it is worthwhile carrying a bag full of scroggin, say about 125 g per day, containing nuts, raisins, ginger, glucose powder, jelly beans, peel, chocolate pieces and chopped, dried apricot pieces. (A little brandy or your favourite liqueur poured all over it is very nice, but don't tell the Mountain Safety Council!)

### Salt intake

The value of salt in water should not be overlooked. The body requires both of these in balance. Dehydration is a really incapacitating condition and makes people more susceptible both to frostbite and hypothermia. The body also needs salt to help it retain fluids. Lack of salt will cause headaches, nausea, loss of appetite and muscle cramps. While tramping it is crucial to keep up one's fluid intake, which should vary from 2 to 5 litres per day, depending on heat, work rate and altitude. (At altitude, dehydration is a real problem.)

### Useful recipes

*Tawhitikuri biscuits*

Lots of good, solid Tawhitikuri biscuits are well worth the effort of a cooking spree before a trip. They don't break up during carrying and you will save food — mainly because you will probably be so exhausted after finishing one that you won't feel like anything else. Besides, all your teeth will probably be broken!

*Ingredients* (for 40 biscuits)

450 g butter  
450 g sugar } Melt together until thick and bubbly  
8 tbsp golden syrup  
680 g oatmeal or rolled oats  
680 g wholemeal  
salt

1 tbsp cinnamon  
1 tbsp ground ginger } Optional  
230 g raisins, peanuts etc.

Mix all dry ingredients with the bubbly mixture — a little water may help. Either roll out on a floured board and cut with a biscuit cutter, or (easier) make little balls and put on to a greased tray and press with a fork.

Bake 15 to 20 minutes at 180°C (350°F).

Some of the biscuits should now be taken to the top of a small cliff and hurled earthwards. If they survive this abuse they are now ready to carry into the hills and rivers to be eaten with care and great pleasure!

*Mangatepopo Muesli*: (1 serving)  
4 tbsp rolled oats  
125 g (1 cup) chopped walnuts, almonds or cashews  
½ tbsp coconut  
1 tbsp sultanas  
½ tbsp glucose  
1½ tbsp wheat germ  
½ tbsp milk powder  
Mix all ingredients.  
Fresh apples and bananas are worth carrying on short trips to chop in to the muesli.

## Survival
### Attitude

Survival is not generally dependent on the equipment you have with you. The important factor is your attitude — your willingness to cope, no matter what.

People with the correct attitude might be able to manipulate situations to their advantage. The correct attitude will also help you cope with everyday problems. (People who don't want to work and would rather collect the dole are probably bad survivors.)

Man is the most successful survivor amongst the animals, not only because he has a large brain and fingers and because he is a fighter, but above all because he is adaptable. He can live and be happy anywhere from the freezing Arctic to the steamy tropics: from the depths of the ocean to the summits of the highest mountains. No other single species can exist in such varied conditions.

A few years ago it was considered impossible to run a mile in less than four minutes or to climb Everest without oxygen. These things weren't impossible because man lacked the strength — they were simply *thought* to be impossible.

Imagine the barriers that may be broken down if people allowed themselves totally free thought. This is the essence of survival — free thought and a minimum of fears. All the textbookery in the world won't help someone survive in the outdoors unless his or her attitude is right.

The survivor needs to develop two types of thought:

a. Lateral thinking — when every possibility is scanned mentally and the correct conclusion is reached.

b. Convergent thinking — when the goal is defined and all other irrelevancies are dismissed. The survivor then heads singlemindedly towards the chosen goal.

Combined with the right attitude, a compact survival kit will give you better than a fighting chance if a survival situation arises.

**The survival kit**

This should be packed in a flat tin or plastic box which is compact enough to be carried in a pocket at all times — especially when you are not carrying your pack. The container should be as robust and as waterproof as possible, and the contents should be inside a sealed plastic bag (preferably the survival bag).

*Contents*: a coil of nylon line
a candle (half)
a notebook and pencil (small)
a tough plastic bag (survival bag — large enough to get inside)
two boxes of waterproof matches
a roll of sticky tape (preferably Sleek)
knife (Swiss army type)
fish hooks
a piano wire or guitar string for snaring animals
aluminium foil for cooking
a few Oxo cubes and barley sugars (in a small box)
a small compass
survival notes

# 4

# The rocks

*A mountaineer, when he meets with a formidable obstacle,*
*does not hold onto the rock by means of his feet and hands*
*only, but he clings to it like a caterpillar, with every*
*part of his body that can come simultaneously into contact*
*with its roughened surface.*

Francis Galton, *Art of Travel*, 1872

WHEN I first began work on the Outdoor Pursuits Centre there was very little rock climbing in the central North Island; in fact, the mountaineers' old excuse that New Zealand didn't have very much good rock was still in vogue. We had climbed a little in the Mangatepopo valley of the Tongariro National Park and also occasionally on the cliffs on the western edge of Lake Taupo, but there were only a handful of relatively unattractive climbs. In the next few years we put up many of the great routes that now bring climbers back weekend after weekend to the beautiful red and yellow volcanic rock.

During Easter 1971, Eric McMahon, Roger Bates, Allan Sheppard and I established a route called "The Skull" on the Karangahape Cliffs. (A final pitch to the climb was added by Noel Sissons and me in 1975.) This was a climb of about 150 m, so named because there was a skull and some bits and pieces of what probably was once a revered Maori near the base of the climb.

Encouraged by this success, and also by the discovery of these relics of the past, Eric and I returned a few weeks later with the talented and well-known pathologist, writer and filmmaker Mike Gill. Mike never gave the impression that he was an active climber, but he has that special "ape-like" build which makes climbing second nature and will allow him to go on climbing until he is 60 or more. Eric is a very quiet and accomplished Scot and tremendously good company in the mountains. It was our intention to try to reach the Karangahape Cliffs by canoe, and our search for a road down to the lake edge was finally successful when we discovered the road to Whanganui Bay — approximately 6–8 km west of Karangahape.

We picked our way down the muddy track, which wound spectacularly down a deep canyon protected on either side by impressive cliffs. Finally the track came out into a lovely hidden bay with the lake stretching away into the misty distance. On the west side of the bay a large stream spilled from a canyon over a waterfall and into a sluggish stream where trout rose lazily as if snapping at the raindrops. On the opposite side stood a very compact cliff about 80 m high. It wasn't as big as Karangahape, but the rock looked so much better — besides, the rain had taken the edge off our enthusiasm to paddle around to that inaccessible cliff. We settled into one of the old shacks near the lake side and, after the usual ritualistic brew, encouraged ourselves to go and have a peek at the cliff.

Me on the first ascent of Park Lane (18) Manga-tepopo Valley. This is a relatively precarious layback — one feels a little like a gate in the wind. If you swing too far to the left you'll be off. (Note the double 9-mm ropes.) *Noel Sissons*

The Whanganui Bay main cliff. Tibia is the chimney on the right. Ray Button and I can be seen climbing "Champagne" (grade 20), just left of the centre. *Corrina Dingle*

"Looks bloody impossible," said Mike, squinting up into the rain.

Eric was quiet.

"Come and have a look at this chimney," I shouted enthusiastically. A vertical chimney split the cliff from somewhere up in the tangled bush.

"The work of an amazing architect," I muttered, bending my neck backwards to get a look at the upper part of the basalt column which had partially separated from the main cliff, leaving the chimney behind it as a possible route upwards.

"I reckon it might go," I said, tearing the equipment from the pack and beginning to tie onto the rope. We cowered in to the base of the cliff trying to keep out of the rain, which wasn't too much of a problem as the cliff was so steep.

I arranged a selection of nuts onto a gear sling, together with a couple of pitons and a hammer. Then off I clambered, initially up a vertical wall covered with pockets; when these ran out I went into the depth of the chimney, which was just the right size, I observed gratefully, to jam with my backside on one wall and my knees on the other. I wriggled upwards towards some blocks which were jammed firmly between the two walls. Eric and Mike watched with interest, looking away occasion-

Inside Tibia — Noel Sissons on the first pitch. *Graeme Dingle*

Inside Tibia — me on the second pitch. *Noel Sissons*

ally to rest their necks (which were bent from looking straight up) and to avoid the shower of grit that rained down, as evidence of my struggle.

"It's more like bloody caving," I shouted down from my dark perch, having no idea, apart from a vivid imagination, of what caving was really like!

I soon reached the first block, and, after hauling myself up on to it, I jumped up and down to assure myself that it was solid — it was. Above me was another block. As I began to clamber on to it I noticed a bone. "Christ, a human femur," I shouted, as if I had discovered the crown jewels.

"What does the pathologist say?" I called, as I threw it down to Mike to examine.

"Ignoramus!" he pronounced. "It's a tibia." So the climb became known as "Tibia".

"God only knows," I thought, "how a human tibia got here. Maybe some poor sod back in Maori times took refuge and got his leg stuck," I thought morbidly, as I continued up the chimney.

There was no chance of using any nuts or pitons in the chimney because the walls were blank, but the rope passing through the chock stones made a perfect runner — not that there was much chance of falling out of the chimney. The biggest problem people have in chimneys is going up, not down. The most common mistake is over-jamming oneself.

Above me, the walls were almost perfectly smooth with the occasional pock-mark to offer a meagre foothold or handhold. I was very excited, particularly because in this upper area of the chimney all sides now appeared to be closed in as if I was climbing up into the top of a bell. However, a shaft of light from above gave me hope of an exit through which I could squeeze. A couple of narrow ledges gave me the opportunity for a short breather, which I felt I needed. I was grunting and panting very hard. I struggled on and, finally, nearly 30 m above Mike and Eric, I squeezed out on to a ledge. I was still confined between the two walls, but was now able to poke my head out of the chimney and look directly down at them. I was filthy dirty from the tunnelling and in a comical mood.

"Hullooo-dere .... Belay on!" And as I brought up the rope I looked out through the driving rain over the huge lake. It looked infinite with the waters disappearing into the rain and mist.

Eric and Mike chimneyed up quickly, although once they arrived on the ledge they complained about their kneecaps being abraded. I noted with some pleasure that they were also breathing very heavily and were extremely dirty. We changed over the belays so I could continue on the sharp end.

I now left the sanctuary of the chimney to do a long, eerie step across a wall, which was greasy with lichen, to reach the relative sanctuary of a shallow chimney with its open side facing the lake — the view was tremendous. Loose blocks prompted me to proceed carefully, and I protected myself with two nuts as I went.

After 15 m the shallow chimney ended, and I scrambled once more behind the detached column and into the continuation of the original chimney. I began to fossick around for a belay when, to my astonishment, I found a very neat stack of bones concealed beneath an overhang in the chimney — all limb bones: tibias and fibulas, femurs and humerae, and so on.

"Bloody hell!" I shouted incredulously. "A whole stack of bones." Mike and Eric quickly came up, and I was relieved to see that Mike acknowledged my find.

I wonder how they got here? By rope ladder from the top perhaps?"

"I hope so, because here we are with all our modern fancy gear — if a Maori in a flax skirt with a bundle of bones in his arms could climb this, I'm giving up!"

The stack was very neat, really a bundle rather than a stack, with all the bones laid parallel — we calculated about four body sets of limb bones.

Mike had a good look around for other bones while Eric arranged a belay, and I pondered the problem of climbing the wall above. It was still raining hard and the walls were covered with greasy lichen. I decided to attempt the wall of the main cliff, but it looked far from easy. To overcome the problem of the greasy holds, I removed one of my friction boots, took off the sock, replaced the boot and pulled the sock over the top of the boot. Thus, I had one rubber sole for dry holds and one woollen one for wet holds. I considered myself pretty smart, but didn't say so as I was still far from the top of the cliff.

I left the sanctuary of the chimney and began up a thin crack, but was discouraged by a hollow-sounding block. I finally struggled around it and reached the base of a dirty but wider crack. Higher, it looked as if I could jam both my hands and feet in this crack and, more importantly, it looked as if I would be able to position a good nut. I decided I needed some good protection before committing myself to this crack, but could not find any from my current position. I therefore calculated the size of the good crack above me and tied a specially selected nut to three or four joined slings. Then, like a gaucho, I spun the nut around my head and let it fly. Miracles happen — the nut shot straight into the desired crack and jammed fast. I clipped in and climbed the crack with only a few grunts. Several relatively easy moves led to the scrub at the top of the cliff.

Tibia was certainly a climb, but we had no idea the climb would become a really popular classic.

On the second ascent with Noel Sissons and Ian Jowett I climbed the chimney direct, which makes a much more satisfactory final pitch.

Ascentionists now climb to the top of Tibia pinnacle then do an airy stride to gain the main cliff.

---

## Summary of rock climb at Whanganui Bay

*The first ascent of Tibia by Mike Gill, Eric McMahon and Graeme Dingle: 75m, grade 16. (Refer to the section on grading on page 91.)*

This climb, although not considered very hard today, was significant in that it opened up one of the best crags in New Zealand.

Today there are dozens of great routes at Whanganui Bay; Tibia is one of the easiest and there are many over grade 20. Many of these hard climbs were established by the Aucklanders Robbie McBirnie and Rick McGregor, who mastered their crack-climbing technique on the lower rocks of Mount Eden Quarry.

I have climbed Tibia dozens of times and it has lost none of its charm, but it has always surprised me that on the last pitch I climbed the greasy crack to the right of the chimney rather than the route that is now climbed inside the chimney. First ascents are always very different from subsequent ascents, particularly if the route becomes a "trade route". No-one can ever recapture that feeling of exploration — the sense of commitment, of seriousness and the joy of discovery and success.

---

# Rock climbing in New Zealand

An experienced mountaineer once said: "Rock climbing is all right, but it is not like the real thing," and for many years the few crags which were climbed around New Zealand were regarded as only practising places for the mountains. These would be used on weekends and the mountains would be visited only once or twice during the year — usually around Christmas.

There was an apathetic attitude to rock climbing in New Zealand, and if Kiwi mountaineers had a choice they would always climb snow rather than rock. Consequently, we generally became great snow plodders and terrible rock climbers: usually the opposite was the case in Britain. A much-used example of this is the first ascent of Kanchenjunga (the third highest mountain in the world) when the British climbers Joe Brown and George Band made the final ascent very much on rock, and Norm Hardie, the New Zealander, and Tony Streather made the ascent mainly on snow — each pair claiming that theirs was the best route.

The common excuse that New Zealanders gave for their snow fetish was, "Oh, New Zilin' rock is terrible, like piled up Weetbix (and nearly as nutritious). Yeah, New Zilin' is just too young, geographically speaking, to have good rock." This is only partly true. We do have reasonable rock in the volcanic areas or where it has been weathered — for example, by pounding seas, like Ti Point and Titahi Bay; also by glacial action. In the central Southern

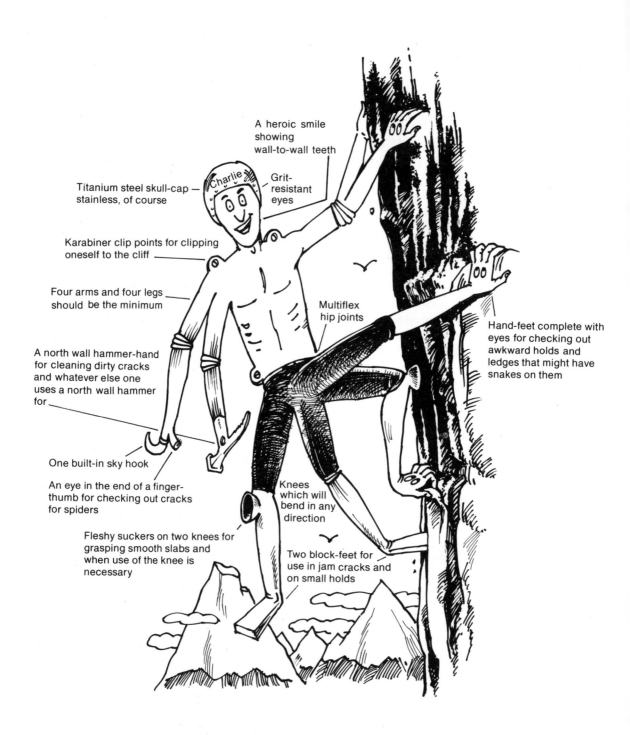

A heroic smile showing wall-to-wall teeth

Titanium steel skull-cap — stainless, of course

Charlie

Grit-resistant eyes

Karabiner clip points for clipping oneself to the cliff

Four arms and four legs should be the minimum

Multiflex hip joints

Hand-feet complete with eyes for checking out awkward holds and ledges that might have snakes on them

A north wall hammer-hand for cleaning dirty cracks and whatever else one uses a north wall hammer for

One built-in sky hook

An eye in the end of a finger-thumb for checking out cracks for spiders

Knees which will bend in any direction

Fleshy suckers on two knees for grasping smooth slabs and when use of the knee is necessary

Two block-feet for use in jam cracks and on small holds

The ideal rock-climbing physique — inside is all guts!

Alps the rock tends to be good where it is red or brown and steep; the darker rock is often bad, but on steeper faces it can be quite tolerable. The main source of crag climbing is in volcanic areas such as the central North Island and Banks Peninsula near Christchurch.

The point is that rock climbing has now become an activity in its own right and no longer needs to be justified as the ugly sister of mountaineering.

Ironically, the best rock climbers are not usually top mountaineers, and vice versa.

## The rock climber's physique

As with chess, there is no ideal rock-climbing physique (unlike rugby, where it helps to be big and white). Although many of the greats have been short and muscular (Brown, Whillans, Chouinard), just as many excellent climbers have been tall and skinny.

When I was 20 years old I was taken by Carlo Mauri (a great Italian mountaineer) to meet the Italian Ambassadress. She took a calculating look at me and said, "Ah ... I have heard Sir Edmund Hillary is number one; this little man is number two. Now I see why. You are just like a squirrel." (All hairy, cross-eyed and buck-toothed, I thought!)

It helps immeasurably to have two strong hands (three would be better!) and two supple legs, preferably with feet on the ends (sometimes feet on knees can be a great aid!), but that's about as far as it goes.

A thinking head can be a help, but it is sometimes a hindrance because of stray thoughts like "What am I doing here?" which usually don't aid the upward passage.

## Finding a cliff and choosing a line

A very experienced climber can often assess the quality of rock and the approximate grade of a line without actually rubbing noses with it. This ability is a reasonable measure of a climber's experience. If holds can be seen from below, the climb will usually be of a relatively easy grade (probably at least below severe — or grade 14).

New Zealand cliffs can be grouped into four main categories: sea cliffs, volcanic, limestone and alpine rock. The rock composition, its history and age are important, but in New Zealand most rocks are geologically very young.

### Sea cliffs

Usually bad rock except where the sea has weathered it, and this weathering usually wouldn't extend more than one pitch above mean sea level. There are many potentially good sea cliffs on the offshore islands, particularly in the Hauraki Gulf — these are mainly unexplored (1983).

Established sea cliffs throughout New Zealand are at Long Beach, Dunedin; Titahi Bay and Baring Head, Wellington; and at Ti Point north of Auckland.

### Volcanic

This rock is usually of the columnar-jointing type where parallel cracks and right-angled corners are prominent; or it is solidified lava where the rock is very rough and holes are abundant. Volcanic climbing areas are common in New Zealand: Mount Eden Quarry and Karangahape Gorge, Auckland; Whanganui Bay and Mangatepopo Valley, central North Island; Castle Rock and Rapaki Rock, Christchurch.

### Limestone

This is probably the most unreliable type of rock to be found in New Zealand. There are no well-developed areas as yet, although there is potential in both the Waikato and Nelson areas.

### Alpine rock

This can be divided into two areas, with sedimentary schists and argillites being common throughout the Southern Alps, and igneous granites offering good climbing in Fiordland and to a much lesser extent in the Nelson Lakes area. Sedimentary rocks, unlike granite, must be well weathered (usually by glacial action) before they are much use for climbing. This is the type of rock that has turned most New Zealand mountaineers off rock climbing.

If a preliminary investigation of a cliff from the ground fails to convince the would-be climber that it is a climbing possibility, the only other option is to abseil down the cliff from above, but this option calls for the utmost caution. There are many dangers — one of these being the possibility of marooning if anchors cannot be found midway down the cliff and if the descent requires more than two abseils.

If such a descent is to be undertaken, those involved should also be proficient in the use of ascender techniques (see page 84).

There are major advantages in this kind of reconnaissance:
1. The rock, including quality, holds, availability of belays and stances can be scrutinised.
2. If there are good abseil points you can be assured of good belay points.

My own approach to crag climbing is more akin to mountaineering — I find it more realistic to approach a crag line from the bottom and to take my chances with the unknown as I go up, just as I do on a mountain wall. However, as I have explained, rock climbing is a different game from mountaineering, and many great crag climbs simply would not exist if first ascentionists had not abseiled down and checked and cleaned (gardened) the route before climbing it.

Generally, you would be ill-advised to embark on a new route with an inexperienced companion, as loose rock, unknown runner positions and belays can lead to complications which would require a competent second.

Me practising aid climbing on a tree. Note how I am standing with my left foot in a sling behind me to aid balance.

## The difference between free and aid climbing

A move or series of moves are classified "aid" (sometimes also called cheating) when artificial means other than the natural rock are used to make progress (for example, pulling up on a nut or piton). This form of climbing is often used to overcome difficult moves on alpine climbs when speed is essential and ethics are of less concern. Aid climbing on crags is gener-ally frowned upon and is considered unethical as someone else may be able to climb the route "free"; besides, one never knows when some smart alec is hiding around a corner waiting to show you that it can be climbed "free".

Many climbs that were previously referred to as aid climbs, or required partial aid, have now been climbed totally "free" — in some cases ascentionists use the piton scars of previous ascents as holds. Often the free ascent is of a relatively low grade, showing that the first ascentionists either were not very good or, more likely, did not try very hard to do the climb free before resorting to aid.

## Movement

This is the single most important aspect of rock climbing. If you move in a careful and calculated way you may go through an entire climbing career without falling off. It is not only your equipment that keeps you safe; in fact, equipment is secondary to movement. In free climbing, anyway, if you follow all the "rules" and move properly, the equipment (rope and protection) need never come into use.

A basic set of movement rules is as follows: (eat a prune each day!)

1. Try to maintain three points of contact on the rock — two hands and one foot, or one hand and two feet. Thus, only one limb should change position at any one time, minimising the risk of a mistake.
2. Try to maintain balance through your feet. This is not always possible (for instance, in laybacking or overhanging moves), but you should always try to take as much weight through the feet as possible. Certainly, never forget your feet, and try to watch them at each move.
3. Try to stand upright with your hands below shoulder level. This ensures that most of your weight is taken by your feet and helps conserve strength in hands and arms. An exception to this rule is on low-angled friction slabs, when it is usually best to stick your bum out to put as much weight over the feet as possible.
4. Always work out the move ahead before launching into it. Sometimes, say on strenuous ground, it will be necessary to work out several moves in advance so that once you commit yourself you don't have to hang around wasting strength.

### Testing holds

If the climber is moving in control there will

**A climber in balance and control**

Try to stand as upright as the angle of the rock allows — don't lie against the rock.
Try to move only one limb at a time. Work out moves first before launching into them.

be plenty of opportunity to test holds before using them. This can be done simply by tapping the hold with the palm or the ends of the fingers. An obvious hollow sound indicates that a hold is loose. Some holds, although loose, may still be used if force is exerted in the correct way. Generally it is better to pull downwards rather than outwards on loose holds. However, make sure you place good runners below loose sections, no matter how many times you have done the climb before.

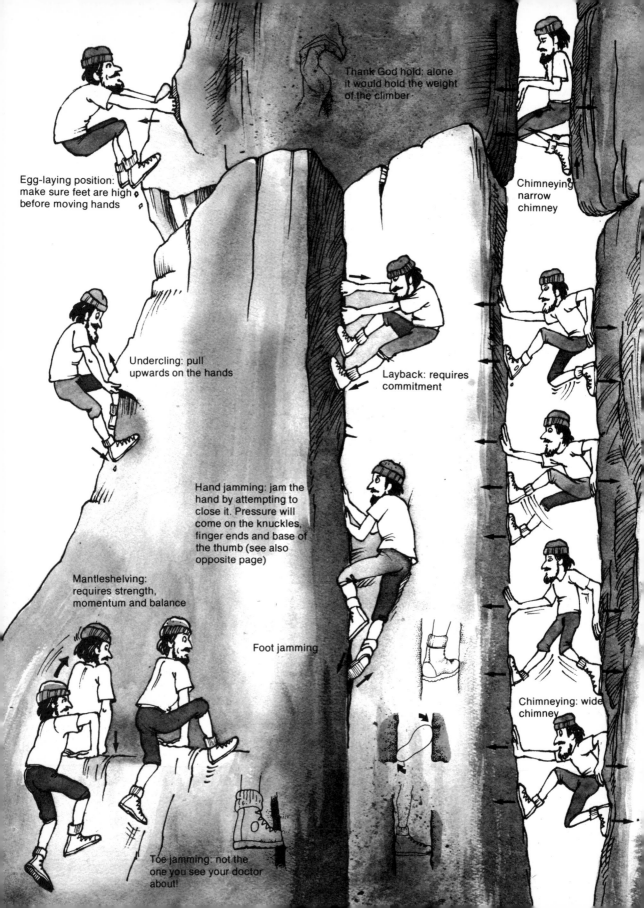

Thank God hold: alone it would hold the weight of the climber

Egg-laying position: make sure feet are high before moving hands

Chimneying narrow chimney

Undercling: pull upwards on the hands

Layback: requires commitment

Hand jamming: jam the hand by attempting to close it. Pressure will come on the knuckles, finger ends and base of the thumb (see also opposite page)

Mantleshelving: requires strength, momentum and balance

Foot jamming

Chimneying: wide chimney

Toe jamming: not the one you see your doctor about!

# Movement techniques

The pinch grip: thumb and fingers are opposed

Bridging: wider chimney

Slab climbing

Bridging

Fist jams: these are best placed just above constrictions in a crack

Hand traversing

Cling holds

off width: yuck!

Finger jamming: often a good hold can be achieved by pulling outwards and downwards on a finger crack, but sometimes it will be necessary to jam the knuckles where the crack constricts and simply pull up on this knuckle jam. In such cases it is better not to have a vivid imagination — *just do it*

# Equipment

Rock climbing, more than most activities I know, has its gear freaks. Some of them don't get far off the ground — they're probably weighed down by too much gear or safety attitudes. Some labour up climbs, encumbered with enough gear to set up shop somewhere on the cliff; and many, it seems, become disillusioned and set up shop at the bottom of the cliff, much to the delight of other climbers who are always on the lookout for cheap gear. At the risk of

**Aid climbing on a roof**

Slings on these aid points will help minimise rope drag by reducing the angle of the rope

Etriers or rope ladders

Boots are more comfortable than friction boots for extensive aid climbing

Haul rope for bringing up gear and to use if retreat by abseil is necessary

sounding "over the hill", my advice is to start slowly and learn to know what you need through experience. You should strike a happy balance between safety and overkill. It is a refreshing experience to climb occasionally lightly laden or even with no gear at all. (Well, at least keep your knickers on.)

To set oneself up well is a fairly expensive business, but, as I have already said, it is not necessary to have everything, nor to have the most expensive gear to start with. The well-set-up rock climber may look like the one in the picture, but there is a minimum equipment list, too:

1. *Rope*: Locally made hawser-laid rope, approximately 35 m long is adequate. However, it must be nylon and you should inspect every centimetre of the rope before buying. If the rope has irregularities of any kind don't buy it. I recommend 11 mm diameter (number 4), although on certain serious climbs, particularly loose, multi-pitch climbs, a double 9 mm rope may be safer.

2. *Footwear*: Rubber-soled sandshoes or cheap road shoes will do (don't buy good road shoes — they cost nearly as much as rock boots). I strongly recommend that a pair of rock boots (E.B.s, P.A.s or similar) be purchased early in your career. It is good for technique to climb occasionally in mountain boots.

3. *Nuts*: A small range of Chouinard hexentrics (say numbers 3–8) and two stoppers on wire (say numbers 3 and 4) are quite sufficient to start with. The hexentrics should be fitted with kernmantel rope slings to the maximum size that the holes in the nut will take (9 mm will be the heaviest rope needed). The rope should fit easily through the holes so that the nut can be moved on the sling if necessary.

4. *Slings*: Half a dozen tape slings (25 mm tape) are invaluable. Each sling will take about 1 m of tape.

5. *Karabiners*: You will require approximately one per article of protection; eight plus two spares would be quite sufficient to match the preceding gear list.

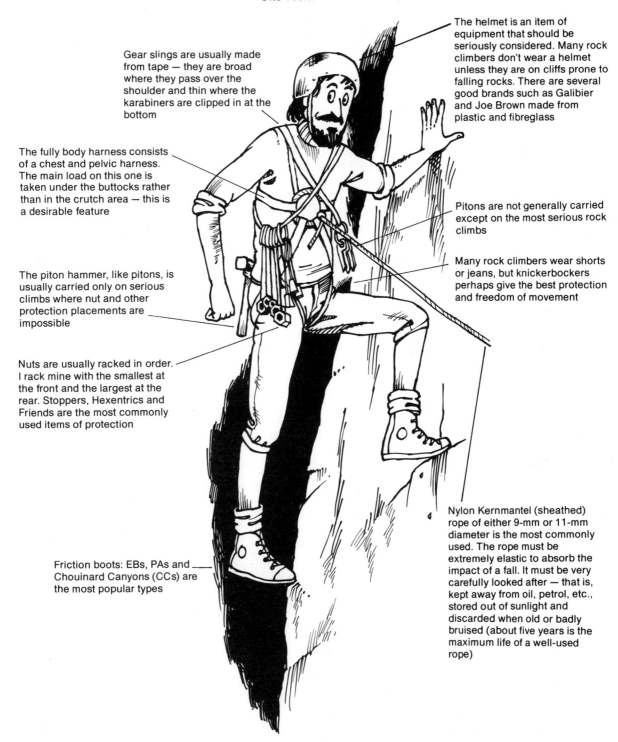

The helmet is an item of equipment that should be seriously considered. Many rock climbers don't wear a helmet unless they are on cliffs prone to falling rocks. There are several good brands such as Galibier and Joe Brown made from plastic and fibreglass

Gear slings are usually made from tape — they are broad where they pass over the shoulder and thin where the karabiners are clipped in at the bottom

The fully body harness consists of a chest and pelvic harness. The main load on this one is taken under the buttocks rather than in the crutch area — this is a desirable feature

Pitons are not generally carried except on the most serious rock climbs

Many rock climbers wear shorts or jeans, but knickerbockers perhaps give the best protection and freedom of movement

The piton hammer, like pitons, is usually carried only on serious climbs where nut and other protection placements are impossible

Nuts are usually racked in order. I rack mine with the smallest at the front and the largest at the rear. Stoppers, Hexentrics and Friends are the most commonly used items of protection

Friction boots: EBs, PAs and Chouinard Canyons (CCs) are the most popular types

Nylon Kernmantel (sheathed) rope of either 9-mm or 11-mm diameter is the most commonly used. The rope must be extremely elastic to absorb the impact of a fall. It must be very carefully looked after — that is, kept away from oil, petrol, etc., stored out of sunlight and discarded when old or badly bruised (about five years is the maximum life of a well-used rope)

**A well-dressed rock climber**

## Knots

The only knots a rock climber needs to know are the figure-of-eight, half hitch, the double fisherman's and the Prusik, although the bowline and clove hitch are also handy. Two others (not really knots) well worth knowing are the Italian hitch and the Bachmann knot.

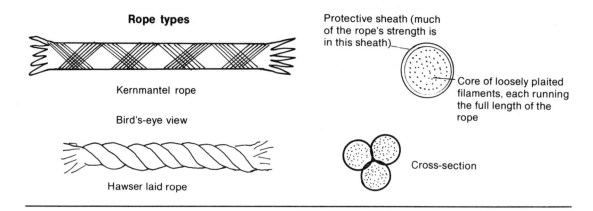

**Rope types**

Kernmantel rope

Bird's-eye view

Hawser laid rope

Protective sheath (much of the rope's strength is in this sheath)

Core of loosely plaited filaments, each running the full length of the rope

Cross-section

The **figure-of-eight knot** is strong, simple and easy to untie after strain. The knot can be tied either on a bight of rope or, if you wish to tie directly onto a harness, it can be tied using a single line. In this case a figure-of-eight should be tied on a single strand about 50 cm from the rope end. The end is then passed through the harness and follows back through the previously tied figure-of-eight.

The **double fisherman's knot** is used for joining two ropes of similar thickness, particularly in preparing an abseil using two ropes. The single fisherman's knot is similar, but has only one loop on each side and is consequently more difficult to untie after strain.

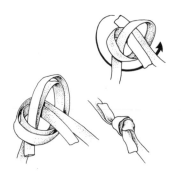

The **tape knot**. The major problem with this kind of knot is that it is inclined to work loose. Therefore it must be continually checked and tightened. Many climbers prefer to use the single fisherman's knot for joining tapes.

The **Prusik knot**. Because this knot tightens readily and can be difficult to work when wet, many climbers prefer the Bachmann knot. For extra grip, especially on Kernmantel rope, another loop is often added to the Prusik.

The **bowline knot** — a particularly good climbing knot as it is very easy to untie after strain. Its main drawback is that it can work loose, therefore it should be finished with a "full hitch" when it is used as the main tie-on knot. The bowline can also be tied on a double rope (bight).

The **Bachmann knot** — a very useful knot for rescue work and for use in ascending the rope.

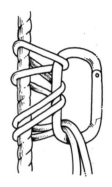

## Coiling a rope

A

This is the normal method of coiling a rope for storage. The circumference of the coil is approximately 2.5 m (i.e. the span of your arms). A knack for twisting the rope with each coil will need to be acquired to avoid getting kinks in each loop. The easiest way to get rid of such kinks is to drop the loose end of the rope over a cliff before beginning coiling. The kinks will then shake down the rope as it is coiled in.

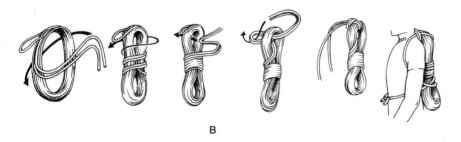

B

This is very useful when the rope is simply being coiled for carriage to the next place of use (for example, the next abseil). It is much quicker than (a) because coiling begins from the centre (the double rope is coiled) and the finishing tie is quicker.

## Protection

Falling off while rock climbing is not necessarily akin to ending your life — in fact, a properly protected rock climber should survive many falls during his or her career. Unfortunately, this is not true in mountaineering, so rock climbers who aspire to alpine climbing should be very careful not to take their psychology with them.

The following methods of protection from falls are usual.

### Roping up

*Tying the rope around your waist* using a figure-of-eight knot is the simplest means of tying on. However, hanging on the end of a rope using this system is not the most comfortable experience on earth (but it is effective in discouraging falls). Certainly, at an early stage, and for most instruction situations, this is probably the best method of attachment to the rope. But it should be remembered that a climber simply hanging on a rope tied around his waist will suffocate after minutes.

*The swami belt* is simply a length of tape wound several times around the waist and finished off with a fisherman's knot. The rope is then tied through all loops of tape. This system has few advantages over simply tying the end of the rope around the waist, but in the event of a fall, the load is a little more distributed.

Tape knot or single fisherman's knot finished off with full hitches

The swami belt — still popular because of its simplicity.

*Manufactured harnesses* come in three main types: *the pelvic harness*, the *chest harness* and a *combination* of both.

Chest harnesses worn without a crutch strap are dangerous because it is possible to fly out of them — and they tend to be uncomfortable on most women. Of the pelvic-type harnesses, the most comfortable for men are the type with

The Whillans harness has many good features such as giving one the ability to cope with the calls of nature without having to remove the harness. The karabiner (A) is a crucial part of the design. When the strain comes on, the weight should be taken on the buttocks. If this does not happen it becomes a dangerous harness for men (some people reckon it should be used in conjunction with a cricket box or Morris Minor hubcap!). *Corrina Dingle*

two thigh straps rather than one broad crutch strap (like the Whillans), which has been known to cause grievous bodily harm and certainly causes me enough discomfort and apprehension to dissuade me from using one. (However, I also recognise Don Whillans as a

Full body harness. The main load will be taken on the buttocks (A). The chest harness and pelvic harness are connected by karabiners (B & C) so the pelvic harness can be removed without untying from the main rope. *Corrina Dingle*

fierce warrior and wish to be most careful with my comments.) If you'll forgive me, Don, most women find the Whillans harness fine. Of all the manufactured harnesses, the one I find best is the combination harness. The main problem with such a harness is complications caused by the need to remove clothing — unless you can down your trousers or remove an article of clothing from the upper body without untying, the harness is of doubtful value. The one pictured allows all these contortions in perfect safety.

*Self-made tape harnesses*, which involve loops around the tops of the thighs, can easily be fashioned and are quite satisfactory although they have limitations when you want to remove your pants!

### Self-made harness

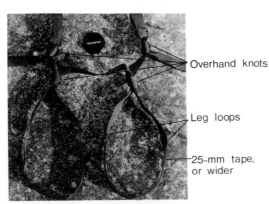

Overhand knots

Leg loops

25-mm tape, or wider

First step through the loops and pull the harness up.

Tape ends are passed around the waist and through the small loops.

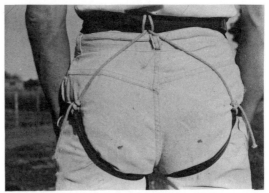

The cord attached thus will stop the leg loops dropping down the backs of the thighs.

Finish off with a tape knot or a fisherman's knot, as for the swami belt. The climbing rope is passed through both small loops and behind the tape which passes around the waist. The load will be taken evenly between the waist, buttocks and upper thighs. *Corrina Dingle*

**Runners** or running belays (described by some as a cowardly second)

These are cunningly designed devices intended to stop the climber hitting the ground, and they fall (humph!) into four main categories: natural runners, nuts, pitons and camming devices.

*Natural runners* include chock stones jammed in cracks with a sling placed round them, natural rock spikes that will take a sling, and trees.

*Nuts or artificial chocks* were developed as the result of British climbers' opposition to the use of artificial aids, namely pitons in this case. There was a saying that "The hand that would knock a piton into English rock would shoot a fox", and some climbs put up in Britain by continental climbers using pitons were quickly reclimbed by the British using their "more pure" technique. The climbing world can be very grateful to the British for this attitude, as it led to cleaner climbing techniques. In those old days (actually, about when I was starting!) British climbers would carry a pocketful of stones of varying sizes and these they would adeptly fiddle into cracks, and around them we would arrange the runner sling. Of course, before long the smart guys began carrying their chocks already attached to the slings, in the form of engineering nuts with the sling through the hole in the middle. These were soon replaced by aluminium nuts, and today there are many varieties. The ones I find most useful are the "Hexentrics" and "Stoppers" made by the American climbing genius, Yvon Chouinard.

---

**"Clean" climbing gear**

Using the tape sling with natural features as runners and belays.

The **tape sling** is usually made of 25-mm tubular of flat tape, tied with a tape knot or a fisherman's knot. The most convenient length is 50–55 cm (long enough to be carried over the head and across the trunk, like a bandolier). Some climbers like to carry one or two slings twice this length, but I find it easier to join two or three together if necessary

In the case of a **nubbin** like this, thread the sling through itself to help grip the rock better. Also note the advice given for the spike runner.

**The thread belay**

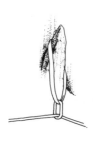

The **spike runner**. Sometimes it may be necessary to weight down such a runner with a nut or several karabiners to stop the sling riding off with the friction of the rope. A longer sling will also reduce this possibility

**Well-rooted trees** can make great runners and belays

**Natural chock stones** are very useful. These first inspired the use of artificial chock stones (for example, nuts)

*Cams*: Many nuts, the Hexentrics included, are designed to cam under load and this is particularly useful when parallel-sided cracks are encountered. The more complex American-designed camming devices called "Friends" can even be employed successfully when cracks are flared, or where you need an urgent placement (as we say in the trade).

## Nut slings used as runners

Hexentric jammed lengthways

A stopper. These are also available with curved sides to assist them to hold in the rock

The Hexentric jammed in a camming position

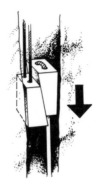

In narrow parallel-sided cracks where stoppers will normally not hold, they can be stacked like this

The slings on nuts are made from climbing rope or tape. Use the maximum-sized sling the nut holes will accommodate (up to 9-mm rope, 25-mm tape). The sling is tied in the normal way (see page 73) and generally needs to be no longer than 30 cm.

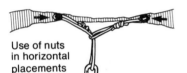

Use of nuts in horizontal placements

Opposing pulls used to guard against a pull from up or down — say in the case of a main belay

Good

Not good because under stress the sling will break easily at the nut

Many nuts, particularly very small ones, and stoppers, are fitted with a swaged wire sling. In many situations it is best to increase the length of this sling by clipping a tape sling between the wire and the climbing rope. This will reduce the chances of the nut being levered out of position by the rope drag

**Friends** — these little demons have revolutionised crack climbing as they can be inserted quickly and will hold even in flared cracks. Care must be taken not to force them into cracks too near their minimum size, or to push them too far into the crack, otherwise removal can be impossible. Their high cost is a disadvantage.

*Pitons or pegs* were developed shortly after the turn of the century, and were used vigorously up until recently, when suddenly piton became almost a dirty word as a result of the tremendous conservation move throughout the world. It is true that pitons do scar the rock badly, and their indiscriminate use, where it will spoil the pleasure of others, should be discouraged. However, on very serious and loose cliffs particularly their necessity is acknowledged. Pitons come in two main types: soft and hard — although soft pitons are almost obsolete because of the difficulty of recovery. With the perfection of nuts, the most commonly used pegs are thin, blade types. These are particularly useful in the Southern Alps.

Some routes do require the use of fixed pitons. These *in situ* pitons should be left in place.

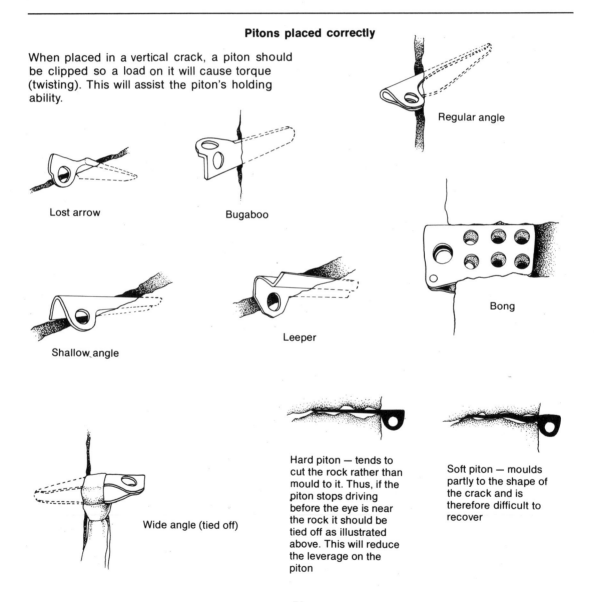

**Pitons placed correctly**

When placed in a vertical crack, a piton should be clipped so a load on it will cause torque (twisting). This will assist the piton's holding ability.

Regular angle

Lost arrow

Bugaboo

Shallow angle

Leeper

Bong

Wide angle (tied off)

Hard piton — tends to cut the rock rather than mould to it. Thus, if the piton stops driving before the eye is near the rock it should be tied off as illustrated above. This will reduce the leverage on the piton

Soft piton — moulds partly to the shape of the crack and is therefore difficult to recover

### Karabiners

These are now made from very light alloys. (Some are even made of hollow tubing.) The strength of the karabiner lengthwise and in some cases across the gate will be clearly stamped onto the metal. Karabiners without this marking should be treated with suspicion. Do not use an aluminium karabiner after it has sustained heavy impact, such as falling onto rock from higher than 4 m. Locking karabiners have their uses in instructional situations, but these are not widely used by the experts. In all cases the gates should be easy to operate with one finger or the thumb.

The D-shaped karabiner allows the strain to be taken as close to the back (strongest side) as possible

The modified D — a well-shaped karabiner giving the strength of the D and the added advantage of a gate that opens wider

The oval karabiner is perhaps not quite as strong as those previously mentioned, but it is convenient to use

### Fixed belays

A belay position is determined by one or more of the following factors: the rope running out, the availability of a comfortable stance and, most importantly, the availability of suitable anchor placements. Before runners were perfected, belays were positioned as close as 5 m, but with better protection the distance between them has grown so that on many modern climbs pitches are as long as 50 m.

Once the anchors (be they nuts, pitons or natural anchors) have been chosen, tying on is then completed by the use of the clove hitch knot, the figure-of-eight or the thread. The thread has the advantage of being fully adjustable (for example, if the anchor point(s) happens to be some distance from the stance, the thread tie-on method is the best). This is done as follows:

1. Place the anchor(s).
2. Clip the rope into the anchor(s) – don't tie any knots.
3. Move to your belay position taking with you rope A.
4. Tie on as illustrated with three half hitches.

**The thread belay**

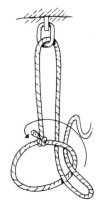
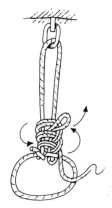

cliff

you

The simplest belay is to loop the rope directly around a spike or tree, but, unless speed is essential, this technique is not good because it wears a metre or so of rope near the tie-on point and this will eventually weaken it.

Generally, you should not rely on only a single anchor, and you should also consider that because of runners, a falling leader may exert an upward force on the belayer. This may send the belayer flying up in the air, so if possible it is a good idea to design the belay to take an upward force. Another extremely important aspect, often overlooked, is that the belayer should always be able to escape from the system in the event of the belayed person becoming unconscious (either because of a fall or being hit by a falling object) and hanging on the rope. This escape should be practised.

The actual belaying of the rope can be effected in three ways:

a. *Body belay*: This could be either a waist belay or shoulder belay as shown. Your choice of method should mainly depend on whether you are tied on to the rope at the chest or at the waist. These belays can be painful, and are mainly superseded by friction-brake belays. However, they are still valuable for guiding or instructing where the second may need some help (hauling) from above, or when the rope is frozen or otherwise difficult to manage.

b. *The Italian friction hitch*: Generally these friction-brake belays should be used from the body rather than direct on to the anchor(s).

c. *The Stitch plate*: This device works in a similar way to the Italian hitch, but is smoother to use and easier on the rope. The small eye of most figure-eight descenders can also be used.

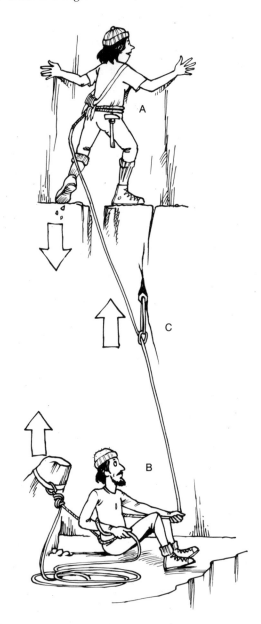

**The spike belay**
These two climbers are dicing with death. If the leader (A) falls off and the single runner holds, the belayer (B) will be pulled upwards and the sling (C) may be lifted off the spike. If the runner then fails with the weight of two people on it, they will be in trouble. B should attempt to find an additional belay which will take an upward pull. If this is not possible A should place more than one good runner.

**The waist belay**
This climber is tied directly onto the rope — an uncommon practice among modern climbers.

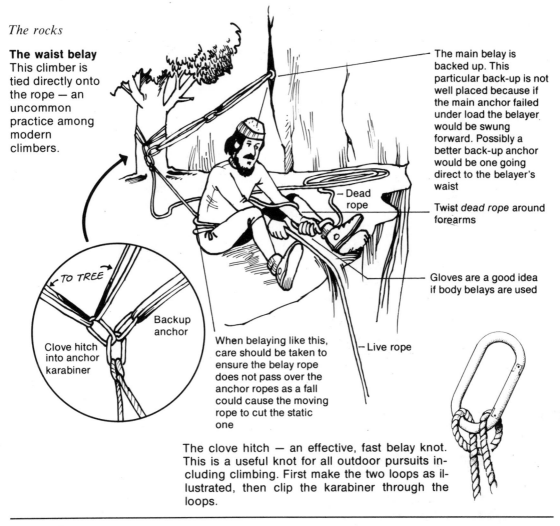

The main belay is backed up. This particular back-up is not well placed because if the main anchor failed under load the belayer would be swung forward. Possibly a better back-up anchor would be one going direct to the belayer's waist

Twist *dead rope* around forearms

— Dead rope

Gloves are a good idea if body belays are used

← TO TREE →

Clove hitch into anchor karabiner

Backup anchor

When belaying like this, care should be taken to ensure the belay rope does not pass over the anchor ropes as a fall could cause the moving rope to cut the static one

— Live rope

The clove hitch — an effective, fast belay knot. This is a useful knot for all outdoor pursuits including climbing. First make the two loops as illustrated, then clip the karabiner through the loops.

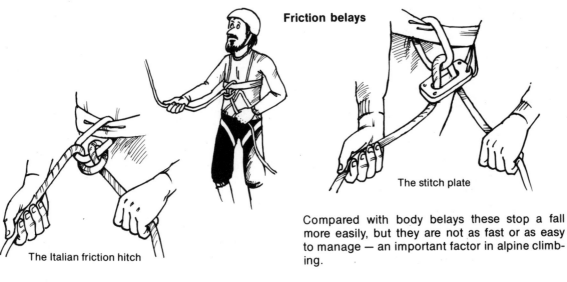

**Friction belays**

The stitch plate

The Italian friction hitch

Compared with body belays these stop a fall more easily, but they are not as fast or as easy to manage — an important factor in alpine climbing.

## SELF RESCUE FOR ROCK OR CREVASSE EXTRACTION

### Shoulder belay

A is leading, attached to the rope by a pelvic harness. B belays in full body harness. When tied on at the chest it is best to use a shoulder belay if you choose a body belay. The dead rope is grasped like a jug handle. Be careful to keep the rope away from the bare flesh of your neck.

### The monkey hang

A has fallen and the runner has failed. Because she is tied on around the waist and is hanging free of the slope it is crucial that the load be taken off her waist. The following steps are made:

1. She turns upside down to take the load off her hips
2. She slips the sling over her feet and brings it down to her upper thigh
3. She now turns right-way up. Meanwhile, B has twisted the dead rope around his foot to free his right arm. He has also readied a sling to fix the rope

## Escaping from the system

(see also previous illustration). A has turned upright so the sling under her thighs is now taking the load. B has let go of the rope with his hands. His right foot is taking the weight. He has fixed a Prusik to the live rope (see page 73) and clipped this sling to the anchor. He can now untie from the system and give assistance to A.

The rescue procedure followed from this point could be as for ascending if A is uninjured and has the equipment (see use of ascenders, page 41), or hauling loads (see page (85).

Another system that is simple and effective is for B to throw down the dead rope with loops tied in it for A to climb. Alternatively, the dead rope can be thrown down with one loop tied in it. This rope is fixed back to the anchor with a Prusik, exactly like the live rope. A then stands in the loop while B takes up the live rope until it is tight. The dead rope is then raised a metre or so, and once again A stands in the loop. This system is slow but not too strenuous.

B has now escaped from the system and can decide which of the following courses of action is best:
1. To do nothing while A uses an ascending technique to climb the rope back to B.
2. To assist A back to the ledge.
3. To haul A back to the ledge.
4. To descend to A and render assistance.
5. To lower A to the nearest ledge.

## Communication

I am continually horrified by stereotyping trends in all outdoor pursuits. In rock climbing this often becomes obvious in the calls climbers use. There is nothing worse than going for a Sunday outing to a crag in the peaceful countryside and hearing 100 climbers all calling out the same jargon: "I'm off .... I'm there .... Hold .... Take in .... That's me .... Climb ...." and so on!

There is, of course, a need for clear communication as climbers often cannot see each other and in some cases hearing is made difficult by wind and other factors. If calls aren't clear, the confusion can be incredible. For example, if the second climber calls, "I'm gripped .... Take in slack", expecting a tight rope, and the leader only hears "Slack", he will feed out a heap of rope making the second's problem worse! Or, when my mate Ray Button called to me, "You got me" while leading a hard climb recently, I thought he wanted me to hold him so I pulled the rope tight thereby wrenching him from the rock.

The British system, which I think overdoes it, is as follows: when the climber leaves the ground or ledge he calls, "Climbing" (so his friend knows he is not going scuba diving!). When he gets his first running belay on he says, "Runner on". The leader can now prepare to be projected up in the air at any moment! The second then calls to the leader, "Six metres," telling the leader that there are 6 m of rope left and to start looking for a belay. When the leader reaches the belay stance he calls, "I'm there", so his friend knows he is not somewhere else, I presume. Obviously, I find a note of ridiculousness in some of these calls, but let me now write again as a responsible adviser, with the safety of my readers weighing heavily on my pen.

The normal recognised calling system is as follows. The leader, after tying on and preparing to bring up the second, says, "Taking in". When the rope becomes taut the second calls, "That's me" so the leader knows that the rope

is not just caught around a rock. The leader, having heard the last cry, calls, "Climb when ready". Once he has untied the belay and is ready to climb, the second calls, "Climbing".

Some other calls that climbers use are "Slack" (not when the climber is unhappy, but when he requires more rope). "Tight" (when the climber needs a tight rope), "Take in" (when the climber wants slack rope taken up) and "Hold" (when the climber hopes that his insurance policy is paid up!). There is also a "Below" call when something is dropped (usually by British climbers on to French climbers!).

If there are other climbers on the cliff it is a good idea to qualify calls with your friend's name, or you may have the wrong climber reacting to your calls.

A rope of climbers should decide on their own calling system; with experienced people this usually becomes fairly cryptic, and a lot is left to the perception of the other rope members. This is the style to aim for.

## Big wall techniques

On difficult multi-day climbs it is impossible to climb with the equipment, food and fluid on your back. Therefore the system most teams use is as follows:
1. The leader climbs the pitch and, at the top, belays himself and the climbing rope.
2. He then hauls up the kit using his trail rope.
3. The second uses ascenders to climb the pitch, taking out protection as he proceeds.

### Use of ascenders

These gadgets are used to climb a rope — for instance, when fixed ropes are adopted on a big climb or expedition, when a climber falls over an overhang and is hanging free, when a mountaineer falls into a crevasse, in seconding some very hard climbs and in reclimbing an abseil. There are several different means of attaching yourself to the rope, such as Jumars, Cloggers, the Prusik knot and the Bachmann knot, but once this is done the climbing technique is more or less the same. I have found the safest and most effective system is the one shown, which was developed in Yosemite, where ascenders are used probably more than anywhere else in the world.

## A climber using ascenders

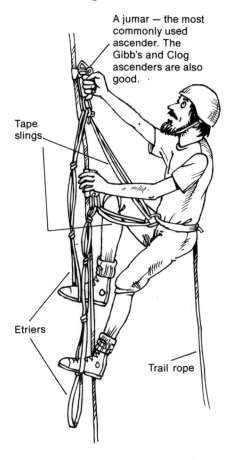

A jumar — the most commonly used ascender. The Gibb's and Clog ascenders are also good.

Tape slings

Etriers

Trail rope

Stand as upright as possible, using the hands on the ascenders for balance, and move your legs alternately. Some climbers use large bands of rubber (for instance, cut from truck tubes) attached to etriers to hold the feet in the loops.

## HAULING TECHNIQUES
(also used for crevasse rescue)

### Hauling a load weighing up to approximately 45 kg

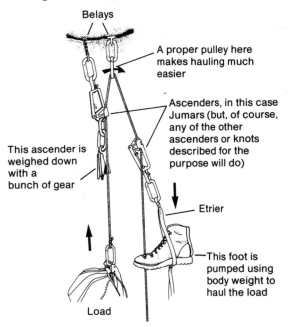

Belays

A proper pulley here makes hauling much easier

Ascenders, in this case Jumars (but, of course, any of the other ascenders or knots described for the purpose will do)

This ascender is weighed down with a bunch of gear

Etrier

This foot is pumped using body weight to haul the load

Load

### Hauling a load weighing more than 45 kg

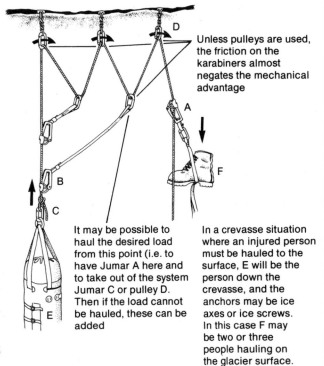

D

Unless pulleys are used, the friction on the karabiners almost negates the mechanical advantage

A

F

B

C

E

It may be possible to haul the desired load from this point (i.e. to have Jumar A here and to take out of the system Jumar C or pulley D. Then if the load cannot be hauled, these can be added

In a crevasse situation where an injured person must be hauled to the surface, E will be the person down the crevasse, and the anchors may be ice axes or ice screws. In this case F may be two or three people hauling on the glacier surface.

# Abseiling

### The Tawhitikuri Stream abseiling incident

Peter met his group of 10 from Te Kuiti on the front steps of the Outdoor Pursuits Centre. It was a clear, sunny day and his friendliness won the kids over in a few moments.

He discussed the day's activities as if they were making the choice. Yes, they were keen to do a navigation exercise to the old Ketetahi Mill then descend the Tawhitikuri stream and, sure, they had all heard about abseiling and wanted to abseil over the waterfall. The headmaster, Ken, who was visiting the centre for a day would accompany them. Although he stifled the group's enthusiasm to begin with, he soon became just another one of them — a big kid enjoying himself in the bush.

They spent an hour learning to abseil, then climbed the Taurewa spur through lush podocarp forest. The sun beamed in shafts through the upper canopy of matai and rimu, but the shadows were still dark on the forest floor. The dampness from rain the previous night made the forest smell mysterious, and from far and near the calls of bellbirds and tuis could be heard — when the kids were too puffed to call out to each other. From every deep, shadowy gully came the low roar of water on its mad dash to the Wanganui.

Peter let them lead in turn, Tracy then Glen, then John. They arrived at the abandoned mill just as their stomachs started to indicate that it was lunchtime. After a leisurely brew and some doorstop sandwiches and cheese, they began to move down the gorge of the Tawhitikuri Stream and soon reached the place where the waterfall plummets nearly 35 m into a pool.

Peter took the rope from his pack, found the middle and threw one end over the waterfall. Peering down into the shadows, he could see that it reached the pool. He tied the middle of the rope to a stout tree and prepared the party for descent.

"Who wants to go first? You will do!" and Bill grinned his delight at being selected. He was to abseil on a single rope while Peter safe-guarded him on the other.

"Okay, off you go." Bill slid over the side and soon swung under the freezing shower. With a groan he jerked his way down the rope — lower, lower, lower ... and then suddenly the belay rope stopped. It had run out. Somehow one end of the rope had become shorter than the other. If it was the one Bill was abseiling on it wouldn't have mattered so much, but it was the one tied to his waist.

There was a muffled cry from Bill. Peter peered over the side. "Oh Gawd!" Bill was hanging 3 m above the pool, the rope to his waist as tight as a harp string and already beginning to strangle him.

"Untie the knot," Peter called down.

"What?"

"Untie the bloody rope," he shouted. Bill finally understood and tried to untie the knot, but this was impossible with his weight on it. Peter tried a few other frantic suggestions, but Bill couldn't hear above the noise of the cold water thundering on his head. The rope cutting into his waist was hurting like hell.

"Four minutes consciousness when hanging with a rope tied around your waist," Peter thought to himself. "Shit! What's Ding going to say?" He looked at the headmaster and at the rest of the group — they didn't realise how serious it was. He fossicked around in his pack until he found a knife, and then crawled to the edge to begin sawing through the rope — then he dropped the knife. Groan!

"Anyone got a knife?" All he received in reply were vague "No's".

Below, Bill was already beginning to feel queer.

"Right," said Peter to the rest of the group. "Follow me." They scrambled through the bush until they reached a track. This was the normal route down — a long, greasy mud-slide — lethal in wet weather and usually requiring a rope. "No sense wishing," thought Peter. He shepherded them down as quickly and as carefully as possible, then hurried across to the waterfall.

"Are you all right Bill?"

A strangled moan was his reply.

"Right you lads. Stand here in this pool." They formed a circle, waist deep in water, clasping each other's shoulders — the waterfall was pouring down on their heads. Peter climbed up and stood on their shoulders. At full stretch he could just touch Bill's feet. "Okay Bill. When I push up, you untie the knot."

With a fantastic effort he pushed up taking Bill's weight. Bill's numb thumbs fumbled with the uncompromising knot, but finally it loosened and undid, and a moment later, with a groan of relief, the human pyramid collapsed into the pool. Peter emerged dripping and looked sheepishly at the headmaster, "All in a day's work at OPC."

---

## Summary of abseiling incident on Tawhitikuri Stream

Peter clearly made a crucial mistake in not making sure that both ropes were long enough. This situation was saved by the actions he took after he had dropped his knife. This kind of quick thinking and strength is often the mark of a good instructor or guide. However, the incident needn't have happened if proper abseiling procedures had been followed.

---

Abseiling is potentially a very hazardous activity, probably because danger is not immediately apparent. Learners think that once they are sliding down the rope in control the danger is over. Most accidents, however, occur when the anchors fail or when the abseiling device fails, which can happen at any time. Other dangers include the abseiler being hit by falling rocks and debris, and abseiling off the end of the rope. Unlike climbing, in abseiling there is no back-up once the anchors have failed.

There are many methods of abseiling, but I have described only the ones I prefer:

1. *The classic system* has a greater application because it may be used by trampers, canoeists, and so on, who have no specialised equipment other than a rope.
2. *Using an angle piton as a brake bar* is simple and quick, but a strong screw-locking karabiner must be used as there is a danger of breaking the karabiner gate open with a force it is not made to take.

Descenders, particularly figure-eight descenders, are good, but for mountain work their weight must be balanced against their usefulness.

3. *The karabiner brake* method has its applications in climbing, caving and rescue. There is no limit to the number of brake points that can be put on to increase the friction (for example, during a rescue when two or more people may be lowered at once). This is a good system because it requires no extra items of gear to be carried. However, it can be a bit messy technically because of the number of karabiners involved and the awkward manner of using them.

Popular conception has it that the abseiler springs around, like a gazelle on heat, on his way down the cliff. (I won't blame the army for this misconception!) It is very unwise to put more strain on the anchors than is absolutely necessary, so please be gentle.

## Stages in abseiling

1. Place the master anchor.
2. Tie the two ends of the rope together with a figure-of-eight knot, or tie a knot in each end individually.
3. Coil the rope loosely back from the end knot.
4. Secure the middle of the rope to the anchor. If the rope is to be attached to a sling that will be left in place, one end should have been threaded through this before the figure-of-eight was tied. If two ropes are joined for the abseil, the joining knot should be a double fisherman's. This knot should be placed to one side of the anchor sling, and the correct rope to pull (to retrieve the abseil rope) should be noted by each of the abseilers.
5. Back up the master anchor with another anchor as illustrated.
6. The first person abseils down. If he does not reach the ground he should anchor himself before leaving the rope. If he needs to stop, several turns of the dead rope around the upper thigh will leave the hands free.
7. The first person down checks that the rope runs (can be retrieved). If not, the person at the top of the abseil should adjust the ropes, slings or whatever is causing the obstruction. The first abseiler should then try again to make the ropes run.
8. The other person abseils down, after retrieving any back-up anchors. If another abseil needs to be made the anchors should be set up before the rope is pulled down, and one end should be threaded through the anchor sling.
9. Pull down the abseil rope. If it catches and repeated attempts fail to retrieve it, one of the options is to climb the rope. If this must be done (as a last resort) the rope that is not being climbed must be anchored.

Setting up an abseil

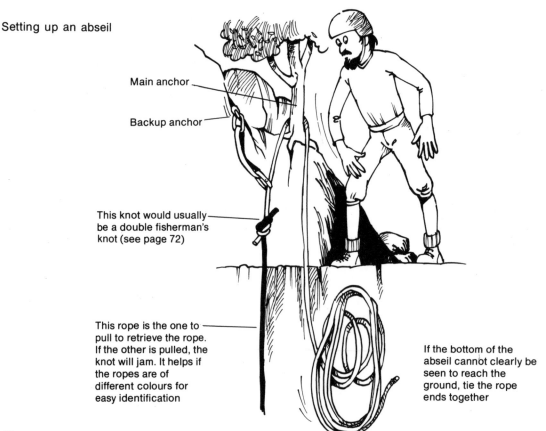

Main anchor

Backup anchor

This knot would usually be a double fisherman's knot (see page 72)

This rope is the one to pull to retrieve the rope. If the other is pulled, the knot will jam. It helps if the ropes are of different colours for easy identification

If the bottom of the abseil cannot clearly be seen to reach the ground, tie the rope ends together

## The classic abseil

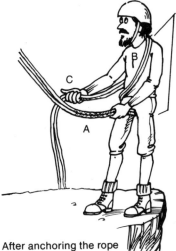

Because the rope must be kept away from bare flesh, singlets and shorts are not the clothing to wear for this system. The more clothing between the rope and the abseiler the better. Nylon clothing may melt with the friction of the rope, so be cautious

After anchoring the rope and so on, step astride ropes A. Pass them around the buttock and across the chest B, over the shoulders and across the back to hand C

Keep your body out from the cliff, holding your feet flat to the rock and a little below bottom level. Keep your feet apart for stability. Hand A shouldn't do too much work. C is the controlling hand. By moving C further around the body to the right, the abseil will be slowed

## The expedition abseil

Very useful when ground is not very steep and when less friction is required than when on a vertical or near-vertical wall.

## The karabiner brake and improvised harness for abseiling

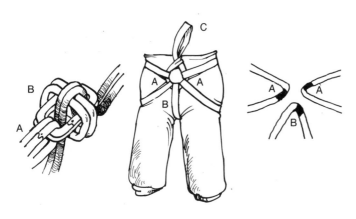

A long sling made from tape or rope can make a good abseiling harness.

1. The sling is held behind the backside with the top side above the rump and the bottom hanging below, while the two end loops (a) are held in front.
2. Now pull a third loop (b) through to the front.
3. Join these three loops with a short sling (c).

If locking karabiners are used they need not be doubled up. It is important that the two A karabiners be used with the two gates opposed. The two B karabiners must be used with gates down.

The karabiner brake is used in a similar manner to any of the other descenders. It can, of course, be used for lowering other people as well as for lowering yourself. The friction can be increased, perhaps for lowering a rescuer and patient, by linking the first karabiner brake to one or two further brakes linked by karabiners.

There have been murmurs in some quarters about banning abseiling as a school activity because of its potential danger. In my opinion, there is, in fact, little danger at this level. The majority of accidents happen to relatively experienced people in serious mountain situations. The most common cause of accidents is the failure of anchors (particularly, old slings breaking) — nylon often deteriorates without any obvious outward sign.

# Grading of rock

Lack of co-operation and international understanding is clearly demonstrated by the number of grading systems that are used for rock climbing. Most of the continents on which rock climbing has been done have their own special grading system. The Europeans adopted a system of 1 to 6, with 6 being accepted as the limit of human possibility. (The limit has now been surpassed.) The British adopted an adjectival system with "Very Difficult" at the top. The top soon became "Severe", then "Very Severe", then "Hard Very Severe", then "Extremely Severe", then "Exceptionally Severe". It has since been modified to include a numerical system.

It is not clear whether the Americans originally intended an open-ended grading system, but that is how it has evolved. They developed a three-part numerical system. The first numbers, 1 to 5, indicate the type of uphill movement; that is, hiking, through scrambling, to roped climbing. The grade of the climb is rated (currently) 0 to 13; thus 5.0, 5.1 and so on. A third rating is introduced — roman numerals I to VI to indicate the overall difficulty of the route. So a technically hard, multi-day climb would be grade VI.

The Australians adopted a similar attitude to grading in that they tried to avoid imposing a ceiling, thus allowing unimpeded development of standards. Currently the Australian grades are 1 to 29.

The Australian system has been adopted on the New Zealand crag scene. Basically, I like the system. It appears to have one main shortcoming, however, as do all the other systems, in that it is inadequate in dealing with mental factors such as exposure, looseness of rock, sustainment and commitment, and so on. The grading is put mainly on the technicality of the hardest move and is then loaded for exposure, looseness, lack of protection, and so on. I would like to see a continued use of the Australian system for grading rock climbs in New Zealand

**Relativity of rock grading systems**

(On multi-pitch climbs of an alpine nature the Europeans and Americans use an additional system to indicate seriousness. See alpine gradings on page 116.)

The relativity of grades as outlined below is approximate only.

| European (UIAA) | British | American | Australasian |
|---|---|---|---|
| 1 | Easy | 5.0 | 8 |
| 2 | Moderate | 5.1 | 9 |
| 3 | Difficult | 5.2 | 10 |
| 4 | Very Difficult | 5.3 | 11 |
| 4+ | Hard Very Difficult | 5.4 | 12 |
| 5− | Severe | 5.5 | 13 |
| 5 | Hard Severe | 5.6 | 14 |
| 5+ | Mild Very Severe | 5.7 | 15 |
| 6− | Very Severe | 5.8 | 16–17 |
| 6 | Hard Very Severe | 5.9 | 18–19 |
| 6+5b | Extreme | 5.10a | 18–19 |
| 7− | Extreme | 5.10b | 19 |
| 7  5c | Grade is | 5.10c | 20 |
| 7+ | now also | 5.10d | 21 |
| 8−6a | broken | 5.11a | 22 |
| 8 | into six | 5.11.b-c | 23–24 |
| 9−6c | divisions: | 5.12 | 25–26 |
| 9 | E1 to E6 | | 27–28 |
| 9+7a | to indicate | | 29 |
| 10− | seriousness | 5.13 | |
| 10 | | | |

with the following modifications to current practice: that the grade of any route is the difficulty of the hardest move and that other factors be noted verbally.

For example:

grade 20 — sustained (on all pitches)

grade 20 — on one pitch only (sustained)

grade 20 — one move

grade 20 — two moves
grade 20 — three moves (more than three
     moves = sustained)
grade 20 — badly protected
grade 20 — loose rock
grade 20 — exposed . . . and so on.

The description of the climb should then take care of whether the climb is grade 20 handjamming or grade 20 laybacking and so on. There is no reason why plus (+) or minus (−) subgrades should not be used with this system (for example, 20+, 20−, etc.).

### Aid·

The American system is good, with grades I to V ranging from easy-aid moves on "bomb proof" pitons or nuts to complex moves on points of aid that only just support the weight of the climber. This cannot be an open-ended system as grade V states that the aid point will only just support the weight of the climber.

# Ethics or the imposed conscience

All games have their rules. But, fortunately, outdoor pursuits are relatively uncluttered by rules and this is why many of us enjoy these activities. I don't wish to have someone blowing a whistle or giving me demerit points whenever I use my knees while rock climbing or every time I fail to 'roll-up' while canoeing.

Of all the activities discussed in this book, rock climbing is probably in the greatest danger of being spoiled by ethics.

I have considered the question of ethics at length, and I have decided that the answer lies in basic philosophy. The old Christian doctrine "Do unto others as you'd have done unto yourself" is no longer acceptable because we don't all want the same things done to us. (God forbid!) I propose a better alternative that suits not only outdoor pursuits but all aspects of life — do exactly what you want as long as it does not adversely affect others ("others" is used here in its broadest sense, meaning not just human beings, but all life). You will need to rely on social conditioning (conscience) to decide whether your action will adversely affect anyone.

As an example, if you apply this philosophy to rock climbing, placing a piton which damages the rock and spoils the pleasure of other climbers as a result is unethical. A brief discussion on the use of chalk is also relevant here. There is no doubt that chalk, which is used by many climbers to assist grip on the rock, is here to stay. On some crags, however, the local climbers don't use it because it makes white patches on the rock and because it marks key holds, thus robbing other climbers of some challenge. Where this is the consensus of opinion at a particular crag I believe it is unethical to use chalk. Other than this, I say climb, canoe, tramp and so on in a way that makes you feel good, and tell the critics to mind their own business.

Outdoor pursuits do not need scrutineers and referees. This is a game of self-adjustment, self-discipline and self-expression, and long may it be so. There aren't many such areas in life.

# 5

# The snow and the ice

*Sometimes a climb is born of a dream, an excitement,*
*a spontaneous desire, often unreasoning; a lovely name, a*
*shape, a story, a memory, and there we are committed to*
*a summit.*  Gaston Rebuffat, *Between Heaven and Earth*, 1962

IF ONE had the gall to talk seriously about an ascent of the Caroline Face in 1968, all but the bravest would catch their breath or think you were a lunatic. Several years later enthusiastic youths would talk about climbing it, or at least the possibility — the route had become a "trade route" or, as Mummery said near the turn of the century after a woman climbed one of his hard routes in the alps, "An easy day for a lady." But this is eight decades later, and I think I'd rather die on a mountain than get beaten to death by a feminist!

The Caroline Face remained inviolate since at least the beginning of recorded history — maybe some adventurers of a long-forgotten civilisation had climbed it, but the people of this age preferred to regard it as an unclimbed and fearful 2,000-m monster that often disgorged thousands of tonnes of ice-like scales, sending its would-be conquerors running for the security of the valleys. Some would-be-suitors had perished threatening its virginity; others had had their wrists severely slapped. However, it was 1970 and the race was on, competition lending bravery to the would-be heroes. Mick Bowie, one of the great Hermitage guides of the 1930s, prophecised in 1970, "For every one who climbs the Caroline three will die."

Modern Kiwi alpinists became concerned whenever an outsider arrived and regarded what they considered to be their preserve — a similar situation, in fact, to the attitude which preceded it by 80 years when New Zealanders feared that Mount Cook might be climbed for the first time by a well-known English mountaineer, Fitzgerald. The locals made an all-out effort, and on Christmas Day 1894 they were successful, much to the annoyance of that English poohbah who vowed he would never attempt Mount Cook. In 1970 it would have been just as humiliating if our modern plum had been picked by an outsider.

The internal competition was hot, too. George Harris, a very influential climber of the '60s, and I made plans to attempt the face with Pete Gough and John Glasgow, two climbers recently back from the Andes, sporting hippylike beards, long hair and ponchos. A meeting was arranged at Mount Cook village on 10 November, so it was with considerable concern that we heard the national news on 8 November: "Two Christchurch men, John Glasgow and Peter Gough, today set out to attempt the notorious Caroline Face of Mount Cook. 'Several people have already died attempting to climb this sheer face,' said the acting Ranger from Mount Cook today. The pair are tonight resting at an altitude of 7,000 feet in preparation to complete the climb tomorrow."

93

Grand traverse of Mount Cook. Harry Ayres, O.B.E. (aged 66, on his eighteenth ascent of Cook) is leading with Lyn Crawford behind as they approach the summit. The east face is on the right. *Graeme Dingle*

"A triumph for long hair." Peter Gough and John Glasgow after the Caroline.

The Caroline Face of Mount Cook from the ridge above the old Ball Hut. The face is extremely foreshortened in this picture. The arrow marks the ice cliffs half way up the face. The route roughly follows the spur between the two arrows (top and bottom). *Graeme Dingle*

Being of a highly competitive nature I desperately hoped they would fail. George said he wasn't bothered — then moments later proved he was by giving his kids hell for nothing!

At 6 p.m. on 9 November Pete and John struggled onto the summit ridge, their emotions summarised by Pete in the words, "You know Glasgow, you're a bit of a prick, but sometimes I almost love you."

For them the pain was over; for George and me it began at Ball Hut, beside the Tasman Glacier, at about 10 p.m. on 10 November. With a day's driving behind us and a night and a day's climbing ahead, sleep was impossible. It was a fitful rest disturbed by visions of effort, pain and death. After two hours, the jangling of the alarm dragged us back to conscious effort — disciplined packing and dressing, choking down a little food and then stumbling forth into the night — feeling far from conquering heroes; in fact we felt more like hunted animals ... hunted by our own drive for success, perhaps?

Above us, rising into the night and eerie in its comparative silence, was the medium we would use to push our lives a little further — maybe to the very brink. One thing I was sure of — we had to do it: we had to try our hardest which maybe even meant dying on that unfeeling monolith. To me, this face epitomised humanity's effort through the ages to raise itself, the irony being from an unknown source to an unknown future.

With head down and feet still uncoordinated in the darkness, I concentrated on the pool of light cast by my headlamp. I was discussing a philosophy of life with myself, justifying this lunacy when I could be snuggled between warm sheets. The roar of an avalanche brought me back to the realm of the hunted animal. Caroline was wreathed in cloud, and above the summit of Mount Cook a large boomerang-shaped lenticular cloud warned us to watch the weather. "We can make our decision on the weather at the ice cliffs," I suggested to my silent friend.

As we gained height on the Caroline glacier, snow conditions became terrible. The soft snow

of the day had begun to freeze over and we broke through the crust at every second step. It was just a matter of being mechanical, and eventually the dreadful plod would end where the face rose abruptly and the real climbing began.

This happened at about 2 a.m. We began up a short snow arête which soon ran into a little rocky step and was followed by a dicy ice step which we both found very awkward in the dark. We still weren't warmed up to the task, our enthusiasm being drawn from the very bottom of the well, but we knew, or at least hoped, that we would soon get going. Steep snow led to another rock step. We climbed this up a crack, which angled diagonally to the right, and soon got into trouble — first when my torch failed and then when George got stuck on small holds and had to reverse down, all pretty hairy stuff in the dark without the rope and with reasonably big packs on our backs.

The next 300 m involved weaving about on steep snow — picking the easiest line up little gullies around bulges and steps and trying to get this dangerous first third of the face out of the way quickly. At the third rock step I skirted around to the left, crossing a very awkward gully with great, tottering ice blocks above it and then traversed 15 m to the left to where a rock knob about the size of a fist protruded from the ice. For speed I simply looped the rope around this knob, and with this miserable belay George had to be content.

On reaching the gully George was forced to make a very wide step across, but he complained that his legs were not as long as mine. After he had made about three attempts to bridge across the gap, I became impatient and a little un-nerved by the tottering blocks above him — if they came down they would sweep him away and almost certainly take me as well. So I screamed at him, "For Christ's sake, George, get a move on." My command was effective, but didn't have quite the desired effect. George reached out his left leg in a violent bridging move; the leg failed to touch the ice and he described a lovely sideways cartwheel and continued gathering momentum in a graceful pendulum beneath me. Once the big swing was over I looked at the little rock knob which, amazingly, still held. But George wasn't so grateful! About 15 m below he was shouting up that he had damaged himself. Apparently in his enthusiasm to get purchase he had attempted to crampon up the back of one of his legs, and the pain (judging from his language) must have been pretty severe. Unfortunately for George, I was not in a pampering mood and told him to get a grip and a move on.

Above us, the face leant back a little, and we soon came over a snowy rise to find that we had reached Pete's and John's bivouac. It was only 6.30 a.m., and we decided to brew up. I am not sure whether George was trying to contrive an extended rest, but before we had melted sufficient snow for a brew he knocked over the primus.

We were away again by 7 a.m., grateful that the cloud was now breaking up and evaporating — even the horrid lenticular cloud that had extended over the summit was now gone and the sun beat down from a clear, blue sky, making us feel as if we were in the middle of the Sahara. The snow reflected back the heat.

We moved in lethargic bursts up a long snow arête which finally met with the dreaded ice cliffs. This was the half-way point. The cliffs were considered the crux, and once above them we knew we had passed the point of no return: but thoughts of failure were far away that day. The blue ice rising steeply above was inviting us to climb, and we couldn't wait to see what was over the top.

I led off enthusiastically up the hard, clear ice, balancing upwards delicately in a shallow glassy groove on the tips of my front points. I continued this way up the gully until I reached a good ledge about half-way up the cliff. Here I belayed George up to me and then continued on ... a little too quickly because I forgot to collect from him the extra ice screws that I would need for runners. I was fully committed on the lead before I realised my mistake

and decided, for the sake of speed, to continue climbing without the security of runners. It wasn't too hard though, at least for the first 20 m, and I was soon jamming my way up an almost vertical chimney in the ice. There were some wobbly blocks of ice in the chimney which gave me a horrid feeling of insecurity. About 25 m above George I was compelled to do some gymnastics — a kind of desperate layback up a fragile flake with no wall against which to brace my feet. Just as I emerged thankfully from the chimney and began to scramble over the brow of the cliff, George shouted out "End of rope."

"Move up so I can get a decent belay," I shouted back. The rope soon went slack and I could hear George climbing up as I took in the rope.

"Okay, off you go," and I scrambled quickly up to a point where I could give him a secure belay. His handsome, grinning face soon emerged over the brow of the cliff, and he shouted enthusiastically, "Great lead, Graeme!"

We moved buoyantly up the steps made by Pete and John, and after only two rope lengths we reached another significant problem — an overhanging schrund wall, 4 m high. We could see the place where Pete and John had surmounted the wall, but their take-off point had collapsed into the blue depths of the schrund and we had to look for our own way over this problem. It was time for another brew!

Refreshed, we looked at the problem again. It was George's turn to lead and he set off balancing out over the gaping hole on a very fragile finger of snow. He reached up a snow stake at full stretch and drove this into the wall. With a sling for aid he was soon scrambling over the delicate lip and calling for me to follow (which I did with much difficulty, shouting vigorously for a tight rope as I tried to remove the snow stake). Above the schrund the going was steep but monotonous. Beneath a veneer of snow our crampons bit into hard ice and this became more and more exposed the higher we progressed. At about 4 p.m. the sun left us. Suddenly our world became incredibly cold.

The rope stiffened and became as unmanage-able as a steel hawser and our damp clothes froze like armour. We had reached a very narrow arête and the base of the final ice field, which glistened green and glass hard above — a horrifying sight to tired bodies. Only about 400 m above, the summit ridge glistened tantalisingly in the late-afternoon sun.

We should have bivvied at this place, but encouraged by the short distance to go we launched on to what turned out to be the hardest part of the climb. The ice was so hard that George's crampons simply would not bite; fortunately I had had razor-sharp tungsten tips put onto my front points and, with about 5 mm of purchase at each kick, I moved up feeling like a burglar on a steep roof. It was nerve-racking progress; the picks of our ice axes would bounce back ineffectively when they struck the ice. At the end of each rope length I drove the pick of my axe in a few centimetres to provide a shaky belay, and George continually protested that I was taking unnecessary risks; I knew I was, but it was a matter of getting up or spending the night on this terribly steep ice field. Several rope lengths above a large ice cliff guarded our final escape onto the summit ridge, but at its base there appeared to be a ledge on which we could spend the night. The question was — could we reach it?

As the light began to fade I started to climb like a possessed man. With a spasm of what has been called "divine madness", I front pointed vigorously up to the base of the cliffs, shrugging off George's cries for sanity. Horrors, the ledge was nothing more than an easing of the angle. We were copybook victims for an accident. With a supreme effort I desperately tried to concentrate. I brought up George, attached him as well as I could and then began to cut out a small stance on which we could spend the night.

The bivvy was one of the most insecure that either of us had experienced (the sensation of exposure was heightened by the meagre belay — a loose snow stake driven in about 15 cm and a couple of shaky ice screws). Our back-sides had sufficient room on two fashioned ledges, but our legs hung down the face which swept 2,000 m clear to the gaping crevasses of the glacier — "Like gaping crocodiles' mouths in a moat," I reflected morbidly. George was a tower of strength once he warmed up. He made soup and tried to get me to nurse the primus in my lap, but I kept nodding off — I was done.

After a meagre but satisfying meal we dozed off in our upright positions and slept the sleep of the exhausted. It was 3 a.m. when I awoke with a start: George had had a nightmare that he was falling down the face. Beside me he was desperately trying to thrust his hands out through the small opening in the top of his mummy-like sleeping bag. Once he had recovered his composure we sat staring at the lights of The Hermitage which blinked a promise of comfort from 3,000 m below. I thought about all those warm bodies down there, particularly the waitresses, and I felt better. Above us, the nor'-west wind moaned across the ridge. We hoped the impending storm would hold off for a few hours.

Shortly after dawn, George wriggled on his little ledge, and my crash helmet, which I had failed to tie on, fell out from behind him and took off down the face — it almost made me sick to see it bound downwards. I looked away before it went out of sight and said nothing. Although our boots had been inside our sleeping bags they were frozen solid, and it was with considerable trouble and effort that we finally got ourselves ready to leave our perch and continue to safety. In a leisurely manner we waited for the sun to warm us before beginning the eerie traverse around the base of the ice cliffs. Three rope lengths of very very hairy front pointing later, we gratefully reached easy ground. All that remained of the Caroline Face was around 100 m of dreary plodding.

We clambered onto the summit ridge at about 9 a.m., right into the teeth of the nor'-wester. Tears of pride rolled down my cheeks.

A little plane, which we later discovered was full of reporters, blew over the ridge and down

The final slopes of the Caroline Face. The bivouac was on the ledge marked X. The route led directly up to it, then led across to where George Harris stands. *Graeme Dingle*

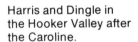

Harris and Dingle in the Hooker Valley after the Caroline.

the Caroline. That night one newspaper billboard announced "Second ascent of Caroline Face", and North Island headlines proudly claimed "Faster time by Wellington pair". Another journalist wanted to know whether we considered our ascent to be a triumph for long hair (as Pete and John had been quoted). Never had there been so much journalistic interest in a local mountaineering event.

---

## Summary of ascent of Caroline Face

*Second ascent of the Caroline Face of Mount Cook on 11 and 12 November 1970 by George Harris and Graeme Dingle. Length: 1,800 m, grade: Extremely difficult, IV (ice). (See alpine gradings on page 116.)*

The climb was quite well executed in that the lower and most dangerous sections of the face were climbed quickly, minimising possible danger. Mistakes of judgment and route finding were made in the top section of the face, probably because of fatigue. It would have been wiser to stop early on the first day at the place where the left traverse was started. Had we done this we would have avoided the dangers of the upper ice field (dangerous only because we were tired) and would probably have taken the more logical direct line to the Middle Peak.

The grading of this climb is difficult because the face can change so drastically. For example, the ice cliffs at the half-way point could be as hard as Grade VI (ice) or as easy as Grade II, depending on recent movements. Also, in some seasons the ice on the upper half of the face can be very hard, making for extremely tiring climbing. Overall, the climb deserves the highest grade because of length, objective dangers and commitment.

---

# Mountaineering in New Zealand

New Zealand mountaineers have always fancied themselves as experts on snow and ice — to a large degree this is true. When our mountaineering forefathers measured two axe handles across the shoulders and could cut steps all day along the summit ridge of old Aorangi we certainly had something to be proud of. Guides like Peter and Alex Graham and, more recently, Harry Ayres and his contemporaries, were certainly world-ranking mountaineers of their time. Following their example at home, and given the means of travel, we had many successes in the Andes and Himalayas during the 1950s and 1960s.

However, with the advent of good front-claw crampons, curved-axe techniques and better protection on ice, we seem to have lost a lot of ground during the mid '70s. However, an amazing revival is currently taking place.

I was at a party in Wales a few years ago where I got involved in an argument about Joe Brown, the legendary British climber. My opponent thought Joe Brown to be the best mountaineer in the world; I argued that his real love was crag climbing. The "Brown" was standing across the room, busy with a pint, so I said, "Let's go and see what he has to say." To approach the king without an audience was unusual, but finally my friend took courage.

"Hi. My antipodean friend here wants to

know whether you consider yourself to be a top mountaineer or not." The "Brown" smiled slowly (but his eyes laughed) and he said, "I know an antipodean who considers himself a pretty hot mountaineer. He thinks that flogging up a 50-degree snow slope all day long is good climbing." At the time this seemed a perfect answer. Brown wasn't interested in the drudgery of mountaineering: he was interested in real climbing — the art of calculating one's chances in a gamble with gravity. Of course, mountaineering and, particularly, snow and ice climbing do involve much more drudgery than pure rock climbing — although sometimes the speed with which one can move on snow and ice make these media more interesting than rock.

Our mountains are an excellent training ground for the development of a sound all-round mountaineering technique: good glacier and icefall climbing, lots of fast up-and-down movement on often dubious snow and ice, carrying heavy loads in difficult mountain country, getting to know the whims of the weather, and so on.

New Zealand mountaineers do not climb many steep and prolonged ice slopes — that is, slopes of over 60 degrees. There is plenty of scope. Very steep ice gullies exist in winter from one end of the Southern Alps to the other; even on Ruapehu and Egmont a few vertical ice pitches are regular visitors in winter.

The most recent surge in New Zealand ice climbing came in the late '60s and early '70s with classic routes being established on the south face of Douglas, the Caroline Face, the south face of St David's Dome and the Balfour Face of Tasman. In *Climbing Ice*, Yvon Chouinard says: "The early 1970s saw the curved pick, front-pointing, and Hamish MacInnes 'Terrordactyl' [a specially shaped ice hammer] universally accepted for climbing steep ice. New routes which were considerably more difficult than any of the old classics were being established everywhere in the world. The word had even gotten to New Zealand, where in 1971 Bill Denz and Bryan Pooley climbed the severe and remote Balfour Face of Mount

Tasman." Strangely, these surges in New Zealand climbing tend to occur at the beginning of each decade, and the 1980s promise a similiar surge in the field of snow and ice, with plenty of interest being shown in steep gullies and faces in the Darrans Ranges under winter conditions.

There are no obvious reasons why the top performers on rock cannot also be the top performers on ice, although until the advent of "piolet traction" it was relatively uncommon for people to be top performers on both. However, with the advent of this technique about 1970 the two climbing arts drew closer together. Previously on ice one had to cut hand holds and rely heavily on sound front-pointing technique and strong hands. Today, comparative novices muscle up classic climbs using curved picks, where previously climbers relied on sound crampon technique built up over quite a long period.

Chouinard points out: "Some climbers claim that using modern equipment and techniques (like piolet traction) diminishes the adventure to be found on the classic ice climbs. What these climbers forget, however, is that the curved ice axe, rigid crampons and piolet traction were specifically designed for climbing steeper and harder ice in better style. They were not designed to 'overkill' the standard difficulties of the classic routes."

It surprises me that it took climbers so long to discover the piolet traction technique for climbing ice — the New Zealand kauri gum collectors were using almost identical techniques to climb giant trees last century.

Protection has also become more sophisticated. It is difficult to protect yourself on snow and bad ice, and it is hard to imagine protection even on good ice ever being as good as rock protection, as the basic material is simply not as strong. MacInnes, that great Scottish character of Glencoe, pioneer of many classic Scottish ice routes, once told me that protection on ice was like protecting rock climbs with rurps (the smallest pitons — the word R.U.R.P. derives from Realisation of the Ultimate Re-

The old kauri gum collectors used techniques similar to those used by modern ice climbers for climbing giant kauri trees.

Piolet traction. Me climbing on Te Heu Heu (Mount Ruapehu) in early winter. The tool in my left hand is out of sight. Often style has to be sacrificed for effectiveness, particularly on bad ice. *Jo Straker*

ality Piton). Today, however, with modern "wart hogs" and "tubes" it's not quite that bad, and you can almost get away with falling off on ice!

Personally I prefer climbing snow and ice to rock climbing because ethics and rules are less sophisticated. You can cut where you wish, rest where you wish, pull up on whatever you like ... and stuff the critics! After all, tomorrow it will all be changed anyway — melted over, or even fallen down. One of the reasons I go into the wilds and climb is to escape our structured society — a society where imposed law is destroying integrity and conscience. In the wilds my own conscience is law and the penalty for the ultimate mistake is sometimes a quick and dispassionate death.

## Equipment

Although much snow and ice climbing equipment is similar to rock climbing equipment, there is really no cheap way to equip yourself for the high mountains. Such environments demand the best of gear.

**Boots** (for alpine climbing)

These should be rigidly soled, relatively high in the ankle and as light and warm as possible. Climbing-boot design had undergone comparatively little change in the last 50 years until quite recently. Now, with the development of plastic boots we have entered a new era of light, warm boots of previously undreamed quality.

## Crampons

These should not be expected to go on flexible boots (and stay in one piece). If the boots flex and the crampons don't, the crampons will eventually fatigue and break. Of course, even the best boots will flex a little, but this can be absorbed by the hinge in the middle of the crampon. Of the types illustrated, there will no doubt be endless arguments about which is best. I have used them all and find them all good, but each has slight advantages over the next. Some criteria to note are:

1. Short points are best on rock and hard ice.
2. Salewa-type front points are best on rock.
3. Chouinard-type front points are best on very steep and hard ice.
4. Simond front points are best on sustained high-angle ice of indifferent or soft quality.

Strapping is not the ultimate way of attaching crampons to boots as it is fiddly and inhibits blood circulation, causing cold feet. Crampon bindings are in the early stages of development and use, and with the wider use of plastic boots, straps will probably become obsolete.

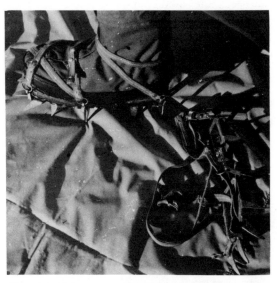

Simond Makalu crampons and Berghaus Yeti gaiters. With the advent of plastic boots, this type of gaiter will be used less frequently. Note the two sets of front points on the crampons and the convenient strapping configuration. The buckles are of the quick-slide type. *Corrina Dingle*

Chouinard hinged crampons with Beck straps and San Marco Himalaya boots. The gaiters are made from breathable Goretex. The crampon straps are of neoprene-coated tape so they will be pliable even in freezing conditions. Note the strapping configuration. The boots are made of polyurethane and this particular model has an inner bootie for added insulation. There are several good makes of plastic boots available, including Koflach and Kastinger. *Corrina Dingle*

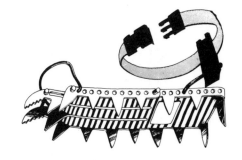

A look into the future — Footfangs are the first real revolution in crampons since the advent of front points. Their main advantages over traditional crampons are that they are strapless, the nylon sole minimises snow buildup (balling) and they are rigid. They also have 18 points as opposed to the traditional 12.

## Rope

On most alpine snow and ice climbs a single 9-mm rope will be sufficient, but on serious climbs a second rope should either be worn or carried in the pack in case of retreat by abseil.

So-called "waterproof" Kernmantel ropes are generally used, but these soon lose their waterproof qualities and therefore I am yet to be convinced that Kernmantel ropes are better than those of the good hawser-laid type. The latter are less inclined to soak up water and become unmanageable through freezing, and they are lighter when wet. Kernmantel rope does have the advantage of generally being more elastic and, being smaller, it has less frictional drag.

## Ice axes and north wall hammers

There are more kinds made than I've got hairs on my right arm, most of them inadequate for New Zealand conditions. Ice tools like Terrodactyls and Hummingbirds can be very effective on technical ice, but may be found lacking as all-round snow and ice tools. So, you "Terrodactyl" fiends out there, I'm sorry, but your preference is not recommended as an all-round piece of alpine implement (he said, ducking quickly!). You may need to try several types to find the combination that suits best.

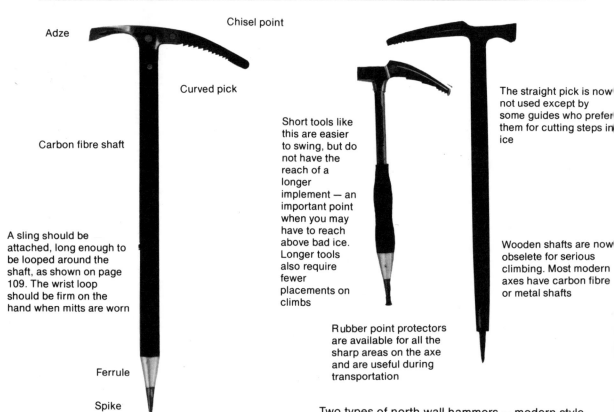

Adze

Chisel point

Curved pick

Carbon fibre shaft

A sling should be attached, long enough to be looped around the shaft, as shown on page 109. The wrist loop should be firm on the hand when mitts are worn

Short tools like this are easier to swing, but do not have the reach of a longer implement — an important point when you may have to reach above bad ice. Longer tools also require fewer placements on climbs

The straight pick is now not used except by some guides who prefer them for cutting steps in ice

Wooden shafts are now obselete for serious climbing. Most modern axes have carbon fibre or metal shafts

Rubber point protectors are available for all the sharp areas on the axe and are useful during transportation

Ferrule

Spike

The Chouinard ice axe. A similar tool is available with a hammer-head instead of an adze, and many climbers use one of each. If two tools are to be used at once, they should be of a similar length, rather than one being long and the other very short. The normal shaft length is 60–70 cm.

Two types of north wall hammers — modern style (left) and the old style (right). The north wall hammer is useful on alpine climbs where rock and ice is to be climbed because the tool doubles as a piton hammer. On difficult climbs many climbers carry one ice axe and one north wall hammer. Axes and hammers should have facility for the fitting of a wrist sling.

North wall hammer

Ice axe

**The well-dressed snow and ice climber**

Original belay used while main anchors were placed (see page 111)

Main anchors placed well apart in case of ice fractures

Head gear — some climbers prefer not to wear a helmet when climbing technical ice (for example, frozen waterfalls); but on alpine climbs where there is a real danger of falling debris most climbers wear a helmet. On cold climbs a woolly hat or balaclava is usually worn under the helmet

Slings from main anchors to the belayer's harness

Shoulder belay

The harness is much the same as that worn when rock climbing, but the need to remove and add clothing is much greater on alpine climbs. This factor must be considered when choosing a harness to avoid having to get out of the system for every call of nature or temperature change

Gear sling — one to hold protection gear is sufficient for most ice climbs. Where the terrain is difficult and mixed, use one sling for ice gear and one for rock gear (worn on opposite sides)

Some climbers wear good-quality ski gloves for technical climbing because they offer the advantage of being able to use the fingers. However, many others wear thin woollen or polypropelene gloves under Dachstein (woollen) mitts. Wrist loops fitted to the mitts will minimise the danger of loss

Holsters (used for holding ice tools). These are usually made of plastic or leather and are attached to the harness. Wear two for steep climbs. One holster is sufficient for easier climbs

Gaiters for snow and ice climbing are usually knee length and made from heavy nylon. They prevent snow penetrating the tops of the boots and contain loose clothing and socks, preventing catching on the crampons

Clothing is an exceptionally personal consideration, so I will describe what I would wear on a cold alpine climb: worn against the skin, polypropelene or woollen underwear with long sleeves and legs and a polar neck; over this a layer of fibre pile or wool. In bad or windy weather I put on a one-piece suit made of Klimate or Goretex, but many people prefer a separate parka and overtrousers. I rarely wear long underwear on summer climbs

Boots and crampons (see pages 102–3)

# Techniques for climbing snow and ice

**The ice axe used as a walking stick**
The axe should be held in the uphill hand with the pick pointing backwards so that if a self arrest is required the shaft can be grasped by the other hand, putting the pick into the correct position for the self arrest.

**Self arresting on snow**
Tuck the ice axe head under and to one side of your chest. Work the pick in gently rather than stab at the snow. Keep the spike up. Force the knees in. Keep crampons clear of the slope.

**Self arresting after a head-first fall**

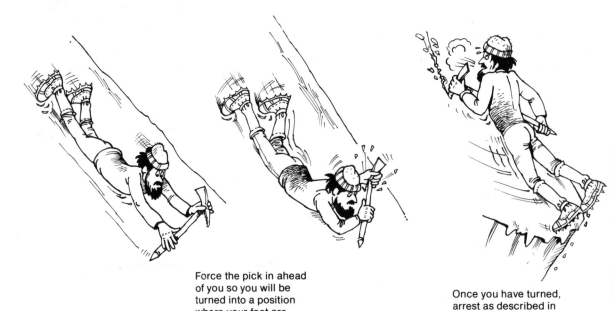

Force the pick in ahead of you so you will be turned into a position where your feet are facing downhill

Once you have turned, arrest as described in the previous illustration

# Self arresting on snow after a head-first fall on the back

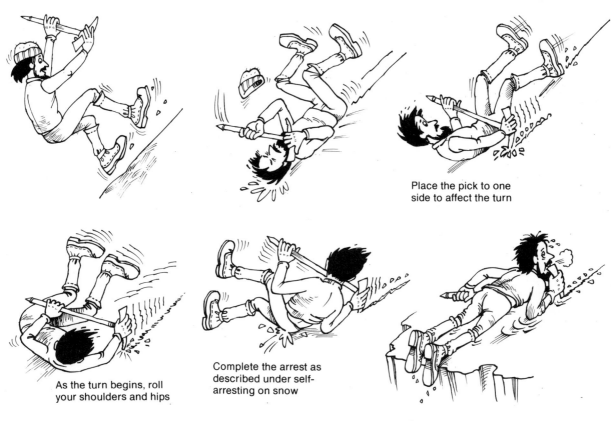

Place the pick to one side to affect the turn

As the turn begins, roll your shoulders and hips

Complete the arrest as described under self-arresting on snow

**Climbing with the ice axe in the support position**

**The glissade**
With knees bent and keeping in balance, use the axe as a third leg and keep it ready to be used for an arrest if necessary.

**Pigeon holing**
Punch the feet in positively. Use the axe as shown or with the shaft horizontal and held by the right hand.

### Cutting steps down

Cut one step at a time before moving. In this case the climber will move his left foot into the step being cut. He will then cut the next step down and back for the right foot. Follow this rhythm: cut one step forward, move, cut one step back and move. Practice will tell you which sequence you feel most comfortable with. I personally feel best stepping down with the opposite foot sequence to that illustrated (that is, the step being cut would be further back and I would cross my left foot behind the right).

### Cutting steps up

If it is steep cut two steps ahead. Then, using the axe for support, step up into them. When you want to change direction cut a larger step. Make steps large enough for standing in comfortably.

### Cramponning

Front pointing using the ice axe as a dagger. Keep your heels low to reduce calf stress. Try to make strikes with the crampons positive and correct the first time. Don't drive the axe pick in too far. It should be used to maintain balance only. The axe will probably feel most comfortable if the shaft is approximately horizontal.

### Cramponning

French technique — the knees are bent and the ankles are at a grotesque angle. The steeper the angle, the further down the slope your toes will point. Move both feet, then move the axe.

### Piolet traction on steep ice

Drive the axes in just far enough to hold your weight between them, then walk your feet up as far as is comfortable and repeat the sequence. Some climbers lash their wrist straps to the shaft of the axe, but the illustrated half hitch is good enough and will be found to be more versatile.

### Piolet traction and hand holds

This is sometimes useful if you have only one axe at your disposal or when climbing hollow ice that may not hold the picks well. Cut two hand holds ahead (usually with the adze), then move up to the top hold. The hand holds become footholds as you ascend.

### An ice bollard used as an abseil anchor

Note the backup anchor, which will be recovered by the last person if the bollard has been satisfactory. Natural ice bollards are usually quite easy to find, but sometimes it will be necessary to cut one with the axe, as shown.

## Protection

As I have said earlier, a climber's best protection is not in the equipment carried, but in the way he or she climbs. On a high mountain where a change in the weather can turn an easy climb into a life-and-death struggle you are often best protected by moving quickly and placing the minimum of protective equipment (ice screws, snow stakes and so on). However, the term "protection" generally refers to "runners" placed to limit the distance of a fall, should one occur.

This section includes special protection techniques for use on snow and ice. For information on roping up, harnesses and so on see Chapter 4.

### Bollards and icicles

Both can be used successfully as runners when nothing else is available.

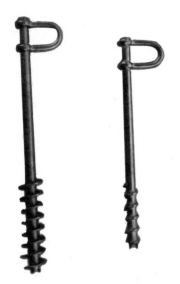

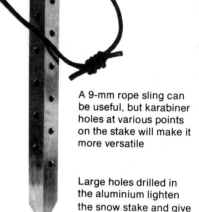

A 9-mm rope sling can be useful, but karabiner holes at various points on the stake will make it more versatile

Large holes drilled in the aluminium lighten the snow stake and give it better holding power

Ice screws — the tube types are the strongest. When screwed in properly, a dowel of ice protrudes from the top of the screw. I have found the best ice screws to be the Chouinard type.

The screw on the left, with its coarser thread and extra length, will be more effective than the one on the right. The cutting teeth are a crucial part of the design.

A wart hog or Dubek ice piton. This type of ice protection, which is driven in and screwed out, is quicker to place than the screw, but it is not as strong. However, in good ice a wart hog will be acequate.

Lowe ice equipment, such as the Snarg, is also very good.

The snow stake made from a length of angle aluminium about 70 cm long can be very useful for belays when the snow or ice is too soft to hold screws or Dubeks. The alternative is Deadmen, which I have generally found to be an unnecessary burden in most climbing conditions. A Deadman is a plate of aluminium with a cable attached.

## Belaying

1. *The New Zealand footbrake*: This is a much-maligned and misunderstood belay overseas, but will be found to be a most useful and effective belay for many alpine situations where speed is essential. There are several rules to observe if the belay is to be sound:

a. If runners are to be used this is the wrong belay. It is designed to hold only a downward pull.

b. The leader must not climb directly above the belayer, and the belayer must face the side on which the leader will fall.

c. If the leader falls from well above the belayer, the belayer should attempt to take in as much rope as possible to minimise the length of the fall.

**The New Zealand foot brake belay**

In the event of a lead fall, the belayer, after taking in as much rope as possible, will support the head of the axe with his or her free hand while the other hand increases the angle of the rope around the boot, thus stopping the fall gradually.

**The static belay**
(see also belaying on rock — Chapter 4)

Hanging from the axe while placing a belay. Another ice screw or one of the ice tools can be used to screw home the anchor. But often it is easier and quicker to whack in a wart hog in such a position. The other anchor will be placed a safe distance away at X in case the ice breaks around either anchor.

The belay anchors are placed. The climber cuts a resting stance.

**Belaying on steep ice**
Often ice climbers use friction brakes (see rock climbing). However, body belays are easier if the ropes are frozen. They will be quicker and may put less load on the anchors.

d. The belayer should not attempt a static arrest. The belay is designed to be dynamic so that the load is absorbed slowly.

e. The leader should attempt to slow his descent by vigorous use of the self-arrest technique.

In many situations, particularly wet snow conditions, this belay will be the strongest that can be found.

2. *The static belay*: The belay will be the same as on rock (see Chapter 4), but the belayer will be tied to snow stakes, ice axe shafts, ice axe picks, wart hogs or tubular screws, depending on conditions. On very steep ice I have found the following system the best:

a. Drive in the pick of the axe(s) securely.

b. If you aren't already attached to an axe sling, attach yourself. If you are not on a ledge or stance, hang from the axe.

c. Place your belays (well apart).

d. Tie on to the belays.

e. Remove an axe and cut a stance. (It is a good idea to make this sufficiently adequate to accommodate your partner when he or she reaches you.)

f. Belay as for rock. (The stitch-plate-type belay device may be difficult to use if the rope is frozen, and a belay around the body may be necessary.)

111

## Glaciers

*Tourist:*   *"Where did all the rocks come from?"*
*Guide:*     *"The glacier brought them."*
*Tourist:*   *"Where has the glacier gone?"*
*Guide:*     *"Back for more rocks!"*

Gleaned from an alpine club newsletter

To travel safely around the Southern Alps and other well-glaciated mountains your glacier technique must be good. In order to stay out of trouble it is perhaps best to understand the habits of glaciers. Try to imagine a length of pliable but brittle material. Now bend it sideways — it will crack on the outside of the curve (lateral crevasses) and crumble on the inside (lateral humps and séracs). Bend it over a lump

**The alpine landscape**

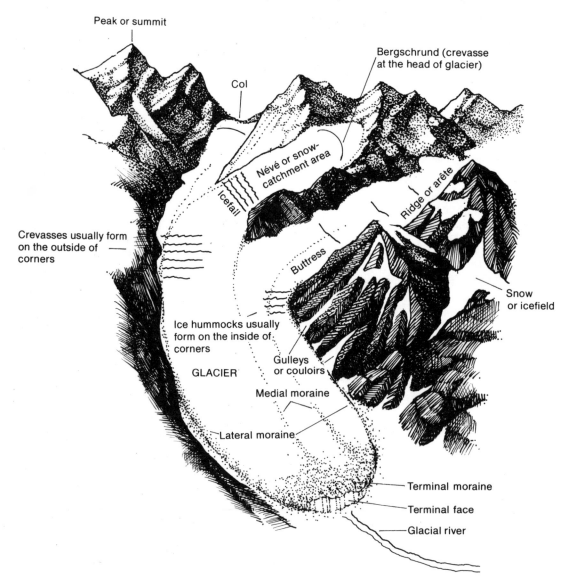

Peak or summit

Col

Bergschrund (crevasse at the head of glacier)

Névé or snow-catchment area

Icefall

Ridge or arête

Crevasses usually form on the outside of corners

Buttress

Snow or icefield

Ice hummocks usually form on the inside of corners

GLACIER

Gulleys or couloirs

Medial moraine

Lateral moraine

Terminal moraine

Terminal face

Glacial river

or a step and it will crack on the top surface (icefall, séracs and so on).

### Crevasse extraction

Ascender techniques have already been covered in Chapter 4. Extracting yourself from a crevasse employs virtually the same technique (see page 85).

If you are trying to rescue an unconscious person from a crevasse there are two alternatives, listed below in order of preference.

1. Lower the victim to a ledge or to the crevasse bottom, then abseil down to give help.
2. Set up a pulley system to haul the person out. This should be similar to the hauling system described in Chapter 4, with the added complication that the hauling rope will pass over the crevasse lip, creating extra friction. The effort and skill involved in this manoeuvre is fantastic — try it and see.

### Snow conditions and avalanches

Avalanches of all kinds are common in the New Zealand mountains, with the wind-slab type being the most common in winter and therefore probably the greatest winter mountaineering danger. In summer, though, the ice avalanche is probably the most common type. Perhaps the best practical way to discuss avalanche dangers is to give some hypothetical situations in the high Southern Alps. You can try to anticipate for yourself the likely conditions before reading my own appraisals.

▲ It is midsummer and the snow of the previous day was wet and knee deep. There was a heavy frost during the night. At 2.00 a.m. the surface is hard and supports your weight.
*Conditions: probably near perfect, but the heat of the sun may make conditions slushy again even as early as 10 a.m., so move fast.*

▲ It is summer and there has been a rain storm and strong winds. The weather clears in the evening and there is a hard frost.
*Conditions: probably okay as long as there is no new snow at a higher level. Rocks may be iced, and there is a likelihood of hard ice, particularly on slopes exposed to the wind during the storm.*

▲ It has been snowing hard for three days with waist-deep powder snow around the hut.
*Conditions (winter or summer): powder avalanches likely. These are very dangerous because of the associated wind blast. Winds may exceed 320 km/h and can snap off large trees. Allow at least one day of warm weather before venturing on to the mountain. If caught, get behind a rock or lie flat. Cover your face.*

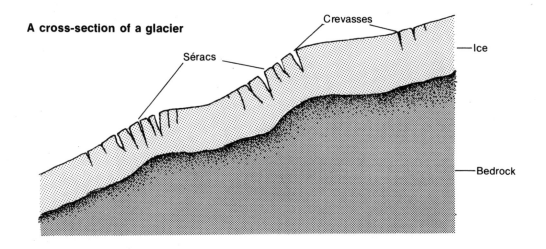

**A cross-section of a glacier**

Séracs

Crevasses

Ice

Bedrock

▲ There has been a snow storm with strong winds and some snow. The weather clears and there is a frost.

*Conditions (winter or summer): probably hard ice and iced rocks on the windward slopes; wind slab on lee slopes. Wind slab can often be identified by the resulting crunchy noise when you walk on it. The surface may have wind patterns (like sand), and it will break into blocks easily. Through a process called firnification a gap will form between the new snow, laid down by the wind, and the old snow slope. Avalanches are usually triggered by the new layer collapsing on to the old slope. Slopes over 20 degrees can be dangerous. Beware, the wind slab may itself be masked by a layer of powder snow. If in doubt, cut a cross-section. (I have seen slabs in excess of 3 m thick, so sometimes a cross-section will not locate the base.) If caught, try to stay on the surface.*

## Avalance types

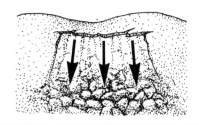 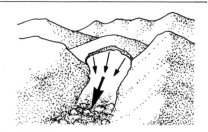

Avalanches can occur on open slopes, but they quickly channel into gulleys. Stay on ridges if there is an avalanche danger

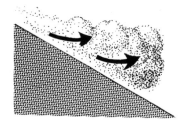 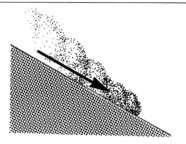

Powder avalanches often become airborne, but if snow conditions are heavy they may flow downhill

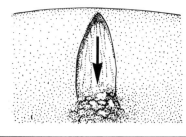 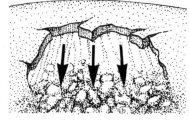

Loose snow avalanche beginning from a single point

Slab avalanche — these can be up to 4.5 m thick

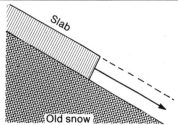  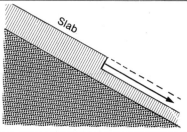

The entire slab has avalanched

Only the surface slab has avalanched

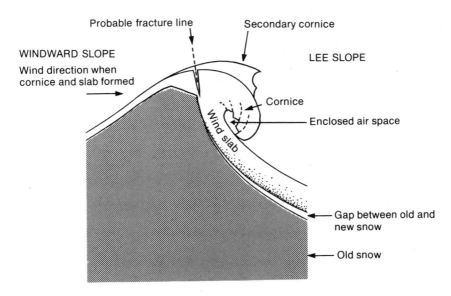

Cornices and wind slab. Great caution must be exercised in walking on cornices or the slopes beneath them. Both cornices and wind slab are formed by wind-blown snow and both usually form on leeward slopes. If you wish to check a slope you suspect may be wind slab, cut a cross-section into it, noting changes in snow consistency and layering. If air gaps exist between layers, avoid the slope at all costs. It is not always easy to make a positive identification of dangerous wind slab, so suspect slopes are best avoided, particularly after bad weather that has been accompanied by wind. Before descending a suspect slope it is a good idea to try to set off any avalanche ready to occur by first rolling a large rock downhill. (Check first that nobody is on the slope below.)

▲ It is summer and the weather has been hot and the snow is slushy. There have been no frosts for a couple of nights.
*Conditions: all slopes over 30 degrees will be prone to wet snow avalanche. This has the consistency of wet cement, and usually moves relatively slowly and in runnels. If caught, move down with the avalanche, staying on your feet and moving to the side if possible. When these avalanches stop they set like cement, so try to stay upright with your arms free.*

▲ It is summer and the weather has been hot and you need to move through an icefall or under ice cliffs.
*Conditions: séracs and ice cliffs are probably the most unpredictable of all avalanche possibilities. Sometimes they will simply fall down through the effect of expansion and contraction and gravity,* but often they collapse. A collapse is usually heralded by a discharge of debris from the base.

▲ You are climbing a vertical ice gully (winter or summer). There has been no frost and there is water running between the ice and the rock.
*Conditions: the gully is probably about to fall about your ears. Vertical ice over rock should be avoided if the ice is not sticking to the rock itself.*

Rock avalanche is not very common, although during summer some gullies can be dangerous because of rock fall. Big rock avalanches in New Zealand have occurred mainly as a result of earthquakes and lightning strikes, such as in the case of the avalanche that crushed the old Pioneer hut. Small rock falls may occur simply through the melting of snow and ice, so the danger is less when temperatures are low.

115

# Alpine grading

New Zealand mountaineers have tended to avoid grading alpine climbs. This is partly because weather and seasonal changes can affect gradings to a large degree, but mainly because of a desire to retain a higher level of initiative and mountaineering judgement. It was felt that if you can't look at a climb and feel confident of climbing it, you probably aren't ready for it. This philosophy has some merit as it is too easy to rob an activity of its charm by over-preparation. There is, however, a good case for grading, if only to right the current inaccurate and haphazard system.*

## Overall gradings

Unlike pure rock climbing (say on small crags) I believe mountain climbs do need an overall grading that takes into account length, objective dangers, isolation and so on. The increasing number of climbers in New Zealand together with higher technical standards warrant the introduction of a grading system. The French system seems to be suitable for New Zealand conditions, and I would like to see a new system based on this be adopted. In this system each separate grade is also divisible into inferior (minus) and superior (plus) classifications. Individual pitch gradings are then added to descriptions where necessary.

To put any grading system into perspective it is necessary to set up some routes as bases for comparison. I have therefore put examples of New Zealand climbs beside each grade. The grades are assessed when the climb is in good condition (usually assessed on the first ascent and clarified on the second). See also the summary of the Caroline Face ascent earlier in this chapter.

*Since this was written, Hugh Logan's excellent guide to the Mount Cook area has been published. It includes his own grading system, and is a good start. Hugh has put one grade on a climb by accumulating all the factors of technical difficulty, remoteness and other hazards. I believe we should bring ourselves into line with the U.I.A.A. (international) grading system as soon as possible.

## Comparison of French overall grading with a possible New Zealand equivalent

| Suggested New Zealand | French | New Zealand example (assessed in good summer condition) |
|---|---|---|
| Easy (E) | Facile | Mt Olivier from Mueller hut |
| Moderate (M) | Peu difficile | East ridge Dixon from Grand Plateau |
| Mildly difficult (MD) | Assez difficile | Linda G1 route — Mt Cook |
| Difficult (D) | Difficile | West face direct Haidinger |
| Very difficult (VD) | Très difficile | South face of St David's Dome (Hicks) via Jones/Dingle |
| Extremely difficult (ED) | Extrement difficile | Balfour face — Mt Tasman (Denz/Pooley) |

## Pitch gradings (rock, snow and ice)

Pure rock climbing and alpine climbing are sufficiently different to warrant totally different pitch grading systems. Probably the main area of contention in the alpine systems is grading ice, because it can change so much from season to season and even from day to day. In Europe ice is graded by its angle: for example the second ice field on the north face of the Eiger is rated 55 degrees.

The major problem here is that climbers almost always overestimate the angle of ice. Hard ice of 70 degrees will feel desperately steep if it is a long slope.

The Scottish system of grading snow and ice (I–VI) is probably the most satisfactory, but there is no reason why this also should not be open-ended to leave room for improvements in technique and equipment.

There is not as much international contention with alpine grading as with pure rock (crag) grading, and the European system has generally been accepted. However, the European system has not dealt adequately with the ice area and I would like to see in New Zealand an integration of the Scottish ice-grading system into the European system as follows: grades I to infinity.

Each grade divided into sub-grades of plus (+) and minus (−), thus: V1−, V1+, etc. The grading should be put on the difficulty of the move with no relationship to objective dangers such as loose rock, lack of protection and so on. The latter are catered for in the overall grading of the route.

## Route description and grading example

The route description below is an example of what I would consider reasonable and desirable for a route in the Southern Alps.

*South face St David's Dome (Hicks), the left hand buttress via Jones/Dingle, 600 m, mixed rock and ice. Grade V.D.*

*Average time*: 8–10 hours (many parties bivvy on the descent).
*Suggested equipment*: A small selection of nuts, blade pitons and ice protection.

About the centre of the face rises a prominent buttress. This buttress is not gained until several pitches have been climbed. Start below and just to the right of the crest of the buttress. Cross the bergschrund (sometimes difficult) and climb two slabby pitches (grade IV+) to a broad snow-covered ledge (snow field). Trav-

**Comparison of ice grading systems**

| *Scottish* | *European (estimate only)* |
| --- | --- |
| I Easy snow slope | 20–45 degrees |
| II Steep snow slope Fixed belays may be necessary but usually no runners required | 45–70 degrees Snow usually would not be steeper than 70 degrees |
| III Very steep ice slope This is the absolute limit of front pointing without the aid of hand holds or curved pick | 60–80 degrees |
| IV Approaching vertical | 80–90 degrees |
| V Vertical with or without bulges | 90 degrees |
| VI Overhanging | Over 90 degrees |

erse left across snow or ice to a gully on the left of the buttress. Climb this gully for one pitch and then gain the buttress at the first opportunity. Approximately two pitches on good rock (grade IV–V) lead to the crest of the buttress. Several pitches up more broken rock on the buttress lead to the top ice field. The route here will depend on the state of the cliff. Sometimes it can be climbed direct, but usually parties skirt the cliff on the left. Depending on the ice conditions and whether the cliff is climbed, the grade of this ice field is II–IV (ice).

(First ascent: Murray Jones and Graeme Dingle, 31 December 1970.)

# Aid climbing on ice

Since the advent of curved picks and piolet traction, aid climbing on ice has become very much a thing of the past. However, some very steep or rotten ice walls are still climbed using aid. This can be related to easy-aid climbing on rock as placements of screws or ice pitons can be made anywhere and are not governed by the availability of cracks. Apart from the different equipment used, the techniques employed in aid climbing on ice are much the same as those employed on rock.

If etriers (small ladders) are carried (for ice alone) the runged variety are best as tape etriers will be easily spiked by crampons.

# 6
# The rivers

*White-water canoeing is like being in an avalanche, but with slightly more control.*

Author

THIS SECTION deals with mastering two aspects of nature's drainage system: getting down rivers (by raft and canoe) and getting across them. River crossing, of course, is normally not regarded as a sport, but as an aspect of the activity known broadly as tramping. Crossing techniques are widely disputed and these disputes usually stem from the natural bloody-mindedness of trampers, and also from their backgrounds (that is, the types of rivers they have been used to). I have three reasons for including river crossing in this section rather than in the tramping section: there is obviously much to be learned about the habits of rivers from rafting and canoeing; there are such violent disputes about river-crossing techniques that I am hoping to escape arguments by hiding this important aspect in this section; if would-be canoeists are blessed with as little control of their canoes as I am they will prob-

Ali Ward canoeing the Rudraprayag rapid — Alakananda River, India. *Stu Allen*

ably be in need of crossing techniques (when they lose their canoes)!

Canoeing is often compared to climbing — indeed, many climbers are good canoeists and vice versa. However, there are always exceptions, and I must admit that somewhere along the way I have missed the canoeing bus. I like canoes; I like the romance of canoeing, but I hate cold water and without a canoe have the greatest difficulty remaining afloat. Despite this, I have probably had more experience than any other incompetent performer. I also have a very strong sense of survival, which makes me react with tremendous strength and singlemindedness when I find myself in a vigorous rapid.

At 18, I wasn't sure whether I wanted to be a runner, a climber, a racing-car driver or anything else. In my desperation, I even considered canoeing! I made a canoe, but soon lost it in an abortive attempt to negotiate a flooded Hutt River gorge. I made another and decided to cross Cook Strait. However, this plan was sidetracked (probably thankfully) by a poster in a Wellington shop window: "Longest canoe race in the world" it read. What splendid training for Cook Strait, I thought, incorrectly, and after completing entry formalities I set off for Taumarunui with my home-made horror.

The train was packed and I spent a sleepless night sharing a couple of seats with several exuberant Maori guys, who drank continuously from a seemingly unlimited supply of brown bottles which they produced magically from somewhere beneath their seats. They removed the tops expertly with their teeth before quickly quaffing down the brown fluid. I staggered from the train at about 3 a.m. and lay down in my sleeping bag in front of the Taumarunui Railway Station.

The race began from Cherry Grove at about 10 a.m. I was horrified to observe sleek Olympic class K.1's, not to mention their muscled paddlers. My 3-m canvas canoe was beginning to look a little inadequate so we both kept a pretty low profile. I pulled on my holey longjohns and tattered hat and prepared for the Le Mans start. At the starter's "Go" we ran for

My first canoe in the Hutt River. This type of wood and canvas canoe is relatively easy to make, but has mainly been outdated by stronger fibreglass canoes. *Dingle Collection*

our canoes and slipped into the stream, most of the canoeists efficiently stretching their spray skirts around coamings and gunning off down the first rapid while I drifted downstream struggling with the dozen press studs that attached my skirt to its coaming — I negotiated the first rapid backwards.

The Wanganui river makes a delightful canoe journey, and I soon learnt to stop racing and enjoy the scenery. In many places the river has cut deep gorges into the grey papa, and salubrious green pools are divided every kilometre or so by mild rapids.

I suspect that I humiliated the very name of canoeing by looking so out of place, and I found the canoeists a very cliquey and unfriendly lot — but in their defence I was probably pretty shy and aloof. I camped that night with a couple of hard-case shooters — Jim and Hori — and we sat around till very late chatting and listening to the yarns of a 90-year-old Maori who had lived beside the river all his life. He had farmed there since being given a returned serviceman's block after the First World War. The wonderful old fellow even tried to teach me a chant to paddle by, and said that if he were in the race he would race all night — apparently in the old days many Maori canoes travelled at night. I went to sleep in my damp sleeping bag at peace with the world. Nearby, Hori and the old man spoke in their musical tongue, their faces lit by the flickering fire. A morepork repeated a lonely cry and the river noise added a final note of timelessness.

I suffered a rather less peaceful awakening. Hori was rattling his hobnails over a piece of corrugated iron as he scuttled about collecting wood for the fire, which was already blazing high. He dumped a can of baked beans into the flames as I began to doze again. Suddenly a report like a cannon blast shattered the frosty morning. The fire was all but destroyed by the exploding can, and baked beans were scattered everywhere. His nonchalant comment was, "Pressure cook 'em, boy!"

The race continued with the keen kiddies battling it out for supremacy, while I continued merely to finish the journey, as I did so bemoaning the fact that I hadn't gone to the alps instead.

At Wanganui I collected my prize (I had generously been given such a large handicap on the last stage that I came in second!) and I hitched back to Wellington determined never again to rush into something I knew so little about and vowing to stick to climbing in future. For the time the Cook Strait crossing was shelved.

Many years later, however, I forgot my folly and my vows. During the summer of 1973 I asked Grant Lupton, one of the instructors from my newly formed baby, the Outdoor Pursuits Centre, to have a crack at the strait. Grant was a very strong, good-humoured bloke and was keen to have a go. We decided to make it a goodwill visit to Outward Bound. On the eve of our departure the party doubled with the addition of Grant's brother, Bob, a tough SAS type, and John Davidson, a newly arrived instructor at OPC. In fact, I think he arrived from Britain that very day, and very pale-faced he was, too — a condition that would be transformed into blisters within the next 24 hours on the straits.

We drove to Makara, near Wellington, and lay on the beach for a few hours' sleep before our adventure. At dawn we stacked a little gear into our boats and I taped a compass on to my spray skirt, as I did so checking the map bearing to Tory Channel. I was surprised to find that you don't paddle south to reach the South Island; Tory Channel is, in fact, due west. "Good things these compasses. I can see why they have them on ships and aeroplanes now!"

From our sheltered bay the sea looked very calm, the South Island showing up as a very hazy blue line on the horizon. We left the beach and paddled out to sea, rather surprised to find that once we had left the bay a heavy southerly swell was running through the strait. Leaving the sanctuary of the land posed a psychological problem, not easily overcome in the conditions, so we turned into the waves and headed for Ohau Point. Near the point we came across a commercial fishing boat.

"Ah, gudday" (very strange looks!). "Air ya goin'? Good. Have you heard a forecast for today? Orr, light to moderate sutherlies — little change I'd say. Where the hell are you goin' in those silly little things — South America?"

We committed ourselves and paddled for the hazy blue line on the horizon, rising up on to the crests of each wave, broaching and sliding down the other side. One moment the other canoes would be out of sight down in the troughs; the next they would be way above. It didn't pay to dwell on our immediate surroundings too long, and I was grateful for the greasy eggs, sausages and bacon I hadn't had for breakfast (we probably travelled further up and down than we did forward). About mid-way across we had a short break. Bob and Grant relieved themselves in their boats (bad toilet training as babies!); John got half out of his cockpit for the operation, straddling his boat like a spider. I saved mine, preferring to suffer, because I was afraid of attracting the sharks and killer whales that had, at the time, been receiving a lot of publicity. One had bitten off an outboard motor; another had sunk a large yacht. Shortly afterwards a flying fish landed in John's lap.

After a few hours the hazy blue line began showing a few features, but nowhere could we see Tory Channel — only a line of white breakers was visible where the waves crashed on the coast. Grant was the first to voice his doubts about my navigation ability: "Even if we find Tory Channel I don't think we can get through. I'm sure it's too narrow."

"Nonsense!" I returned, "the bloody ferries go through there." Bob and John weren't sure and I began to rack my brain. I couldn't remember with any certainty, even though I was sure I'd been through dozens of times on the inter-island ferry. The only other choice was to paddle north around Arapawa Island into Queen Charlotte Sound, but it was a very long way and our party appeared to be tiring somewhat — I couldn't understand why!

To add to our worries we were about 8 km off the coast when we appeared to stop making progress — "Maybe a tidal rip or something." I considered the return journey to the North Island, but soon gave that idea away. Some steady paddling was in order and that soon paid dividends. After about an hour of effort we surged forward and covered the last few kilometres to Tory Channel in no time at all. Six-and-a-half hours from Makara we finally slid through the narrow gap that was Tory Channel into Queen Charlotte Sound. We immediately crawled up on to a beach and went to sleep.

Like Hansel and Gretel, when we woke we were very hungry.

"Right Grant, where's the tucker?" Grant produced a small bag of dehydrated vegetables and some very soggy peanuts.

"What?"

"But you buggers have eaten it all," he pleaded.

Bob wasn't going hungry — he fashioned a fishing line, made a hook from a fork prong and, armed with these doubtful items and our good wishes, set off to catch dinner. Two hours later he returned with half a billyful of sea lettuce and some snails — it was a foul meal!

Next day we paddled to Outward Bound at the head of Queen Charlotte Sound. The only excitement during the day resulted from trying to rig up a makeshift sail from a ground sheet and trying to sneak a free ride by surfing on the wake of passing ferries. Neither was very successful, but helped to pass the time.

## Summary of Cook Strait crossing

*A kayak crossing of Cook Strait during December 1974 by John Davidson, Grant Lupton, Bob Lupton and Graeme Dingle.*

The trip was badly planned and prepared for, but carried out with the energy of survivors. Our main mistake was insufficient knowledge of tides and insufficient experience at Eskimo rolling or deep-water rescues. John Davidson was the only one who could Eskimo roll with certainty.

# The OPC staff Mohaka trip

In the five years that followed our Cook Strait adventure, canoeing had taken a firm hold as an activity at OPC; most of the instructors were now actually pretty competent in the silly fibreglass shells. The team comprised John Davidson, still as buoyant as ever and capable of as many tricks in a canoe as a performing monkey; Ray Button, our neat all-rounder and centre chief instructor; John Watson, the bearded mariner, known to the centre staff as Grandad because of his advanced years — 38!; and Joe Straker, our blue-eyed blonde British bomber, who had recently joined us from the UK. But the one with the real push and enthusiasm for canoeing and a staff river trip was Stu Allan. Less than 12 months before, when at his peak as a climber, Stu had fallen from a cliff in the Mangatepopo Valley, breaking his pelvis in five places, fracturing a couple of ribs, breaking his tail bone in two places and throwing in a few other mischiefs for good measure. He was now putting his previous climbing zest into canoeing — with much success.

It was a cool January day in 1979 when we all set off down the Mohaka river. This wonderful river has its source in the Kaimanawa Ranges, and it flows more or less north-east for 120 km into Hawke Bay, south of Wairoa. As we left our camp beside the Napier-Taupo highway, mist hung low in the valley, but the exceptionally warm river water filled us with a pleasant anticipation of getting wet.

Also with us was Colin Abbott, an ex-OPC instructor. His exceptionally gaunt, lined face and straggly beard earned him the name Rasputin, the rascally monk. In the raft a merry crew of Rodger and Jan Pardy, Tony Parker and Maggie Button sang and splashed their way down the river, claiming as they went to be the last of the "Mohakans".

For about 15 km from the highway the river was gentle and shallow with only the occasional flurry of white water. Most were soon getting bored by the lack of excitement, but I felt sure that before the trip was through they would have their fill.

John Davidson soon began to fool about to ward off the boredom. He played a little game, the aim of which was to do a full roll without getting his crash helmet wet. He took his helmet off, jettisoned his paddle and tipped over his canoe, while holding the helmet out of the water. His other hand now came up from the other side of the upturned canoe and received the helmet. To finish he then rolled up, with one hand still holding the helmet aloft — tricks fit for a circus. "If I could do that, I'd be world champion," I moaned jealously.

The scenery soon became more interesting as we passed an area of conglomerate pinnacles called "the Surface of Mars". Here, Stu was practising weird helicopter rolls and Ray was rolling with Maggie clinging to the deck of his canoe. A short distance further on we had lunch beside an abandoned attempt at a copper mine. Geologically, the valley was a gem.

After lunch the canoeing became more exciting as the river began to fall quickly through a rocky gorge. John Watson and I were finding things very interesting. Following Ray down through the rocky rapids, we watched him intently for the correct line as he picked his way through the narrow rock-studded shoots with the occasional small drop to give the party a burst of adrenalin. After about an hour of this exhilaration we reached a derelict camp fashioned from New Zealand Railways tarpaulins. Nearby lay two abandoned canoes of about the same vintage as the one I had used in the Wanganui River race. Their owners had apparently "psyched" and walked out — not surprising; they had done very well to get this far. "Bloody heroes," said Ray, looking at the battered antiques.

We paddled on and were shortly taken by surprise by a very rocky grade 3–4 rapid. Chatting and drifting along we blundered into the first wild water and things went quite well for a while until suddenly Colin Abbott and I shot into a narrow channel together — a dreadful combination in a tight spot! I lost my cool, fought to get into an eddy, the canoe swung around against a rock and I tipped in. It would have been an easy roll, but my confidence deserted me and I abandoned ship. The unfortunate canoe and I then shot down over a 1-m fall and I floundered in the pool for a while until Ray rescued me. Earlier, Ray had also come to grief, but managed to roll up. John Watson was the only other casualty.

The rafters were now enjoying themselves immensely, and Rodger's silly songs were exchanged for whoops of joy.

The river continued to provide the entertainment for a further two hours, cutting through narrow slit gorges and presenting the odd good rapid. In one of these the raft nearly flipped, tipping Maggie and Jan into the water, where Jan had tremendous difficulty staying afloat. (It is often hard to tell whether a floundering person is laughing or drowning — maybe even both.)

At about 6 p.m. we began to look for a camp site, and soon found one not far above the Te Hoe river junction. The only problem with the little river flat we had chosen was an unreasonable sheep that had hung itself in a scrubby Manuka bush and was smelling badly. As we had a considerable amount of drying to do, I stacked some dead wood around the tree and set fire to it. Both the sheep and the tree burned admirably. "Roast mutton for dinner," grinned Rodger. Remarkably, most of us had kept our sleeping bags dry, by the copious use of plastic bags or thoroughly taped plastic containers.

It was a pleasant evening sitting by the fire with friends, chatting about the day and drinking coffee laced with rum.

Day two was the big day. Somewhere below us we knew the river thundered through a gorge, which was said to be grade 5. John Davidson was in a crazy mood and paddled off alone, not to be seen again for the rest of the trip. However, that removed one problem — there is now only one John for the narrator

Me breaking through a small stopper on the Mandakini River, India. *Tony Parker*

to describe!

We paddled for an hour, passing en route the Te Hoe River flowing in on the true left and adding greatly to the Mohaka's volume, before the confining walls and increased roar of water heralded the much-dreaded rapid. We beached the canoes and raft and went for a look. The rapid was fairly straight and about 400 m in length, but wild water cascading around and over large boulders made it an intimidating place. The first 200 m looked relatively easy: water dropped in a series of short cascades studded with rocks to a deeper section about 100 m long.

The final 100 m was frightening. It began with a horribly undercut rock stuck right in the middle of the current. To be caught in this would mean sure death. The flow then broke evenly on each side, which presented two possibilities. On the right a small fall led to an aerated eddy before two gaps, one of which was too narrow to go through and the other just wide enough to take a canoe (if it went in straight). At the end of this gap a final fall would take the canoe into a large pool. On the left the water swept into a broken area, then around another undercut rock before finally plunging over a drop, which we had previously heard measured 2.5 m, but was in fact nearer 1.5 m. Ray was keen on trying the right-hand side, while Stu and Jo decided on the left. Colin also decided to give the rapid a go on the left. The place frightened John and me, and we were torn between the challenge and the fear, finally giving in both to fear and lack of motivation. The rafters also decided to miss the rapid because of their lack of control.

The portage of gear was a very strenuous business because of the maze of huge boulders that littered the bank. Once this was completed we cowardly ones stood in wait, me with a rope to effect a rescue if it was necessary. The rapid was to be shot in three sections.

Down came Ray, his green capsule bobbing up and down, cutting in and out carefully, sweeping to the far right and then to the left and finally emerging unscathed into the relatively easy water. It looked almost easy, and I was beginning to regret not giving it a go. The others followed: Stu, Jo, then Colin. Now they got out and surveyed the next section — too dangerous in the main flow where the current swept under the rock was the consensus, so all three took a shallow "chicken-run" on the extreme left.

Jo led the final section, being too scared to wait. She broke from behind a rock into the main flow, drawing the boat vigorously to the left to avoid being swept against the rocks. She just managed it, then straightened up for the final shoot. The onlookers were scarcely breathing, and hearts pounded. Down the fall she was fired like a rocket. A cheer of relief went up from everyone as she emerged upright in the pool, smiling nervously.

Both Stu and Colin got tangled up in the first lot of rocks through not paddling positively enough, and then were almost swept against the final rock, but recovered in time to be fired down the shoot. Colin tipped in this final sec-

tion, made a hurried attempt at a roll and then bailed out.

Ray's attempt was last and the most spectacular. He had chosen the right side, but probably wasn't too sure of his decision and didn't commit himself properly to the run. He shot over the first little rocky drop and into the boiling eddy. He failed to line up properly for the next section, had second thoughts and desperately tried to backpaddle. The water piled up on his back deck and over he went. The situation looked very bad. In a moment he had rolled up, but seconds later he disappeared into one of the narrow gaps. From where I stood, rope at the ready, all I could see was his paddle blade waving around in the air and I was sure he had become jammed across the gap. I dashed about like a blue-arsed fly, getting nowhere, trying to work out whether I could jump the gap to effect a rescue. Maggie was shouting, "No, Graeme; no Graeme!" and I wasn't sure whether she was frightened for me or Ray. I later found out that she was afraid that if I jumped and missed I would have pulled her in, too! However, after what seemed an age, Ray suddenly popped out through the hole and dropped into the pool. A final cheer went up and the tension slowly subsided as the dregs of adrenalin were absorbed.

On the rocks above the final fall, three well-known canoeists had desecrated the place by painting their names boldly in yellow on the cliff face.

Below "long rapid" some broken bits of canoe made us wonder at John Davidson's fate — we were really annoyed that he had carried on without giving us any clear understanding of where we would see him again, an extremely courageous but stupid action, I moaned to myself and Stu. But we need not have worried about him; he's a survivor from way back!

The remaining 15 km of the journey is perhaps the most interesting, as the river desperately tries to cut out through the hills to the coast and continues to throw out surprises. We found ourselves cutting through mazes of giant boulders and through gaps just wide enough for the canoes — a nerve-racking experience for the rafters who had to backpaddle hurriedly and portage on a few occasions.

As we grew tired, epics and casualties became more common. John capsized and lost his paddle, which was replaced by the only spare. A little further on, through lack of concentration, I got caught side-on to a rock in the main current. The canoe was pinned in place and quickly filled with water through a hole in the bottom. It then folded neatly around the rock with my legs trapped inside. There followed what seemed to be several minutes of panic and violent rocking before the canoe broke almost in half and I tumbled down the rapid backwards, still in my crippled vessel. After cracking my helmeted head hard on a rock, I abandoned ship and pushed the remaining pieces of fibreglass across the current to the side. My paddle was still folded neatly around the rock, but Rodger expertly retrieved it as the raft rushed past.

Old faithful cellotape and a length of manuka wood jammed down the paddle shaft effected an amazingly good repair job to both canoe and paddle. I had to empty my canoe after every couple of rapids, but, considering that it had been virtually broken in half, I was lucky not to be walking. Later I dropped my paddle which went straight to the bottom of a deep pool, but I amazed myself by recovering

it with a dive. (I told you earlier that I had trouble staying on the surface!)

A little further on a particularly nasty rapid caused another sensation. Stu went first and made a pretty good job of it until he relaxed, went sideways over a large rock and tipped into the stopper beyond. After an effort he rolled up, but the canoe was sucked back into the stopper and this time he abandoned the hapless vessel. He was bundled around a few times in the stopper before being spat out, but his canoe was held there for a further 10 to 15 minutes.

Jo's effort superseded even Stu's. She capsized over half-way down and lost her paddle, then valiantly tried to hand roll before leaving her boat. It seemed she was under water for ages even before she entered Stu's stopper, but now she appeared to be trapped for ever, bundled around as if in a super washing machine — only on what seemed every second revolution did a gasping mouth appear from the water sucking vigorously. Just as I was considering making the "big swim" she popped out. "Thank the Lord!" I groaned. We were tired. As the light faded we bumbled on, John and I getting rather sick of tipping in.

It was nearly pitch black when we thankfully reached our destination — Willow Flat. It was a great adventure, and I consider the Mohaka a river well worth protecting if the N.Z.E.D. set their beady eyes on it for power generation.

---

## Summary of Mohaka River trip

*A descent of the Mohaka River during January 1979 from the Napier/Taupo highway to Willow Flat by staff of the OPC. Grade: Difficult, IV sup.*

Looking back, it would have been better to have spent three days over this section of the river, particularly with low water and a raft.

John Davidson had a responsibility to the rest of the group to state clearly what his intentions were. If he wished to go solo on the second day he should have made that clear to the rest of the group instead of burdening us with concern for his safety.

These factors aside, the trip was well planned and well executed.

# Canoeing and kayaking

The sport of canoeing takes many forms and in this section I have touched on only two of these — sea canoeing and river canoeing. There are many other possibilities including whitewater racing and various types of flat-water racing, canoeing in open and competition Canadian canoes, singles (C1) and doubles (C2), and so on.

There are two main types of craft: those designs based on the Eskimo kayak and those based on the North American Indian canoe. Kayaks employ a double-bladed paddle while canoes require a single-bladed type.

There appears to be much confusion about the naming of the various modern vessels that are used. For example, the organisation representing the sport in Britain is called the British Canoe Union, and in New Zealand the New Zealand Canoeing Association, despite the fact that by far the major percentage of members own vessels based on the Eskimo design — that is, kayaks. For this reason I refer throughout this section to canoes and canoeing and when I wish to differentiate between canoes and kayaks I will write C1 or C2 and K1 or K2. (K2 is also the name of the second-highest mountain on Earth, but if I mean that I will precede the reference with the word "supercalifragilistic"!)

In New Zealand the sport and, particularly, the running of wild rivers have become popular only quite recently, unless one wishes to consider runs supposedly made by Maori dugout canoes. Most of the North Island rivers have now been canoed. The few remaining uncanoed sections are steadily being "knocked off", either by canoeists or the N.Z.E.D., but in the South Island there are still many wild rivers awaiting their first descent. For those North Islanders keen to make a name, there is the horrifying Huka Falls which have now been successfully swum, rafted and canoed. There is a colourful Maori legend which tells us that the amazing Tamatea Arikinui went over the falls in a war canoe together with his warriors, many of whom drowned in the attempt.

There are many good sea journeys to do around the New Zealand coast, too. A few years ago a Greymouth man, Paul Caffyn, completed an amazing circumnavigation of both islands over two separate summers — a truly great effort.

Surfing (in canoes) is also a popular offshoot of the sport and this can be a very successful way of developing general technique and having a lot of fun.

Potentially, canoeing is very dangerous and there have been a number of drownings of novices, particularly in lakes. However, the mortality rate in canoeing accidents is low as yet, although it should be remembered that there are relatively few people canoeing really hard rivers. Canoeing has more potential in New Zealand than just about any other vigorous recreational activity (apart from some indoor sports) as most people live near a river, a lake or the sea.

## Equipment

Canoeing is a relatively expensive game in which to become involved. However, it is certainly not as expensive as alpine climbing or skiing.

A good canoe currently costs about twice the average weekly wage. For yet another week of sweat and toil you should be able to buy the rest of your gear, but the costs won't end there (unless you live near the sea and do all your canoeing there). Canoeing is highly dependent on transport, and there will be lots of repairs necessary to your canoe. However, both factors are reducible if you join a club or share transport with friends. Clubs often own canoe moulds, which enable members to reduce costs considerably.

The advent of plastic canoes (tupperware boats, Stu Allan calls them) has made repairs much less problematic, but the initial outlay is greater.

## Types of canoes and kayaks and their uses

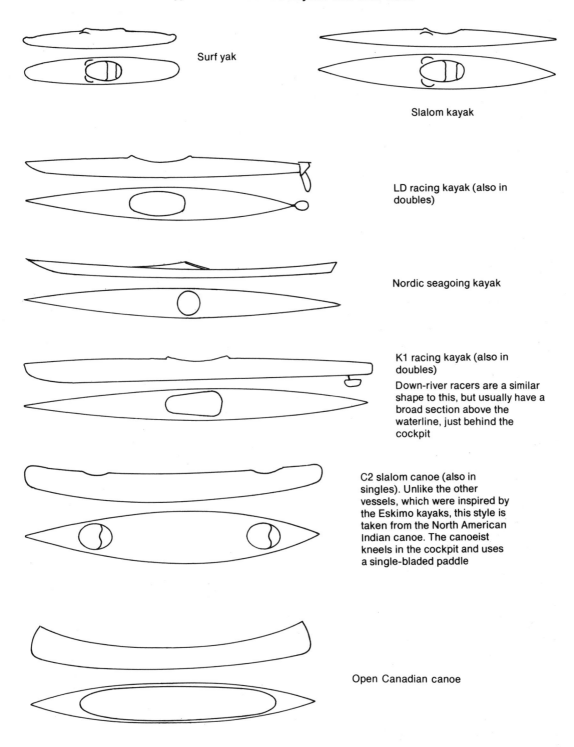

Surf yak

Slalom kayak

LD racing kayak (also in doubles)

Nordic seagoing kayak

K1 racing kayak (also in doubles)

Down-river racers are a similar shape to this, but usually have a broad section above the waterline, just behind the cockpit

C2 slalom canoe (also in singles). Unlike the other vessels, which were inspired by the Eskimo kayaks, this style is taken from the North American Indian canoe. The canoeist kneels in the cockpit and uses a single-bladed paddle

Open Canadian canoe

## The well-dressed canoeist

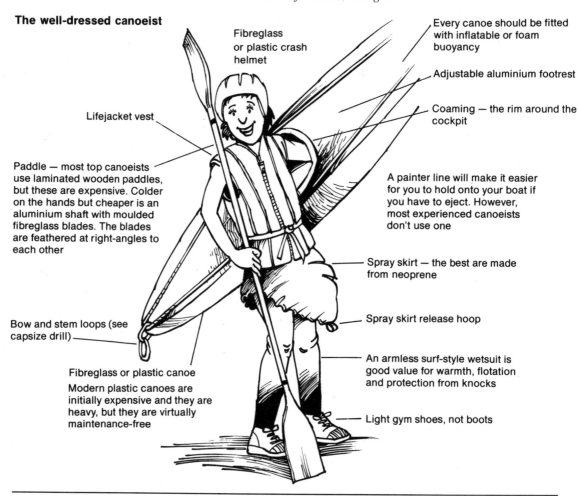

Fibreglass or plastic crash helmet

Every canoe should be fitted with inflatable or foam buoyancy

Adjustable aluminium footrest

Coaming — the rim around the cockpit

Lifejacket vest

Paddle — most top canoeists use laminated wooden paddles, but these are expensive. Colder on the hands but cheaper is an aluminium shaft with moulded fibreglass blades. The blades are feathered at right-angles to each other

A painter line will make it easier for you to hold onto your boat if you have to eject. However, most experienced canoeists don't use one

Spray skirt — the best are made from neoprene

Spray skirt release hoop

Bow and stem loops (see capsize drill)

An armless surf-style wetsuit is good value for warmth, flotation and protection from knocks

Fibreglass or plastic canoe

Modern plastic canoes are initially expensive and they are heavy, but they are virtually maintenance-free

Light gym shoes, not boots

### Carrying the canoe

Avoid carrying a canoe full of water or equipment. When two people are carrying an empty canoe it should be held with one arm around the vessel rather than by the end loops (which may be required when you capsize!)

# Canoeing techniques

The canoeing skill is a highly complex one. Unlike most outdoor pursuits skills, it involves the co-ordination of four separate factors.
1. Your own body and mind.
2. The canoe.
3. The paddle.
4. The water — usually moving.

To become expert you will, of course, need to understand all of these. Whether you use a double-bladed paddle to paddle a kayak or a single-bladed paddle to paddle a canoe, most techniques are similar.

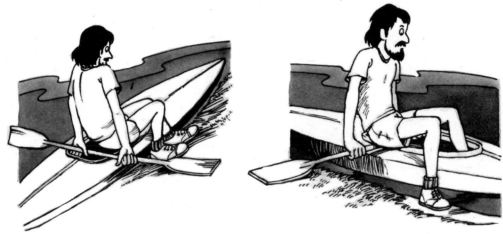

**Getting in and out of the canoe**
Place the paddle blade on dry ground and the shaft across the back coaming. Grasp the shaft and coaming while transferring your weight to the canoe. Work your feet into the canoe and place them comfortably against the footrest. Move your hips into the cockpit. Fit the spray skirt if you are wearing one. When leaving the canoe follow this procedure in reverse.

**The paddle sequence**
Feathered paddles are difficult to use initially, but the tecnhique will soon become second nature.

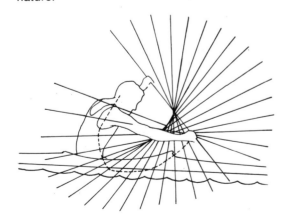

1. Decide which hand is the master hand.
2. Grip the shaft centrally with the hands a little wider than shoulder width apart.
3. Assuming the right hand is master, reach forward and, with the right arm straight, dip the blade into the water close to the canoe. Draw it back until it is just behind your body.
4. At this point the blade is raised from the water and the left blade is dipped towards the water. The left arm is now straight and the right arm is bent with the right hand near the right side of your face.
5. The right wrist is now cocked back, which will rotate the shaft in the left hand until the left blade is in the correct position.
6. Now dip the left blade, draw back with the left arm and drive forward with the right arm.

Lean forward when paddling forward and lean back when paddling backwards.

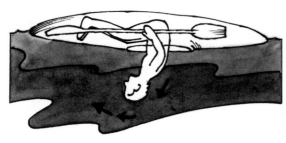

### Getting out of the canoe under water
1. Try to keep hold of your paddle.
2. Release the spray skirt by pulling the release loop.
3. Push your body out of the cockpit by pushing on the deck with your hands.
4. Roll forward. Try to avoid kicking your legs or twisting as you may get caught in the cockpit.

### Floating with the canoe
1. Don't turn the canoe upright — it will float better with the air trapped inside.
2. Move to the upstream end of the canoe. Grasp the end loop. In this respect a painter line (see illustration of well-dressed canoeist on page 128) will assist you to keep hold of the canoe while moving to the end.

Pressing on the paddle

Hanging on the paddle

### The slap for support
Practise this recovery stroke until it becomes second nature. Tip the canoe slowly and, just as it is about to tip completely, slap the surface of the water vigorously. As you become more proficient you will find that a more gentle strike is effective.

Don't forget to use your hip flick as well as leverage off the paddle.

## THE MAIN TURNING STROKES

### Low telemark — pressing stroke

This is probably the first stroke to learn after the paddling stroke. Both telemark turns are used when the canoe is moving in relation to the water.

*Remember that whatever turning stroke you use, lean the canoe in the direction of the turn as if you are riding a bicycle. This is crucial for success.*

### High telemark — hanging stroke

This stroke is more effective than the low telemark, but more difficult to execute. With both strokes, the canoe rotates around the blade.

### The sweep stroke

This turning stroke is generally used when the canoe is not moving in relation to the water.

Place the blade as far away from the canoe as possible, with the shaft angle low (almost horizontal). Sweep the blade in a wide arc. The direction of the sweep will depend on the way you wish to turn the canoe. By rotating the blade a little so that it planes, you can use this stroke for support.

131

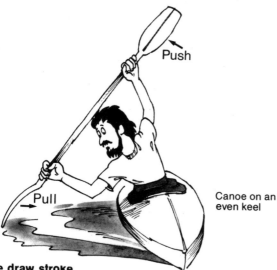

Push

Pull

Canoe on an even keel

### The draw stroke
This stroke is used to move the canoe sideways. Beginners should do it gently as it is easy to tip yourself in if the blade release is not done properly.
1. Pull yourself towards the blade without tipping the canoe too much.
2. When the blade is close to the canoe, rotate it 90 degrees and push it back through the water to the starting point.
3. Repeat.

### The bow rudder
This stroke is used to turn the bow quickly.

A *stern rudder* can be used for turning by placing the paddle, driving face inwards, 60 cm out from the stern.

### Sculling
This is a good confidence-building exercise as a preparation for rolling. With your body on the surface of the water, stroke the paddle blade back and forth on the surface and maintain this position for as long as possible.

### Swimming to the pool edge
On reaching the edge roll up as illustrated in the next diagram.

### Rolling up
Rolling up or using the side rail or pool edge as if it were the paddle shaft. Develop the hip flick in preparation for Eskimo rolling like this.

### Swimming in the canoe
Another useful confidence-building exercise in the pool is to cast the paddle away and swim to it, then if you can roll up as described over the page.

### The Pawlatta roll

While learning you may find it useful to use a diving mask or at least a nose clip. The instructor should stand in the water beside the canoe so the student can be assisted up if necesary.

As you strike, watch blade A and try to keep it on the surface. Avoid striking downwards (this will probably be your major problem). Blade B will be more vertical than illustrated.

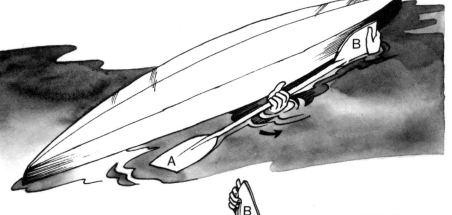

The paddle is held as illustrated with blade A mo or less sitting flat on the deck. Blade B will be almo vertical. Lean forward. The paddle should be locked i this position so that when the canoe is upside down the blade is sitting flat on t surface of the water.

Blade A is now drawn back in a broad arc. At the same time, rotate the canoe with your hips. This is the strike and should be done with aggression and power (at least to begin with). Don't be tempted to get your body out of the water too quickly.

The canoe should be almost righted before the body (arched back as far as possible) leaves the water.

Once you have mastered this as a set up exercise, try setting yourself up underwater (without presetting the paddle).

### The screw roll
This is executed in the same manner as the Pawlatta roll, but the grip on the paddle is the same as for any other stroke. This means that leverage is not quite as good as with the Pawlatta, but the roll can be done more quickly.

### Rafting up
This is done on a lake or sea for communication, to assist one or more members, or simply to rest. Note the way the raft can be manoeuvred by the canoeists on the outside using their paddles in only one hand.

The raft is kept together by grasping overlapped paddles or by holding the neighbour's coaming.

## Deep-water rescue with three canoeists

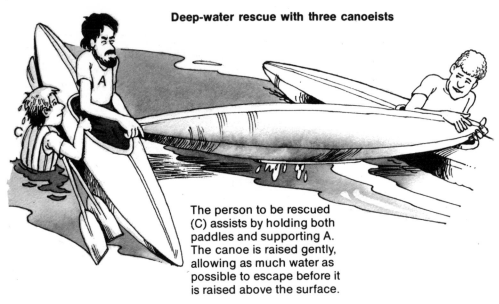

The person to be rescued (C) assists by holding both paddles and supporting A. The canoe is raised gently, allowing as much water as possible to escape before it is raised above the surface.

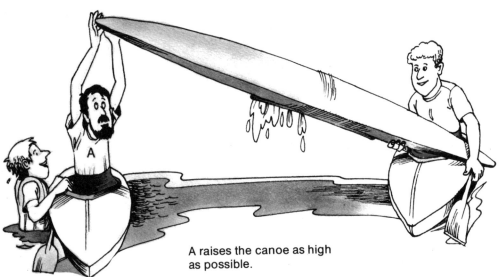

A raises the canoe as high as possible.

C's canoe is turned upright and supported with the assistance of linked paddles and the hands of A and B gripping the coaming of C's canoe as well as their own paddles. C then climbs astride the stern of his canoe and slips his legs into the cockpit.

## Deep-water rescue with two canoeists

The upturned canoeist signals to the other canoeist by raising both hands out of the water and banging on the side of his canoe. If it is necessary to take a breath, do so as in the illustration on page 133.

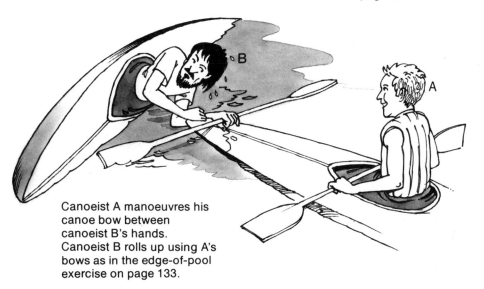

Canoeist A manoeuvres his canoe bow between canoeist B's hands. Canoeist B rolls up using A's bows as in the edge-of-pool exercise on page 133.

## Packing the canoe

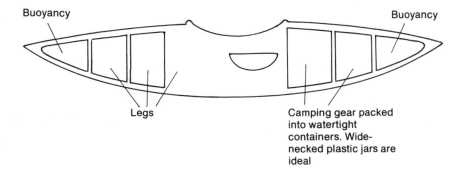

Buoyancy

Buoyancy

Legs

Camping gear packed into watertight containers. Wide-necked plastic jars are ideal

# The laws of moving water

Water reacts exactly like air in the way it flows and swirls. The stopper in a river is very similar to a ridgewave as the air flows over a mountain range. As with air, cold water sinks and warm water rises. While the water of a wild river may look chaotic, its reactions are reasonably predictable, and an understanding of the habits of water is a crucial part of the white-water canoeist's knowledge.

**The loop**

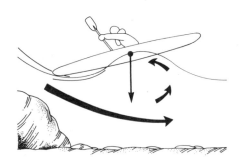

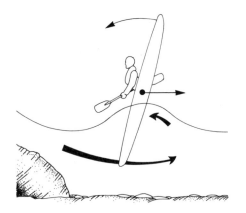

The canoeist drives the canoe into the trough behind a wave.

The bow dips and the stern comes up. By leaning back you will slow the loop. By leaning forward you will speed the loop and be in a better position to roll up again.

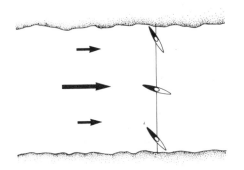

**The ferry glide**

On a straight section of river the current will often be strongest in the middle, while on bends the current will be strongest on the outside of the curve.

The ferry glide is a method of moving across the current without losing ground and with the minimum of effort. You should provide the forward momentum with your paddle, and the current will push the canoe sideways. Point the bow into the current and towards the opposite bank. The angle will depend on the strength of the current — in a gentle current, as at the water's edge, form a steep angle; where there is a strong current the angle should not be as great. Lean downstream to avoid water piling up on the upstream side and tipping you in.

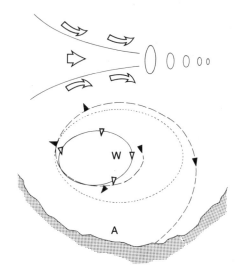

### Escaping from a whirlpool
There has been at least one tragedy I know of and untold epics that have taken place in whirlpools.

If W is the eye of the pool and you want to get to point A, the instinctive thing to do will be to swim direct towards A, as the unsuccessful canoeists marked ▷ are trying to do. It is generally more successful to swim outwards from the eye of the pool, as those marked ▶ are doing.

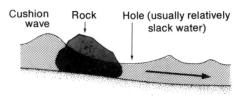

**Cushion wave** **Rock** **Hole (usually relatively slack water)**

### Cross-section of an obstacle in a river

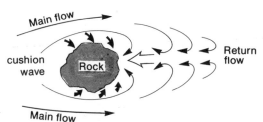

Main flow

cushion wave    Rock    Return flow

Main flow

### A bird's-eye view of an obstacle in a river
(The holes behind the rocks can make good resting places. Practise cutting in and out behind them.)

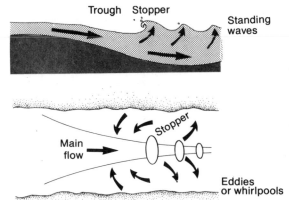

Trough   Stopper   Standing waves

Main flow   Stopper   Eddies or whirlpools

### The formation of waves in a river
When water rushes over a drop, waves form below it. Depending on the severity of the drop, the first wave(s) is known as a stopper(s). The most severe will hold a canoe and its passenger(s) in the trough upstream of the wave. Below the stoppers are standing waves.

## Grading

Canoeists have landed themselves in a similar problematic situation to mountaineers by imposing a ceiling on the ability of future canoeists. The existing systems were designed for canvas craft, but modern materials have widened horizons considerably. For example, grade VI in Europe canoed in K1 (single kayak) racing canoes has been a hitherto inconceivable idea.

Looking at the river gradings and canoeists' attitudes from an outside position, I see a very messy situation. I think climbers as a group understand better than canoeists the value of grading, and canoeists could learn much from looking at the climbing systems of gradings and attitudes. The best I can do here is offer my opinions and suggest thinkings that may tidy things up a little.

A worthwhile grading system should strive to give two types of information:
1. The *overall* commitment of a canoe trip (seriousness).
2. The *technicality* of individual rapids.

To set grades the following factors must be considered:

*Overall* (section grading)
a. The number of rapids: the greater the number of rapids in a section the higher this grade.
b. The objective danger in rapids: snags, log jams, current sweeping under the bank, rocks and holes.
c. Remoteness — here there are two areas: the difficulty of escape from the river and the distance that the river is from the road.
d. Flooding potential.
e. Cold: this will, of course, sap energy quickly, making a section more serious.
f. Colour of water.
g. Length of journey.
h. Whether rapids can be portaged or not.

*Individual* (rapid grading)
The technical grade of a section of river should be placed on the hardest rapid in that section (which, ideally, should be identified).
a. Volume and power of water.
b. Complexity of the course through the rapid.
c. The drop: a waterfall in a low flow might be as difficult technically as a less steep cataract with a much greater flow.
d. The length of the rapid.
e. The wave forms in the rapid: shape of stoppers and waves will vary with the river bottom and flow.
f. Danger (or seriousness).

The technical difficulty of individual rapids, as described in The New Zealand Canoeing Association *Canoeists' Guides*, are generally accepted, but once again, as with climbing, the developers of the system have imposed a ceiling.

I feel that these grades should range from I to infinity with VI being the hardest canoed in New Zealand to date.

**I** Scarcely any white-water except for waves little more than ripples. The current is slow moving to moderate and the course through is obvious.

**II** Straightforward with regular standing waves, rock dodges and small falls of up to 30 cm which need no specialised paddle techniques. Water may slosh over the deck, but with no real force. The course of the river is easily recognisable.

**III** Requiring deliberate guiding of the canoe down the chosen route. Higher irregular waves of up to 1 m in height. Falls of up to 1 m in which the canoe may disappear for a few seconds in foam. Draw and recovery strokes will be needed to combat unexpected conditions.

**IV** There will probably be big, powerful waves, varying in position and irregularly spaced. Powerful backlash and moderate stoppers may exist, all requiring anticipation. Water will splash well over your head. Falls of up to 1.5 m.

**V** Long stretches of very powerful water, foaming and boiling making a planned course extremely difficult to follow. Very powerful backlash and high, varying waves with stoppers that are difficult to break through. Too fast and difficult for most paddle strokes. Support strokes and rolling important, but stoppers require full speed. Falls of up to 2 m.

**VI** Horrific! (to me, anyway).

The technical division of the grading system also uses plus (+) and minus (−) sub-gradings as shown below in the grading examples. Reference to gradings is often meaningless unless reference is also made to flow − gradings can change considerably with river fluctuations.

**Grading examples** (based on the international system of overall and technical gradings)

(E.) *Easy*, I: e.g. Tongariro River from State Highway 1 to Lake Taupo.

(M.) *Moderate*, II−: e.g. Tongariro River from Red Hut Pool to State Highway 1 bridge.

(M.D.) *Mildly Difficult*, III−: e.g. Tongariro River from Poutu Intake to Red Hut Pool.

(D.) *Difficult*, IV−: e.g. Mohaka River from Napier/Taupo Highway to Willow Flat.

(V.D.) *Very difficult*, V−: e.g. Rangitikei Gorge to Pukeokahu.

(E.D.) *Extremely Difficult*, VI: Kawarau from Nevis Bluff to Clutha − only partly canoed by 1983!

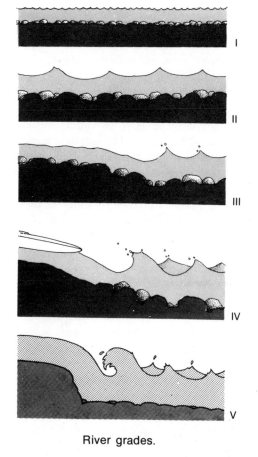

River grades.

Approx. scale: 1 cm = 2 metres

An easy river with one hard rapid or waterfall in it could be graded "Moderate, VI". The verbal description that followed would then qualify what was meant.

# Rafting

*If a traveller has one hide only at his disposal he should make a coracle, if he has two, a punt.*

Francis Galton, *Art of Travel*, 1872

Rafting is a great sport for young and old and can be a tremendous social activity, particularly if you want a group to shed their inhibitions and begin operating as a team. It is most unsophisticated compared with canoeing, and it seems that the less control there is the more fun may be had. Everyone is captain, and when a large rock in mid-stream has to be avoided "sods' lore" determines that 50 per cent of the crew will shout "right" and paddle right; the remainder will shout "left" and paddle towards the left. The usual outcome is that the raft goes straight over the top of the rock!

Good river rafts are very expensive, but just as much fun can be had by tying truck tubes together. If you do wish to bring skill into the game you'll have to know the habits of the river. These will be the same as described in the canoeing section, but the raft, of course, will react much less positively. Any required movement across the current must be anticipated well in advance; to date no-one has been successful at a full Eskimo roll, although half rolls are common.

If you are determined to get technical about rafting you will probably consider two styles of control.

*Paddles*: An inflatable raft of the "Avon" style with up to 10 people plus gear on board is, of course, very heavy and unwieldy and can be a desperate beast to control unless the group works as a team and paddles effectively. The paddling strokes are similar to canoeing strokes, and four of these will be particularly effective: the draw, the drive, the sweep and the stern rudder. I also often use the bow rudder.

*Oars*: A frame, usually tubular steel, is lashed to the top of the raft, and one person (sitting in the centre of the raft) does most of the work.

A commercially produced raft in the upper Tongariro. Crew, *front*: Ian (right) and Roy Jowett; *back*: Lynn Jowett (left) and Corrina Dingle.
*Graeme Dingle*

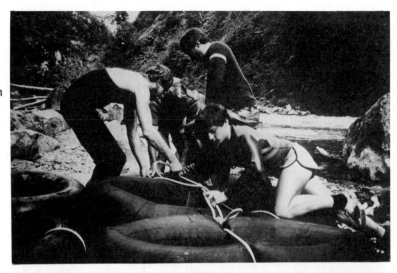

A raft being made from tractor tubes. Crew (right to left): Aaron Hall, Bill Hall, Grant Johnstone, Me.
*Corinna Dingle*

A raft made of tubes in the Tongariro River. Crew, *front*: me; *middle*: Rangi Lord; *back*: a hitchhiker.
*John Blunt*

Sometimes the other people in the raft have paddles for added power. In rapids the oarsman will usually face downstream and row against the current. In this way he or she can manoeuvre back and forth across the current by ferry gliding.

Oars in the hands of an experienced and strong person are perhaps the most effective method of control, but they rob the activity of much of its social charm. Paddles are probably best in smaller, more constrictive rivers. Another advantage of using paddles is if the raft tips there is no heavy frame that will injure and sometimes entangle the occupants. And with paddles, once the raft has tipped the paddlers can clamber back on and continue paddling until the raft can be beached.

In rafting the same safety procedures and equipment (i.e. life jackets and crash helmets) apply as in canoeing. Would-be rafters should read the canoeing section as many aspects will be similar, and the habits of rivers as well as grading systems are common to both activities.

# River crossings

*In crossing a deep river, with a horse or other large animal, drive him in: or even lead him along a steep bank and push him sideways, suddenly into the water: having fairly started, jump in yourself, seize his tail and let him tow you across.*

Francis Galton, *Art of Travel*, 1872

Drowning, mainly in rivers, was once the New Zealand way of dying — many of our pioneer forefathers tried to cross bridgeless rivers on foot or horseback. Rivers are still one of the greatest potential dangers in the outdoors and should be treated with the utmost respect.

It is important to remember that if a crossing looks dicey it may not be so a little further upstream or downstream. Similarly, if it has been raining the river will probably reduce in volume fairly quickly once the rain stops. (If it's Sunday evening and you have to be at work on Monday, what the hell! Safety is more important than saving time, and the country won't grind to a halt without you.) Remember, you do not hurl yourself off a cliff hoping to land in a soft bush at the bottom; similarly, it would be crazy to hurl yourself into a river hoping to emerge on the other side.

I was crossing a river in the Tararuas years ago with a group of friends — all great big muscular trampers. We were crossing on a pole. Because I was the smallest I was put on the downstream end of the pole and we ploughed into the mad, swirling river. The big muscular fellow on the upstream end of the pole stumbled and the pole slowly began to turn in the current. Soon I was the upstream man and all my big mates were systematically plucked from the pole downstream from me. To cut a long story short, I was left standing in the middle of the river holding the pole and finally managed to battle my way to the other side while some of my friends finished up on the wrong side of the river — I was delighted!

## River classifications

It is very difficult, if not impossible, to classify a river as any particular type as most rivers experience many changes on their journey to the sea. Generally a river begins steeply and levels out as it nears the coast. However, its course

The Baru Sahib crossing. Those people (usually of high breeding) who dislike wet feet should find two bearers. A stout pole lashed between them makes a tolerable seat. *Maggie Button*

The pole for support — a technique often used by hunters and musterers who work alone. The pole should be placed securely upstream, then the feet are moved carefully while the pole supports much of the weight.
*Graeme Dingle*

may be complicated if it has been forced to change direction and cut through a seam of rock or a hill that has been thrust up in its path in some wild, bygone age.

Sections of rivers can, however, be broadly categorised. The descriptions below will help you to recognise river types and thus choose a crossing technique.

### Bouldery

Most mountain torrents go through this stage. They are usually steep rivers, often with wild rapids, gorges and falls. Most West Coast (South Island) rivers are of this type as they descend quickly from the Southern Alps.

### Shingle bedded

Glacial rivers usually become braided (divided into several channels) as they cross the glacial plains to the sea. Most East Coast (South Island) rivers, particularly in Canterbury, are of this kind. Gorges are rare once they have reached the plains. Glacial rivers rise with the heat of the day. They are generally at their lowest first thing in the morning.

### Sluggish

These rivers are often deep and gorgey with mild rapids every so often. They are mostly found in the North Island. The Wanganui River is such a river. These rivers often rise very quickly after the onset of rain.

## Choosing a ford and a crossing technique

If the water is clear, relatively slow and less than knee deep you can usually make a solo crossing. If the bottom is difficult or if the water is relatively swift a pole may be used for support. If the river is deeper and swifter, the most effective crossing method is usually one of the *mutual support systems*. However, the problem with any of these systems is that if something goes wrong and people get swept away there is no back-up. If there is any danger from the river below the crossing point this system is unacceptable, particularly with an inexperienced group. With such a group mutual support systems should be used when the crossing is safe.

When some of the members are diffident and perhaps frightened, or if they are much smaller than the rest of the group, there are several alternative mutual support systems which may be employed. They are listed here in order of effectiveness (the last being the strongest): the clothing grip, the pack strap grip, the pole and the log.

If possible, the crossing place should conform to the following factors: it should have a good run out in case anything goes wrong (that is, it should not be above dangerous rapids, waterfalls or where the river sweeps under banks and log jams); a reasonable entrance into the water (not straight off the bank and up to your neck); a reasonably even bottom and a good exit on the opposite bank.

# MUTUAL SUPPORT SYSTEMS

Mutual support — the clothing grip.

Mutual support — the shoulder strap grip.

The log system. There is a source of argument about which way to wrap your arms around the log. In this shot the trampers are using both possibilities. I have always liked to use the technique followed by the six downstream people — that is, facing slightly upstream. The strongest people should be upstream. *Graeme Dingle*

It is most important to work as a team and to stay with the log regardless of the depth of water.

The pole system is similar to the log system, but when a thinner pole is used the party links arms and grasps the pole with both hands. *Graeme Dingle*

The New Zealand Mountain Safety Council *Bushcraft* manual states: "In entering the river, move side-on to the current to present the least resistance by the body to the water. Mentally plot the course to be followed so that the downriver movement is not mistaken for progress across. Steps should not be lifted but you should feel for obstacles or changes of slope on the bottom. Cross directly or diagonally downstream, the course depending upon the strength of the current and its depth. Avoid giving way more than you have to, as stability is affected while moving with a strong current. Keep moving steadily, preferably looking ahead. Do not alarm yourself by staring down at the water rushing by. Be aware of the increasing force of the current against the body as water becomes deeper and swifter.

"With a good ford and water at waist height or more, progress towards the opposite bank may be made by a competent party with a trotting movement downstream partly supported by the water."

If you are forced to retreat do not turn around, but rather back out of the river.

I would use *roped crossings* with an inexperienced party whenever there was any danger of any members of the party being swept away. There is much argument about whether one should be tied on to the rope from around the waist, or simply whether a loop of rope should be held in the hand. Personally, I strongly prefer the first method, particularly if youngsters are involved, because it is important that you (the instructor or guide) remain in control. You do not want them letting go of the loop when they feel like it. Once this problem has been resolved, the only other decision left to make is whether the first person across should swim or walk steadily using a pole for support — there is a case for both, and sometimes even a combination of both (for instance, if the last part of the crossing traverses a very deep section the leader may opt to throw away the pole and swim for it).

The rope should be made of terylene rather than nylon as nylon will stretch, which is a hindrance when people are penduluming. The thinner the diameter of rope (7 mm is about the optimum) the less drag will be created by the water on the rope. An ideal length is 35 m.

The crucial essence of the rope technique illustrated overleaf is the pendulum:

1. If the first person across slips, he or she should pendulum back to the bank. If this is impossible you have chosen the wrong crossing place.
2. Once the first person is across, the party's troubles are over; the remaining members of the party should simply pendulum across on the end of the rope. If the current makes this difficult you have chosen the wrong crossing place. Find somewhere else where the current is an aid rather than an interference to the pendulum.

Of the many don'ts in river crossing, one of the most important is *don't* put a fixed rope across a river and get the party to cross attached to the rope by a karabiner or any other fixture. If you do and if the person crossing slips, the pressure of the water will usually make it impossible for a footing to be regained.

A further technique, which is strongly promoted in Canterbury and is effective in most rivers in that area, is the Canterbury trot: cross by going with the current. Holding the bottom of your pack against your back with your thumbs, lean back on the pack and move diagonally across and down stream with a kind of trotting gait. The system is suitable only where the river bottom is relatively smooth and consistent. With all systems, make sure you can get out of your pack if necessary. Unfasten waist bands and sternum straps and loosen shoulder straps. Some people prefer to slip off one shoulder strap.

The Canterbury trot.

**Crossing a river on a rope**

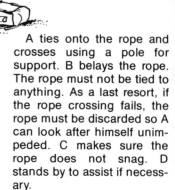

If crossing with an inexperienced group it is crucial that all members understand the system. If the group is made up of inexperienced members except for the leader, it is probably best that the leader stand at position B.

A ties onto the rope and crosses using a pole for support. B belays the rope. The rope must not be tied to anything. As a last resort, if the rope crossing fails, the rope must be discarded so A can look after himself unimpeded. C makes sure the rope does not snag. D stands by to assist if necessary.

After crossing, A takes up a belay position. B continues to belay from the starting point. C faces A and, *with the rope tight*, pendulums to the far bank. D stands by ready to assist if necessary. Finally D pendulums across. Some people prefer not to tie onto the rope and instead hold a hand loop, which can be released as a last resort if trouble occurs.

148

# 7

# First aid and rescue

*Though there is a great difference between a good physician and
a bad one, there is very little between a good one and none at all.*

Old proverb

We cramponed quickly down the last steep slope and hurried across the glacier in Indian file: Graham McCallum, Bill Stevenson, Rob Mitchell and I. We were eager to see the end of an eventful day during which we had climbed Mount Arrowsmith.

The sun had gone; it would be dark in an hour. We scrambled down the exposed slabs beside the glacier, tired and keen to get back to camp. But that was much further away than we thought. At about 1,800 m we discovered Pete Smith, a Dunedin medical student, lying on a ledge, the side of his head smashed in and bloody. Beside him was the culprit, a large block of rock, and his friend, seemingly at his wits' end. He had stuck some zinc tape over the wound, adding considerably to the mess.

I had met Pete Smith a few years before in Malte Brun hut. I remembered him best for his mad streak and a particularly interesting alarm clock he had fashioned from a candle and a load of tinware (mugs and so on) that he had found in the hut. He had marked the candle in inches. Estimating that the candle burned at the rate of 1 inch per hour, he tied a string at the 8-inch mark to activate an alarm after eight hours. This string went up and over a rafter. At the end of it, which was reasonably close to his pillow on the bunk, he tied the mass of tinware.

Eight hours before he wished to wake up he lit the candle and peacefully went to sleep. His awakening, or at least the awakening of the whole hut, was not quite so peaceful — a few minutes before 2 a.m. the bunkroom exploded to the crash of enamelware as the string was released.

Pete Smith now lay in an unconscious bundle and we guessed his skull was fractured. There was a hurried debate about how to handle the problem, with me opting for the careful approach, which meant protecting him as well as possible where he was and getting help. Graham McCallum, who probably had more experience in the mountains than all of us put together, won the day with a more brutal but effective treatment. He figured it was crucial to get Pete Smith lower down the mountain and into some shelter. We dragged the poor wretch down, supported between two climbers with safeguarding ropes going up to climbers above. It was probably about 11 p.m. when we reached a large boulder on the moraine walls, which had been excavated underneath to form a good shelter

The next morning three climbers left for the road end with an urgent message for the police to the effect that a climber had a suspected skull fracture and needed helicopter evacuation urgently.

Later that day we carried Pete the relatively short distance down to Cameron hut, then began what seemed a very long wait.

A chopper or light plane could be expected

Carrying a body down the Ngatiawa River, Tararua Range, *circa* 1962. The position of my head is marked. *Barry Durrant The Dominion.*

Carrying Brian Carey down the Hutt River, Southern Tararuas, *circa* 1965. I am at the front, on the left. A carrying frame has been made from long poles. This system requires a broad path or open country. *The Dominion.*

during the afternoon, but there was nothing, and finally we all settled down for another night. Sometime during the night I awoke to the noise of several people arriving at the hut. It was a doctor accompanied by some army blokes from Burnham. The doctor shone a torch at Pete's head and exclaimed, "Goodness, he's got a fractured skull. I think we need a chopper."

"O.K. then," said someone. "Let's get on the radio and call up for a chopper."

"Radio? We haven't brought a radio."

It was decided to despatch a couple of runners so that a helicopter could get in first thing in the morning.

Peter Pohl (I called him Peter Pohl and Mary) and I left the hut at 3.00 a.m. and jogged off toward the road end about 25 km away. Before long we came across several more soldiers with a stretcher, groping around in the ancient moraines trying to find the hut. We showed them the way and cantered off again into the darkness.

The night passed quickly as we chattered and jogged. It was shortly after daylight when we saw an amazing apparition: ranks of uniformed men marching through the matagouri scrub on a river flat. We wiped our eyes and stared as they approached, crashing in ranks through the matagouri in cotton uniforms with the sleeves rolled up. And they didn't have a radio. The seeming lack of any common sense search and rescue procedure seemed to us Tararua demons unbelievable. We greeted the officer in charge, a sergeant I think.

"Hi there. Going to Cameron hut are you? Do you have any food?" we asked rather stupidly, not expecting them to have stuffed it up their trouser legs!

The NCO held up half a packet of gingernuts. "We don't need any," he said. "We'll be there by morning tea time!"

We recommended that they get some food and a little more gear, suggesting that if the weather changed and the river came up they could be up the valley for a few days. They decided they knew best and we went our separate ways.

From the first farm house Peter telephoned to request a chopper. But the reply came back that the cloud ceiling was too low on the West Coast (where the only available chopper was) and it would not be able to fly until there was a clearing. "Be good chaps and dash back up the valley and ask them to carry."

So off we went again, sidling over 25 km of river crossings and matagouri. We took pity on the army, knowing that it marches on its stomach (I had seen this on a movie once — soldiers with small bushes on their hats were creeping up on other soldiers with bushes on their hats) so we carried with us a few ration packs and these we left on a boulder half-way up the valley.

Meanwhile, at the head of the valley, it had been decided that Pete Smith wasn't in such a bad way after all, and those at the hut had already begun carrying him down. Peter Pohl and Mary (!) and I met them near Top hut (about 2 km below Cameron hut). After a complex and verbose mountaineers' greeting, "Gidday", we announced that we had left the food on the rock half-way up the valley. Unfortunately, while the army carried the climbers fled to the food and had eaten almost everything except the dried milk and porridge by the time the lads in khaki arrived. (This incident nearly flared into something worse than the Boston tea party! I heard later that the army had seriously considered taking the alpine club to court for stealing their food.)

Anyway, to make a long story longer, the doctor now requested that Peter Pohl and Mary and I should run down the valley again to cancel the chopper (we were very conscious in those days of wasting taxpayers' money). Our brains must have been a little woozey by then because we agreed and pounded off down the river bed again — after all, what was the difference between 50 and 75 km? All in a morning's work, as the OPC instructor had once said.

It must have been near midday. Heat waves rose off the stony river bed ahead, and Lake Heron looked like a mirage in the Sahara. We were about 800 m from the road when we heard a strange chop-chopping noise. Over our heads flew a weird bubble-like thing full of people. We threw ourselves down on the stones and screamed obscenities to the sky.

As far as I know, Pete Smith recovered to make more Heath Robinson alarm clocks. However, I was so annoyed by the shambles that could have been averted if very basic search and rescue procedure had been followed that I wrote querying letters to the officer in charge of the rescue party. The only acknowledgement came from a very angry Bill Bridge some months later. He said he had just had a call from an angry commissioner of police demanding to know who the hell this fellow Dingle thought he was. Dingle had apparently claimed £5 10s for loss of wages due to search and rescue — obviously an attempt to rip off the taxpayers!

---

## Summary of rescue attempt

*The rescue of Pete Smith from Mount Arrowsmith, Easter 1968.*

The action of the climbers was almost faultless, and the decision to drag Pete down to a low camp was crucial. It was a dangerous decision, but, in the event, the correct one. On the other hand, the action of the authorities was almost unbelievably incompetent, the major omission being radios. With the danger of sounding wise after the event, the logical sequence of action to be taken by the police officer in charge of search and rescue should have been:

1. Notify search and rescue teams.
2. If a chopper was available, send it to the scene. If not, arrange for one to be available as soon as possible and send a light plane to drop off a message to the climbers telling them what action was being taken.
3. If a chopper was not available send a fast, radio-equipped ground party to the scene to make contact and report back.
4. Send in the main ground party.

Helicopters and mountain rescue are, of course, synonymous, and the marathon carries of little over a decade ago are now very rare. However, this art should not be forgotten as people can walk when choppers cannot fly and there is a tendency amongst modern search controllers to put too much reliance on the chopper to the exclusion of ground parties. Reaching a patient, even an hour before the helicopter, may well save his or her life.

In the case of Pete Smith, the soldiers did a great job, getting quickly up the valley and doing much of the carrying to bring him down. I believe that the forces could do many more of the mountain rescues necessary in New Zealand. They have much of the equipment, the right sort of organisation and the right kind of men. With a little training and more equipment they could do a very worthwhile civilian job, at the same time gaining tremendous military training.

People who are involved in dangerous activities should remember that rescue is not their right — if you are rescued from a dangerous situation you should consider it a bonus. If you feel that search and rescue is inadequate in your area, I suggest you do something about it by offering your services for S.A.R. If canoeists, trampers, sailors, mountaineers and so on feel they would welcome a rescue attempt if in trouble themselves, then it is up to them to offer up their own services for search and rescue, as I am sure most do.

Doctors are relied upon too much in our society. People with minor ailments (such as grazes, small burns, sprained ankles and so on), and often purely imaginary ailments, visit these men and women as if they were gods with miraculous healing powers — so they have become gods. Their magic potions are the almighty tranquiliser and antibiotic. Unnecessary medication costs the New Zealand Government millions each year while the drug companies laugh all the way to the bank. We have a responsibility to understand our bodies and bodily functions, and we should know when we really need a doctor, when we don't and, in the case of incapacitating injury to ourselves or others, how we can best prepare for the doctor's arrival and possible hospitalisation.

It is very important for anyone involved with inherently dangerous and isolated activities, such as outdoor pursuits, to have a good knowledge of first aid with as much practical background as possible. It should be understood that someone with a good understanding of first aid can be of as much use at the scene of an isolated accident as a doctor, for without medical equipment a doctor's scope is severely reduced.

At many mountain and other isolated accident scenes you will often have to be relatively brutal to save a life (as we were with Pete Smith). Usually the most important requirements are shelter and warmth — for what is the use of fixing injuries if your patient dies of hypothermia? I have been on many mountain rescues and have often broken conventional first aid rules, but no patient I have yet come across has died after help has arrived.

Many rescues can be carried out by the rest of the party without bringing in a separate rescue team — sometimes, if you are to save a person, this will not only be desirable but necessary. However, before such action is taken you must be certain that what you are about to do is the best procedure under the circumstances. Remember (as a sobering thought) that movement of patients with spinal injuries, for example, may kill them or cripple them for life.

# Arriving at the scene of an accident

Much of the information contained in this section is taken from a course of advanced first aid conducted in Bangor, North Wales, by Dr Ieuen Jones.

Before arriving at the scene, slow down and compose yourself. Consider what your routine will be when you get there. On arrival, check the patient's breathing and heart. If these are not functioning correctly immediate action must be taken. Also, if there is severe bleeding this must be stopped immediately. Find out the levels of expertise in the party. If on a cliff or steep snow slope or other dangerous ground make sure that everyone, including yourself and the patient, are secure — arrange belays if necessary.

Choose someone in the party to make notes of injuries as you make your examination of the patient. If the patient is conscious be careful not to cause alarm by being dramatic about any injuries. Accurate notes on injuries will help the rescue authorities assess urgency and rescue procedure, particularly if the accident is in an isolated situation.

Now do a full body check. If the patient is conscious, your job is much easier. Take note of the patient's comments, but don't be too distracted by these or by an obvious-looking injury — it may be hiding a more serious and much less obvious injury.

Begin your examination at the top of the head and work down towards the feet. Examine two sides of the body simultaneously using one hand for each side and continuously comparing. Ask someone to make notes of injuries as you proceed. Assuming that the patient is lying on the back, proceed as follows:

## The human skeleton and main arteries

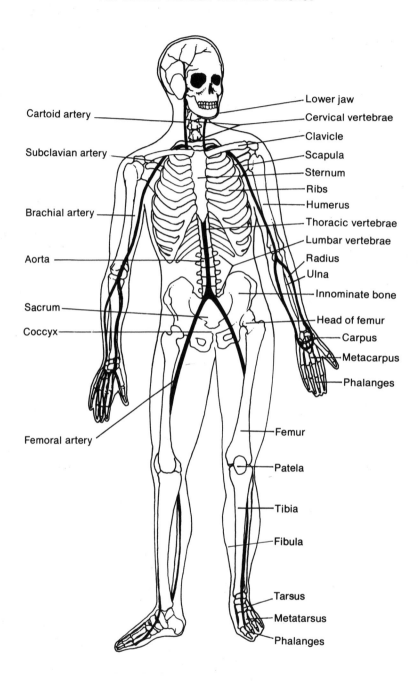

Cartoid artery

Subclavian artery

Brachial artery

Aorta

Sacrum

Coccyx

Femoral artery

Lower jaw

Cervical vertebrae

Clavicle

Scapula

Sternum

Ribs

Humerus

Thoracic vertebrae

Lumbar vertebrae

Radius

Ulna

Innominate bone

Head of femur

Carpus

Metacarpus

Phalanges

Femur

Patela

Tibia

Fibula

Tarsus

Metatarsus

Phalanges

1. Lift the head slightly and slip one hand under it. Any bleeding from the scalp will leave blood on your hand.
2. Run your fingers lightly over the scalp to check for obvious depressions.
3. Check for bleeding from the ears, which will usually indicate a fractured base of the skull. Make sure that any bleeding is from within the ear and not from an injury outside, causing blood to run into the ear.
4. Note black eyes developing, and bleeding in the whites of the eyes (which indicates a possible fracture of the front of the skull).
5. Check pupil size and reaction to light. Different-sized pupils and/or non-reaction will usually indicate concussion.
6. Check for loss of contour and tenderness of the cheekbones and nose. Fracture of either could well mean bleeding down the back of the throat of an unconscious patient.
7. Check the line of the lower jaw.
8. It is very difficult to detect a fracture of the cervical spine, but a swelling or irregularity in the mid-line of the back of the neck may give an indication.
9. On the front of the neck, surgical emphysema may be detected (bubbly feeling skin) pointing to a serious chest injury.
10. A fracture of the scapula (shoulder blade) shows only as bruising and tenderness. Fracture of the scapula or clavicle (collarbone) should make you suspect a more serious underlying injury to the chest.
11. Comparison of the collar bones will readily show up a fracture.
12. In dislocation of the shoulder there will be an obvious step at the point of one shoulder when compared with the other.
13. A fracture of the upper arm is usually obvious and freely mobile.
14. In the elbow there are normally three bony prominences (one on each side and one in the middle) which form the points of an equilateral triangle when the elbow is bent to a right-angle and a straight line when the elbow is straight. In minor injuries of the elbow involving one of these points the above relationship is disturbed.
15. Fractures of the shaft of the radius and ulna (forearm) usually have an obvious angulation without much mobility. The Colley's fracture has a typical dinnerfork deformity (see page 159).
16. Fractures and dislocations of the wrist usually have considerable swelling. Also check radial pulse (at the wrist) at this point.
17. Check for minor fractures in the hand by getting the patient to clench it over your own fingers. You should be able to feel any irregularities.
18. Return next to the chest and spring the two sides evenly, front to back and side to side. Pain at the site of injury when springing pressure is applied to two other points usually indicates a fracture of a rib, rather than bruising. Note also any sucking wounds or flail segments (badly broken areas of the chest which are without support).
19. Examine the abdomen with the flat of the hand and note any guarding or tenderness. Examine the loins at this time to check for tenderness over the kidneys. Stiffness of the abdomen will sometimes indicate internal bleeding.
20. Moving down the pelvis, feel for tenderness over the pubis. If there is tenderness here, diagnose a fracture of the pelvis and examine the pelvis no further. Otherwise, apply a hand to the crest of the ilium (upper pelvis) on either side and spring the pelvis lightly, diagnosing a fracture if there is pain on movement.
21. A dislocated hip is usually characterised by shortening of the limb and the knee is brought a little upward and inward.
22. Start the examination of the knee with the kneecap. This may have slipped over to one side or other, or it may be obviously fractured with overlying bruising and a transverse gap. An almost infallible test of a less-obvious fracture is to ask the patient to raise the knee unaided off the ground. Failure to do this at all means a fracture. Any fracture into the knee joint or a recent tear

of a cartilage causes bleeding into the knee; this may be detected as a horseshoe-shaped swelling around the kneecap. Other than a displaced kneecap as above, the only common cause of loss of ability to straighten the knee is a torn cartilage. A dislocation of the knee proper is rare and is an obvious and severe injury.

23. Fractures of the tibia and fibula (lower leg) are usually obvious, except in young children.

24. Injuries to the ankle are very common. Swelling and tenderness over the bony prominence of the inside or outside of the ankle usually means an undisplaced Potts' fracture (see page 159). Similar swelling and tenderness just below these bony prominences usually means an injury to the ligaments or a sprain.

25. Pain and swelling over the heel itself means a fracture of the heel bone. A fracture of the other heel and in the lumbar spine should also be suspected in these cases.

26. Generally there is no need to remove the boot to check for foot injuries unless there is bleeding. Most of the above examination can be done by loosening the laces and lacing up again afterwards.

27. A final quick check of an apparently uninjured leg can be done by giving the heel of the boot a moderate tap. Any break would be indicated by a stabbing pain at the point of the break.

28. Finally examine the back. Remember that when the patient complains of pain in the back, this usually refers to the full expanse from one side to the other, not just the spine. If the patient must be turned over to make an examination of the back, turn pelvis and shoulders simultaneously avoiding a twist. Slip your flexed knee in under the pelvis to hold the position and use one hand to hold the shoulders in position. Examine the spine with your free hand by passing a finger slowly along the bony prominences of the spine, noting any irregularities in the alignment and any loss of prominence from swelling. Also, in a conscious patient, note any tenderness.

29. Then examine any part of the back of the chest which you were not able to examine fully earlier.

If the patient is in any other position than on the back, the examination of the spine should be done first. If there is no fracture it may then be easier to turn the patient on to the back for the remainder of the examination. If there is a fracture of the spine, the remainder of the examination must be done in the position in which the patient is lying. It is usually best to slip your hand under clothing rather than undress the patient when making an examination.

Don't overlook the possibility that the patient is suffering from an allergy, heart condition, diabetic coma or other illness that shows no immediately identifiable outward symptoms. Often such patients will wear a disc on the wrist or around the neck.

# Treatment

**Personal problems**

People with allergies, heart conditions or any other medical problems should make the party leader aware of the problem and the treatment before the trip gets under way. If members of a group are young and/or inexperienced it is the leader's duty to find out in advance about allergies and so on. At OPC we ask parents to fill out medical information forms relating to their children.

## Diabetics

If a patient is suspected to be suffering from insulin shock or is in a diabetic coma, administer sugar (if unconscious place under the tongue). If the collapse is due to insulin shock the patient will recover immediately, otherwise diagnose diabetic coma and administer insulin.

---

### Artificial respiration

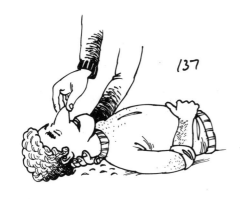

137

138

Rescue breathing — if the patient appears not to be breathing, perform rescue breathing as follows:

1. Extend the neck by tipping back the head. Do this gently by lifting the neck with one hand and tilting the head back with the other.
2. If the mouth is badly damaged you may wish to breathe in through the nose, in which case you will have to seal off the mouth. If rescue breathing through the mouth, pinch the patient's nose closed.
3. Take a deep breath.
4. Seal your mouth tightly around the patient's mouth or nose.
5. Blow in air until you see his chest expand.
6. Remove your mouth and allow him to exhale automatically.
7. Take another breath and repeat this cycle once every five seconds. Remember, the patient's lungs must expand. If they don't, open the mouth and check there is no obstruction. Also check that the neck is stretched and the head is tilted.

If the stomach rises when you breathe into the patient, press the stomach to force it down. The patient may vomit, in which case he should be turned on his side and the vomit should be cleared before you proceed.

---

### Cardiac massage

Rescue breathing is of value only if the heart is pumping to carry oxygen to the vital organs. Therefore you must determine whether the heart is pumping. Often it is difficult to find a pulse in the wrist, so check the cartoid, brachial or femoral arteries. Be careful that you are not feeling your own pulse in your fingertips (you can check this by feeling your own cartoid or femoral artery and comparing the beat).

Cardiac massage and rescue breathing (cardio-pulmonary resuscitation) should be learned together, and training with an experienced person and equipment is recommended.

If you have decided that the patient requires cardiac massage, you will obviously need to do rescue breathing, too. One person trying to do both is somewhat like being a one-armed paperhanger. Preferably, two people should co-operate — one doing rescue breathing and the other cardiac massage.

## Cardiac massage

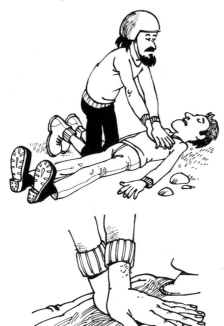

1. Open the airway as described for rescue breathing. If the patient is not breathing, blow four full breaths into his lungs in quick concession.
2. If there is no pulse, place the patient on a firm surface, face up and kneel close to his chest.
3. Place your hands as illustrated (with fingers locked) on the lower sternum (not right at the end).
4. Keeping your arms straight and using the full weight of your shoulders, smoothly depress the sternum 3.5–5 cm. If you are alone do this at the rate of 80 times per minute. When two people are working the rate should be 60 times per minute.
5. If you are alone make 20 compressions for every two quick lung inflations and continue to alternate 20 compressions, two inflations and so on. When two people are working together the synchronisation should be five compressions to one inflation, five compressions, one inflation and so on.

The ventilator should begin to blow as soon as the compressor begins to release pressure. Continue until the patient begins to breathe normally or until advised by a doctor to give up.

---

## Treating a major wound

Bleeding from an artery can cause death within minutes, so urgent action is necessary. If the wound is spurting blood, an artery has been severed. Bleeding from veins is not so serious, but treatment should be quick to minimise shock. If the bleeding is severe, don't worry about hygiene. The bleeding must be stopped by pressure applied directly to the wound. Jam any wad of fabric or even your hand into the wound and, if it does not succeed in stopping the bleeding, continue to add compresses on top of the originals, and further pressure.

Sterile compresses are best, but don't let the bleeding proceed while you find them. Once the bleeding has been controlled, elevate the bleeding area if feasible. Apply a tourniquet (strangulation of the limb above the wound) only if all else fails.

Cut adhesive tape and fold over

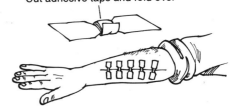

1. Wash your own hands before cleaning the wound.
2. Remove foreign matter without probing too much.
3. Clean around the wound.
4. Close the wound if necessary with "butterfly closures" made as illustrated.
5. Cover the wound with a sterile dressing.

## Minor wounds

Cleanliness is important.

### Fractures

If the fracture is open and bleeding, first treat the bleeding. If the bone is protruding through the skin, pad the bone end and wound before splinting.

Don't attempt to relocate the deformation caused by the fracture. Splint it in the position most comfortable for the patient and with whatever you have at your disposal. An ice axe and torn-up shirt may make almost ideal material if you are in the wilds. Don't remove more clothing than absolutely necessary.

Secure limbs in the most convenient and comfortable place. (With an arm injury this is usually against the chest. Legs are usually most comfortable when tied together.)

### Fractured pelvis

A very serious injury often caused by falling onto the backside. You should also suspect internal injuries. The patient must not be allowed to walk and should be placed on his back with the legs in the most comfortable position — this is usually with the knees flexed.

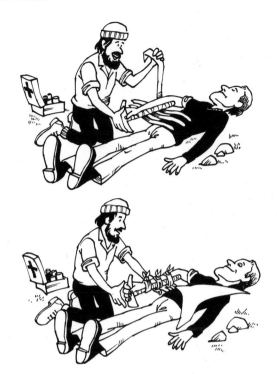

**Splinting a fractured lower arm**

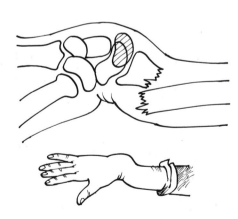

**A Colley's fracture**
This is the common impact injury of the wrist, often caused when a falling person puts down a hand to stop the fall.

**The Pott's fracture**
This is a common injury of the ankle, often caused when a falling person lands on the feet.

### Treating collar bone (clavicle) injuries

The idea is to take pressure off the affected collar bone by drawing back the shoulders and immobilising the arm on the affected side.

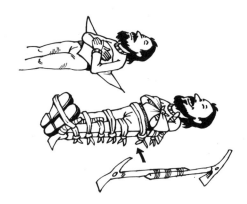

### Splinting a fractured thigh

This is a serious injury which requires careful immobilisation, particularly if the patient is to be moved. Because this fracture usually causes much tissue damage and internal bleeding, the application of traction is worthwhile if the correct equipment is available.

*Lower leg fractures should be treated in a similar manner.*

If a badly injured person is to be carried or transported any distance, it is usually a good idea to immobilise the arms as illustrated.

Completely immobilise the injured leg by carefully splinting it. Pad it carefully between the legs and behind the knees.

### Immobilising the head

Take a section of stiff material such as closed-cell foam (a pack hip belt a strip of a sleeing mat). Tie this around the neck and under the chin.

An alternative method is to place a large pad on the back of the neck, pass a sling around the forehead and chest (as illustrated) and tie this firmly over the pad. Move the patient only on a rigid stretcher. If you must, roll the patient carefully, keeping his legs in line with the body.

## Chest injuries

Fractured ribs are very painful and usually difficult to diagnose. If the bone ends are still in place there is little that can be done, although binding one arm across the chest may reduce the pain associated with movement. If the fractures are inward the condition is potentially much more serious as lung puncturing could result from bad handling. The patient should be immobilised and carried out on a stretcher.

## Spinal injuries

If the patient has pain in the neck or back following an accident, suspect a fracture of the upper spine and immobilise the head. Lay the patient down with the head in the most comfortable position and splint it in one of the two ways illustrated.

## Fractures of the back

These are extremely serious. Check by asking the patient to move his or her legs and toes. Inability to do so, or loss of sensitivity (for example, when the feet are tickled) indicate a thoracic or lumbar spinal injury. Don't move the patient unless absolutely necessary. If you must, roll the patient carefully, keeping the legs in line with the body.

## Head injuries

1. The patient can be allowed to walk if:
   a. unconsciousness has not occurred or has been very brief.
   b. he or she has improved and appears normal.
   c. bleeding is controlled.
2. The condition is fairly serious and the patient will probably need help if:
   a. unconsciousness has lasted for 5 to 20 minutes.
   b. no improvement is apparent.
   c. there are symptoms of nausea.
   d. there is a generalised throbbing in the head.
3. The condition indicates urgent evacuation if:
   a. the patient has been unconscious for more than 20 minutes.
   b. the patient drifts back into unconsciousness.

## Dislocations

These are usually very obvious and should be treated as fractures (immobilised) unless the patient has experienced the problem before and knows the treatment. If an attempt is to be made to relocate the bone, it should be done immediately.

## Sprains and strains

Torn and damaged tissues and associated internal bleeding usually cause much swelling. This will generally be over a wider area than the localised swelling associated with fracture. It is often difficult to tell the difference, so if in doubt treat the injury as a fracture. A gentle tap designed to push the (possibly fractured) bone ends together will often determine the injury (for example, with the lower leg and ankle, tap the heel).

## Shock

This is a condition caused by loss of body fluid, either internal or external. It will be associated with almost all major injuries and is often fatal. It should be treated as follows:
1. Lay the patient down.
2. Keep warm and treat for hypothermia.
3. Reassure the patient — lots of tender loving care is the way it is described in *Mountaineering First Aid*.

## Blisters

Blisters, usually on the feet, can be painful and incapacitating. They are probably the most common injury you will have to deal with. Prevention is much better than cure. Avoid them by:
1. preparing the feet in advance by wearing the footwear before the outing or rubbing the feet with methylated spirits.
2. wearing light footwear until your feet become tough.
3. stopping and covering the areas as soon as an embryonic blister is felt.
   If the blister is in the pre-blistering stage, a good wad of adhesive tape will often ward off the real thing.

Once you have got a real blister you have two

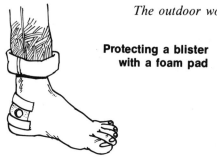

**Protecting a blister
with a foam pad**

choices of action if you wish to remain comfortably mobile.

1. Make a small hole in the surface skin with a sterile needle, scissors or knife. Apply antiseptic and cover the blister with a plaster. This alternative is best if you have stopped for the day.
2. As illustrated, make a pad with a hole in it from closed-cell foam or the like and tape if over the blister.

### Objects in the eye

If the object cannot be dislodged with water

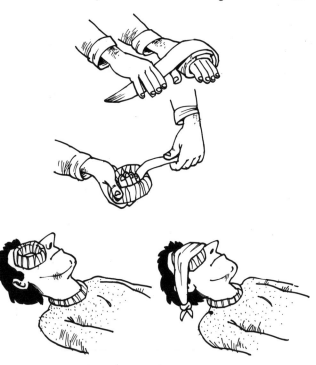

**Ring bandages**
Treating for an object in the eye. A paper cup or similar is useful in place of the ring bandage.

and the corner of a handkerchief, no attempt should be made to remove it. Instead improvise a ring bandage to encircle the whole eye, then cover both eyes with a bandage. If you are in the wilds, the patient will need to be closely assisted or carried out.

### Snowblindness

This is sunburn of the eye surface caused by over-exposure to ultra-violet light. The condition will heal in a few days and there is no quick first aid treatment unless special medication is carried. Sunglasses should be worn whenever travelling on snow, particularly in misty conditions as mist does not cut out ultra-violet light and burning will still occur.

### Burns

Treatment is urgently required and the burned area should be placed immediately in cold water or, if this is not available, use snow. With bad burns follow this treatment by covering the affected area with clean dressings and treat for shock.

### Sunburn

Protection by the generous use of special ointments such as "U.V. Plus", zinc oxide and so on is best. Beware of skin-care lotions such as Nivea which can cause blistering.

### Hyperventilation

Young people, particularly, sometimes over-compensate in anticipation of a big effort (such as going up a hill) and breathe in too much air. The body system becomes saturated with oxygen causing a gas imbalance. The condition can be alarming to see as the patient will have trouble breathing and a temporary paralysis of the extremities will take place. Treat by telling the patient what is happening and encouraging him or her to relax and breathe shallowly. If the condition does not improve, a bag pulled over the head will cause the patient to breathe exhaled carbon dioxide and an improvement should soon occur.

### Frostbite and hypothermia
See Chapter 2.

# Evacuation

After treatment of the patient you must work out what following action should be taken. Consider these factors: daylight, current weather and probable weather, manpower and other available resources.

If you have decided that the patient must stay where he or she is, give as much warmth and shelter as possible and despatch two people to the nearest road with accurate information (written if possible) on map position, injuries, resources at the site and needs. Now put out a ground-to-air sign (in case fixed-wing planes fly over). A large vertical stroke means "Require doctor, serious injuries". If there is one in the vicinity try to locate a helicopter landing zone and here put out a large"H" sign. A windsock (a piece of light cloth) will also help the pilot. If the patient has nothing more than superficial injuries or minor breaks he or she may be evacuated by one of the illustrated systems.

**CARRYING SYSTEMS FOR PATIENTS WITH MINIMAL INJURIES**

**The tape or sling carry**

163

**The coiled rope carry**

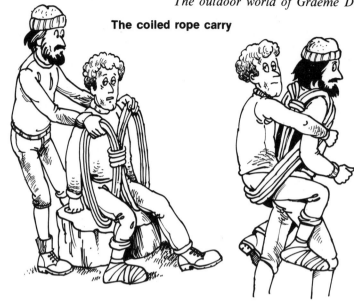

A loop of tape tied under the patient's arm and around the carrier will negate any need for the patient to hold on.

If there are suspected back injuries, serious head injuries, pelvic, upper leg, serious chest or internal injuries a stretcher carry will be necessary. Some huts are equipped with Neil Robinson stretchers. This type is best used for lowering and winching situations, but will be adequate for most carries. If you have to improvise, one of the illustrated systems will be satisfactory. If you have the choice, the sapling stretcher is better as flexing of the rope stretcher may cause the patient much discomfort and even further injuries.

*Immobilisation of fractures is crucial before moving the patient.*

## CARRYING SYSTEMS FOR THE SEVERELY INJURED

**A stretcher made from saplings**

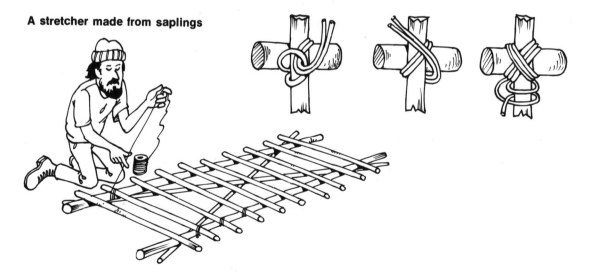

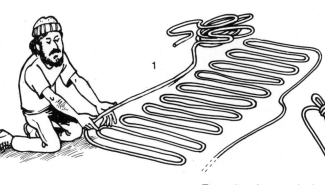

## A rope stretcher

Construct the stretcher beside the patient to ensure the size will be correct. At the completion of stage 2, poles can be inserted through the loops to make the stretcher rigid. These longitudinal poles should be braced apart by a cross-member at each end. Pad the stretcher with a sleeping bag or clothing.

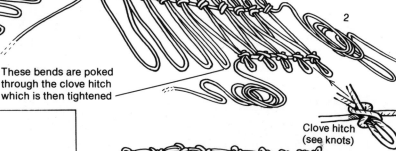

These bends are poked through the clove hitch which is then tightened

Clove hitch (see knots)

## Further carrying systems

These can be used for lowering a patient in a cliff-rescue situation or for carrying. The main problem will be in supporting the head. The most successful way to do this is to incorporate a pack frame or board behind the back and head and to tie this into the system.

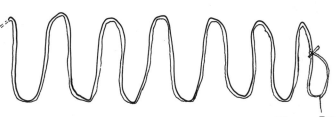

Begin with a foot loop, then bring bights of rope around the legs. Each bight is passed through the next

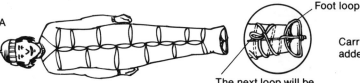

Foot loop

Carry loops may be added to the basket

The next loop will be passed through this one

These arms should be supported in slings

This system is similar to A, but each loop is threaded through its opposite number and tied off with a couple of half hitches. The remaining loop can be used to hold one long pole (longtitudinally) or several shorter poles or ice axes for carrying

Tie a locking knot here

Both these systems can be finished off at the chest like this

165

## Lowering a patient down a cliff

If a lower is necessary and the patient can walk, he or she can be put into a harness and lowered with a karabiner brake from above. (See also rock climbing and abseiling.)

If the patient is being carried or is in a stretcher, the illustrated systems can be used, lowering the rescuer and patient on a double karabiner brake.

Lowering a rescuer and patient.
*Graeme Dingle*

Lowering a stretcher
in the vertical position.
*Graeme Dingle*

Prusik loop tied into chest harness

Main rope tied into pelvic harness

**Lowering a mobile patient** (see also Chapter 4 for knots and improvised harness)

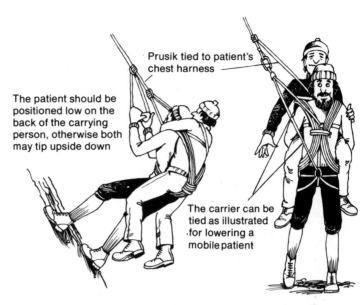

Prusik tied to patient's chest harness

The patient should be positioned low on the back of the carrying person, otherwise both may tip upside down

The carrier can be tied as illustrated for lowering a mobile patient

**Lowering an immobile patient**

Main rope

**Lowering a seriously injured patient**
The stretcher is most easily managed if it is tied on horizontally. The rescuer should clip separately to the main rope and walk down on the outside of the stretcher, keeping it out from the slope and guiding it down the best route.

# First aid kit

Many people actively involved in outdoor pursuits carry very small first aid kits, and often much of the contents are of a survival nature (dry matches, fish hooks and so on). This is because there is not only a limit to what can be carried but also a severe limit to what can be done in an isolated situation. The best first aid facility is medical knowledge. Even on the longer trips I make in New Zealand I carry only the following in my first aid kit:

Roll of zinc oxide tape
Swiss pocket knife — with scissors, tweezers, etc
Length of dressing strip
Packet of Aspirin
Packet of safety pins
Length of nylon line
One bandage
Medication for a special problem in the party — say antihistamine for bee-sting allergies
A notebook with medical notes as well as some blank paper and a pencil.

# 8
# A centre for the outdoors

*Your children are not your children.*
*They are the sons and daughters of life's longing for itself.*
*They come through but not from you,*
*And though they are with you yet they belong not to you.*

*You may give them their love but not your thoughts,*
*For they have their own thoughts.*
*You may house their bodies but not their souls,*
*For their souls dwell in the house of tomorrow, which you cannot*
*visit, even in your dreams.*

*You may strive to be like them, but seek not to make them like you,*
*For life goes not backwards nor tarries with yesterday.*
*You are the bows from which your children as living arrows are*
*sent forth. . . .*

*Let your bending in the archer's hand be for gladness.*

Kahlil Gibran, *The Prophet*

ANOTHER day in the dingy studio: I hear the roar of traffic through paint-speckled windows and see a few more clients who couldn't pay their accounts, had closed up shop or plain never intended to pay. The rat race was getting to me, gnawing at my soul. I was becoming sick of chasing after dollars — dollars to pay one middle man so he could pay another middle man; dollars to buy a little respect in a society where dollars had become more important than life itself.

I had the mountains to fall back on and it was nearly Easter — I would go to Fiordland with Ian Jowett and Noel Sissons, climb some rocks and ice and come back refreshed enough to chase more dollars. But life couldn't go on like this; I knew that. There must be more purpose to it all. Even if there wasn't I was going to try and prove that there could be more purpose. I had to do something positive: establish an outdoor training centre where young people could have the opportunity to experience adventure together, to appreciate themselves, others and their environment — natural and otherwise. It would be my positive contribution to modern civilisation.

"Futile," a friend told me.

"Maybe, as far as the advancement of man

168

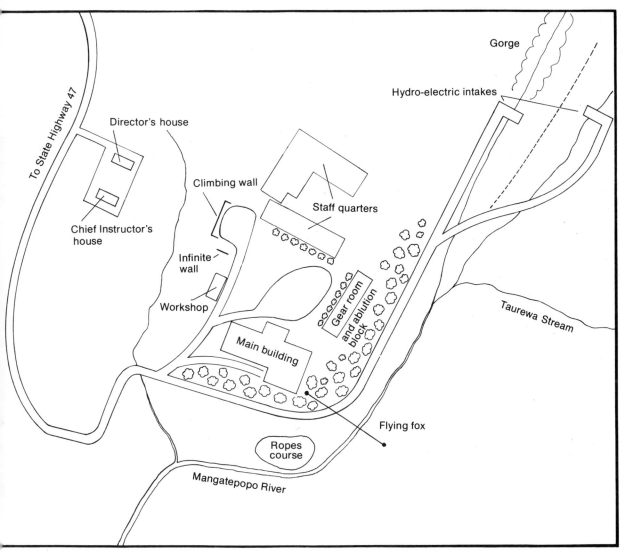

Tawhitikuri.

goes," I said, but for me trying was the important thing — "Dreams are much more important than memories".

I sat down in my pokey little tearoom, pushed the pile of overdue accounts aside and began to write. "Education is living, not preparation for a living." I have often found that to get a good look at something complex (as education has become) it is usually easiest to go right down to the nitty gritty.

At grass roots, if we didn't have some form of education we couldn't select the proper foods or provide warmth. We have progressed a long way (or maybe "proceeded" is a more appropriate term) since the times when such obvious basic needs were the important elements of education, but many people would argue that the sooner we turn back in that direction the better for all life. Once again, we must all see a clear objective to formal education — an objective that motivates people, for without motivation true education becomes impossible.

We must accept education as a lifetime effort, otherwise there are bound to be problems and huge dissatisfactions, and educational methods will never catch up with the needs of

The Outdoor Pursuits Centre with Tongariro (left) and Ngauruhoe behind. *Graeme Dingle*

the time.

The imposed discipline of the church has been broken down. The foundations of society are crumbling and, to some prophets of doom, we appear to be on a terrible downward spiral. But what an exciting age this really is — now we can rebuild on a basis of faith in ourselves and faith in the beauty and pleasure in all life, instead of in fear of what might happen in another life. Our educational institutions should be at the forefront of this renaissance, not wallowing in the dregs of a dead age.

One of our biggest educational bogeys must surely be that epitomised in this statement: "What is more important: the collection of individuals who are the State, or the State itself?" Early in his or her career every teacher must answer this question. Surely the true teacher must answer, the individuals, for what is the State without the individuals?

The majority may agree on this, but our education system puts the State ahead of the individuals. Schools and universities are churning out as quickly, cheaply and as painlessly as possible (for the State) a work force to sustain the State. Most often the ones who make it in our system become the complacent professionals — the doctors, lawyers, teachers and so on. The ones who drop out often become the factory workers.

Many State schools have become big, impersonal, stereotyped production lines! For the majority of kids the classroom is a dead bore — a ridiculous set-up. Kids aren't made for sitting cooped up in a classroom; they are made for running, jumping and exploring their world and themselves.

A few independent educationalists discovered this long ago; names such as A.S. Neal and Rabindranath Tagore immediately spring to mind. Others were and are bound by the system to prepare religiously our youngsters for the almighty school qualifications (School Certificate, University Entrance and so on) even though most wouldn't get them anyway.

Possibly out of desperation to curb behavioural problems, or maybe because of plain good luck, many overseas educationalists have discovered that the outdoors makes a pretty reasonable classroom. Out there everyone relaxes a bit; the teacher is down off the pedestal and somehow the majority of kids instinctively feel that this, rather than textbooks, is what life is about. The teacher notices new talents in the kids — Johnnie, who is never very good in the geography classroom, actually observes that the big river has a tiny source and that it cuts into the land when it meets an obstruction; Judy comments on how dependent on cars the hawk has become to squash animals for its food; and dumb Charlie delights in scrambling up the hillside (because of his enjoyment he will learn about the hillside and about himself, and then about the others around him). Learning, after all, is just a matter of motivation.

I looked at what I had written and wondered whether I was being a little extreme. I realised there was little chance of changing the whole structure of education, but I hoped that by providing an outdoor centre I could embellish education and maybe provoke some of the necessary changes.

I had learned enough about politics in my short life to realise that it would be dangerous to circulate this paper, so I filed it away and drew up the blurb on the proposed centre in very simple and straightforward terms. The paper was headed National Outdoor Training Centre (this name was rejected by the Registrar of Companies, so I later called it the Outdoor Pursuits Centre of New Zealand).

My objectives were these: to offer courses in outdoor activities to secondary school pupils, school teachers, youth leaders, physically disabled people, teacher trainees and all those interested in the outdoors and outdoor activities, with a view to achieving one or more of the following:

1. An introduction to outdoor activities, particularly mountain activities.
2. To cultivate an awareness of the total environment and, particularly, the preservation of natural things.
3. An opportunity to experience adventure, challenge, social interaction, physical and mental satisfaction.
4. To offer opportunities to dispel personal aggressions and frustrations through achievement.
5. To provide a range of alternative lifestyles, both for staff and course members.

Courses would be aimed at as wide a group as possible, and there would be an effort to involve:

1. Non-achievers.
2. Apparent social misfits.
3. Disabled persons.
4. Particularly, there would be an effort to attract Maoris and Polynesians to outdoor education.

In very general terms the course priorities were laid out as follows:

1. Enjoyment of activities.
2. To create a valuable and lasting outdoor and social experience.
3. To provide a sound basis of technique through instruction.

Deciding on the best location took much pondering. After considering accessibility to the main population and a range of natural facilities such as lakes, rivers, forests and mountains, I had to concede, reluctantly, that the central North Island was the only real possibility — a decision that many of my South Island friends found difficult to understand.

I decided that the next step was to gain a little support for my new project — ironically this support would have been very difficult to gain only a year before, but now I had received some public acclaim from my winter trip through the Alps with Jill Tremain. I was considered, wrongly, to be an expert on outdoor education. I therefore dashed off letters to Sir Arthur Porritt, the Governor General (who had not long before honoured me with an award for service to the community), my old friends Ed Hillary and Darrell Ramsey and the Upper Hutt Jaycees, who, I knew, had previously been interested in setting up a school camp. All of these brought positive replies and gave me great encouragement. Unfortunately, similar encouragement was not forthcoming from Government Departments — perhaps I was threatening a few empires! One influential civil servant told me with apparent sincerity, "Look Graeme, a leopard never changes its spots. You'll lose interest in this idea in a few months." I decided that a sign of chronic old age was to think that young people weren't what they used to be.

The Easter trip to the Darrans with Ian and Noel was a great success, and I came back to the city more juiced up than ever. My major hurdle, of course, was that of finance and was partially overcome when the Upper Hutt Jaycees bravely took on the task of raising enough money to buy the initial buildings.

I shared the scheme with my friends: Noel Sissons, a law student and at that time my climbing partner; Mary Atkinson, who later became married to Noel; and my girlfriend who was a really sweet young lady from a thoroughly poohbahish family. Her parents vigorously opposed their daughter's association with me — one of such low breeding, whose father was neither a doctor nor a high-country farmer, and who, on his first meeting with them, wore tight purple jeans. "Oh darling," they said, "just listen to his diction!" Until her family put an end to our wonderful relationship

she was a great ally, and the affair made me grow up very quickly. Before this I had been blissfully unaware of the underlying class structure which does still exist in New Zealand.

During July 1972 I journeyed to the North Island to look for a potential site for the centre. One of my first stops was Roy Turner's place at National Park. Roy is a legendary character — a great, kindly bear of a Yorkshire man and a thoroughly intriguing mixture of capitalist and socialist. He has an unbelievably generous streak, which prompts him to take total strangers into his home and treat them like kings. He also has a great way with ladies, who appear to enjoy his bearlike character. Previous to running his ski business in National Park, he set up the National Downhill Rope Tow on Mount Ruapehu, and scenes of Roy's hairy apparition, growling and chasing delicate little nymphettes across the ski slopes, were quite common! Hence the tow became affectionately known as "Turner's Rape Tow".

Roy took me to look at some sites in the central plateau area. We discovered three that particularly took my fancy. These were occupied by an Italian tunnelling firm — they were Whakapapa on the Whakapapa River, due west of Mount Ngauruhoe; Tawhitikuri at the junction of the Mangatepopo and Tawhitikuri Rivers, due west of Mount Tongariro; and Wanganui which was near the headwaters of the Wanganui River. All three were good possibilities, but it was Tawhitikuri that I most liked because it was surrounded by indigenous forest and hidden away in an isolated little valley.

I returned to Christchurch in high spirits and, with more enthusiasm than before, embarked on the accumulation of written matter — objectives and philosophies, letters and so on.

Sir Arthur Porritt was a great help to me — in his heart he must have thought I hadn't much show of establishing my centre, but he would listen patiently, offer advice and probably even remove a few walls behind the scenes.

I found Government Departments desperate to deal with. I would almost be on the brink of success when my contacts either died or retired. However, Forestry gave me a lot of help with advice and possibilities about leasehold land.

The Jaycees worked steadily on plans to raise funds. They set up a sub-committee including Kelvin Strong, Wayne McCarthy and several other keen young businessmen.

We didn't seem to be having too much luck in our attempts to negotiate with the Italian contractors, and then we heard that the Justice Department wanted Tawhitikuri as a detention centre. I was quite sure by now that Tawhitikuri was by far the best of the sites, and I didn't want to concede it easily to the Justice Department. (It seemed they had the attitude that because they were the Justice Department and the land was owned by the Forest Service, little turds on the pavement like us wouldn't stand a chance.)

During August things with my girlfriend's family came to a head. It was a lost battle from the start. In the final showdown her father did most of the negotiating while her mother sat in the background like a whimpering terrier snapping out the odd derogatory comment about my breeding or my English and so on.

"This centre of yours will be a total financial crapout," her father said, using a word bordering on rude for him.

"I'll not marry a high-country farmer with hairs growing out of his nose," screamed my young lady. A few weeks later she went overseas. Our hearts had taken quite a battering.

By September everything was getting me down. One frosty morning a buoyant Noel came bouncing around to my flat.

"God, you look terrible! Let's go and do a climb."

"No," I protested weakly, but soon began packing. By 3 p.m. we were on Ball Pass and beginning the first winter ascent of the South Ridge of Mount Cook. Two days later we emerged delighted on to the windy summit, and I couldn't remember what my problems were.

During October I gave 50 lectures on the proposed centre to schools and service organisations. Of crucial importance, I met Rex Giles. This important encounter began at Roy Turner's shop. I had called in after doing a lecture in Hawke's Bay.

"Hello Graeme! I had a bloke in here called Syd Reweti. He reckons he knows a millionaire who is interested in putting some money into an outdoor training scheme."

"Likely story," I thought. "Too much of a coincidence; you don't get free lunches anymore." However, a few days later I was at my father's house in Upper Hutt, thinking about Syd Reweti when the phone rang. "Is Graeme there?"

"Speaking."

"Syd Reweti here, Graeme." We met in a Wellington coffee bar and talked about the scheme. After a time Syd rang Rex.

"Yep," said Syd enthusiastically. "He says come and see him." Ten minutes later I was standing in a very tasteful and large office, faced by a tall, very strong-looking man with a large nose, piercing eyes and a very loud voice. He had a small chin, which seemed rather incongruous. For 15 to 20 minutes he fed me his ideas on the avalanche danger in the Southern Alps that coming summer, then, abruptly, he questioned, "Okay, what do you want?" I told him about the centre and he listened carefully — then, in an "I've got other things to do" tone, he boomed, "Okay, I'll give you 20 percent of what you need!"

He opened the door and I reeled back into the street, dazed by my first encounter with this fascinating man.

During November, Noel, Mary, Roie Wardell, Margaret Sissons (Noel's sister) and I ran three experimental courses at the old mill village of Taurewa, near Tawhitikuri. Despite terrible weather these courses were a great success, and we found out much about our needs at Tawhitikuri. I also learnt a very important lesson about outdoor pursuits: that regardless of the best supervision there is no safety guarantee. An adventure, after all, is only an adventure if there is an element of danger — the challenge is in keeping the dangers within an acceptable level. An adventure, therefore, is a potential disaster, or a series of potential disasters, kept under control. The more predictable our lives become the more contrived adventures we are likely to attempt. Synthetic adventure is potentially one of the biggest businesses.

On one occasion during the period of experimental courses I set up an orienteering course in a pine forest near Taurewa. My group was in the forest doing the course while I sat in Roy Turner's Land-Rover timing them. Near the end of the course and on the edge of the pine forest was a 10-m cliff around which I anticipated the students would walk. The first little character emerged from the trees, compass and map in hand, and walked to the edge of the cliff. He looked right, left, looked over the cliff, looked at his map again and then suddenly leapt over the cliff. On impact his knees folded up and he crashed on to his chest, his map and compass flying in opposite directions. I let out a pained moan and began to get out of the Land-Rover, but the inert form picked itself up, took a look at the map and compass and continued to the end of the course!

It wasn't long before Rex Giles became more than 20 per cent interested. With his help the Justice Department problem was resolved through Sir Roy Jack, and we were conceded Tawhitikuri. The problem with the Italian contractor wasn't quite so easily resolved. They didn't appear to sympathise with the objectives of the proposed centre and wanted much more than we could possibly pay for the buildings at Tawhitikuri. Back in Wellington I bemoaned this problem to Rex.

"There's only one way to handle these bastards," he boomed. "Make them think there are several outfits interested, and that they all want to pay about the same ... say $10,000. We'll also ask them if they want the money in a bag, and we'll tell them we know the bloke who built the place and that he says the buildings are worth bugger all."

In early December Rex became annoyed by the Jaycees and in a fit of anger withdrew his support. One week later he phoned and asked to see me. We went for coffee, and I found him, as usual, a really entertaining and warm character — I am sure he liked me. When we returned to his office he phoned his nephew in Rotorua and told him to set the wheels in motion for the purchase of the buildings I required from the Italians. He then told me to have a break and phone him in a fortnight. I floated into the street on cloud nine, and headed for Mount Cook where Noel and I celebrated the end of stage one with the first ascent of the right-hand buttress on the south face of St David's Dome.

On 20 December 1972 I drove to Turangi in my old red Commer van. There I met Rex's nephew at the contractors' office. A cheque for $16,000 purchased three buildings: one of about 300 m² at Tawhitikuri and two, each 150 m², at the Wanganui site. I then asked the Italian who made the deal how I would turn the power on to the building at Tawhitikuri. He was very annoyed that we had tried (and I believe succeeded) to trick them about several companies being interested in the buildings, and I was told very coldly, "You haven't bought ze power."

I drove eagerly out to Tawhitikuri — over the beautiful Te Ponanga Saddle, past the western end of Lake Rotoaira with snow-capped mountains rising beyond and then down access three, for the first time experiencing a really warm and comfortable homecoming feeling.

I had to admit that it didn't look very much like an outdoor pursuits centre. In the middle of a desert of clay stood one very grubby and run-down building; the others were previously removed by the Italians. What absolutely infuriated me was the senseless damage that had occurred to all that couldn't be sold — all the drainage had been buried and in places ripped up, the water supply ruined and the concrete cool storage area flattened. I had stupidly hoped that all those involved would be sympathetic to what we were trying to do.

Tawhitikuri, January 1973, shortly after the building on the left was moved there by truck. *Upper Hutt Jaycees*

The Outdoor Pursuits Centre in 1978. *Graeme Dingle*

I parked the van and walked across the bare clay to the back door. After pushing aside a heap of rotting garbage and wine bottles, I unlocked the door and walked into a large run-down kitchen. There were two other large rooms in the building — one apparently used as a dining room and the other for recreation. The placed reeked of fat and oil which liberally coated the walls. A few postcards depicting Italian places were stuck to the walls — it really was a mess. But I was far from depressed about it; one of the mountaineer's virtues is being able to push from the imagination visions of pain, storm and toil and to see ahead only summits glistening in the sunshine.

I lay my sleeping bag on the floor, collected

some water from the Mangatepopo Stream and got my primus going for a brew — the first of many at Tawhitikuri.

The next day I began the lonely task of installing a water supply and cleaning up. After Christmas my father, Bert, joined me, then Noel and Mary and later in January an Australian couple, Colin and Bev Abbott.

Also about this time Dick arrived from borstal where he had been serving time for his involvement in a gang fight. We all felt that a year at the centre helping with maintenance and so on would give him the opportunity to sort himself out somewhat.

During the next couple of months we all worked with tremendous enthusiasm, moving in buildings, relaying pipes and power cables — with not much more than a vision as our goal. We clubbed possums for food and press-ganged hitch-hikers into helping us.

Jaycee and other service-club groups helped to paint, and my brother-in-law Dan Martin worked like a Trojan doing much of the building.

We used loads of good old Kiwi ingenuity and number 8 wire, and slowly something like my idea of an outdoor pursuits centre emerged.

During March 1973 the first party arrived — a noisy group of 30 from Wainuiomata College. It was a very exciting Sunday night that they arrived. We picked up the group in a bus at National Park Railway Station at about midnight and drove them to Tawhitikuri where they were introduced to the staff and made welcome. It was an amazing course with a tremendous atmosphere, and many of the people from that course have remained closely identified with the centre — in fact two of the students, Colin Parker and Peter Mansfield, later became instructors.

The first year was very hard going. Noel and Mary shared a single $3 \times 5$ m room, as did Colin and Bev, while Dick and I had the luxury of a room each to ourselves. The walls were thin and very little was private — particularly Dick's stereo which we all shared without enthusiasm,

particularly when it was played at 3 a.m. The area is extremely wet (it receives about 4,000 mm of rain per year) and cold (frosts measuring minus 10–15 °C are common), but we were a really together group with a purpose and for a time this overcame all.

One of the really exciting aspects of the centre's early days was the exploration of the surrounding area. There were gorges, waterfalls, caves, cliffs, mountains, forests, rivers and lakes, and the excitement of going into these new areas rubbed off on the group members. On the first morning of the first course we set off up the gorge of the Mangatepopo Stream. We were soon wading waist deep in the freezing water and feeling our way up the most spectacular gorge with vertical walls rising above us. It was dim, and the trees above hung over almost spanning the slit in places, while beyond the clouds raced across a blue sky. We had to shout into each other's ears to make ourselves heard as the river noise bounced along the vertical walls — altogether it was an intimidating place. After about 200 m we came to a large pinnacle standing in the middle of the stream (the Bowling Pin) and here I psyched out and herded my charges reluctantly back down the stream.

Back at the centre, Dick was aghast: "What did you give up for?" As soon as his day's work was over he set off alone up the gorge. He was away for a couple of hours and came back looking most impressed, walked straight to the notice board and pinned onto it a $5 note. "It's impossible," he announced, "$5 for anyone who can get up there."

The race was on! The following Saturday Colin, Noel, Roie and I set off resolutely. We reached the Bowling Pin in a short time, waded across the stream and continued upward, executing hairy little traverses to avoid getting wet. In the middle of one traverse Roie pulled out a hand hold and plummetted backwards into a deep pool. After that she elected to swim rather than climb as she is a very good swimmer. Her talents were soon well employed. When we reached one of the gloomiest parts, where the full current swept under the cliff, we decided to send her through first, tied to the rope. She plunged in and was soon through the boiling current and scrambling out on to a small ledge. We all followed with the help of the rope and gathered on the little ledge.

For a moment this looked like the end of the road. We were surrouned by dark, greasy cliffs about 20 m high. Over one of these cliffs cascaded the Mangatepopo Stream. Even Roie couldn't swim up there, but maybe this was my chance to be famous. I tied the rope around my waist and began up a greasy ramp, traversed left, did a hairy little swing out over the waterfall and "voila", I was soon tied to a tree at the top and bringing up the others. The reward money was ours! It was so good to emerge from the dark confines of the gorge and into the warm sunshine.

The course fee at this time was $30 per head for a five-day course, which included transport to and from the centre and any school between Auckland and Wellington, accommodation, instruction, food and transport in the area.

Financially, the centre could be described as desperate or, probably more accurately, as having a hand-to-mouth existence. To protect the embryonic organisation we all worked on a percentage of the income: if the course was only half filled we received only half wages. We learned a very good lesson from our encounter with one school. The headmaster rang to tell me that the group who were booked in could not afford the cost of the course and it was particularly important that they did such a course because they came from under-privileged backgrounds. I spoke to the instructors who agreed to work the course without any wages. We then agreed to charge the group only $10 instead of the usual $30. On the first night of the course the shop takings for chocolate and other goodies were $45. We never extended our generosity that far again.

During July a course was unexpectedly cancelled so Mary, Noel, Roie and I, together with Mary's brother Richmond, headed for the Southern Alps. Here Noel and I completed one of the early winter ascents of the south face of Douglas. It was obvious to me, though, that if I was going to continue running the centre my hard climbing dreams would have to be shelved. However, I considered it important for the instructors to continue to be actively involved in their chosen activity — I didn't want them to die slowly, dreaming of their past great days. Consequently, instructors' holidays were important to me and I had to argue vigorously with Rex Giles in defence of plenty of time off for everyone. He wanted to treat the place as any other industry — three weeks' holiday per annum.

The idealism of the staff during 1973 was fantastic and absolutely crucial in those early days, but impossible to sustain. During August Noel and I had a row, and he and Mary left the centre. The contributing reason was almost certainly my lack of administrative experience. I had been dashing in all directions attempting to be director, chief instructor and caretaker, but doing none of the jobs very well.

Noel and Mary were a sad loss to the centre because good instructors were hard to find in those days. Roie wept bitterly over the loss, but I kept my emotions back like a good New Zealander. A short time after I made Colin Abbott chief instructor and I began to spend more time administrating and less time with groups.

I was keen from the beginning that the objectives of the centre were seen as pure, not as a cover-up for a concern that would fill some fat cat's pockets; I was also keen that in the long term the centre didn't stand or fall on me. Noel and I had decided that the best way to ensure these objectives was to set up a charitable trust. I will probably never know whether Rex Giles agreed with my motives. The only real indication I had of his feelings was shortly before the signing of the trust deed. He looked over to me and said, "Are you sure this is what you want?" My answer was a firm "Yes," but I was left feeling that it wasn't what he wanted.

At the end of 1974 Roie Wardell and I were

A centre for the outdoors. Note the aritifical climbing wall (left background) and the infinite wall on its left. This is a 3.5-m high, smooth wall to be climbed over by teams using neither edge. The obstacle is said to go indefinitely in each direction.
*Brian Dingle*

married. We built a beautiful A-frame house on the hill above the centre and settled down to a life of bliss. (I had been reading too many fairy tales!) Later in 1975 we both went to Nepal. Roie and Mary Atkinson went off trekking while Noel and I went to tackle the north face of Jannu.

We returned to New Zealand towards the end of the year and slipped back into the centre routine. The blow-up with Rex Giles came in early 1976. We had just completed our first course for the physically disabled and it had been a great event – in terms of personal satisfaction it was probably the best course with which I had ever been involved. When the course members had all left I relaxed and opened my mail. There was a crucial letter. It told me in fairly plain language that I was fired. I was incredulous as Giles had only visited the centre briefly, for about one hour during 1973. For a moment I was stunned, but then I retaliated. My written reply questioned his authority to take such an action, and his reply came promptly. "If I don't have my money by 31 March," it said, "I'll put in the liquidators."

Our total debt to Consolidated Traders was now approximately $42,000, being mainly the original setting-up costs plus a chief instructor's house. Giles had also agreed on behalf of Consolidated Traders to write off $5,000 of the initial advance as a contribution to the Jaycees fund-raising efforts and "as a public expression of confidence in the centre".

The debt wasn't a great amount, but to an organisation with no security (the centre is on Forestry leasehold land) it indicated that the end was near. However, the Ministry of Recreation and Sport leaped to the rescue with a grant of $35,000. With the addition of some of our own funds the loan from Consolidated Traders was soon repaid in full.

In the end, all these troubles were blessings in disguise. As soon as the whole centre administration came to Tawhitikuri the place was transformed – the spirit was refreshed and the flesh responded immediately. Every aspect of the centre improved. By the end of 1978 the centre assets were considerable. There was a stable staff of 10 and nearly 3,000 people annually attended courses.

# OPC philosophy of instruction and leadership

It has not been easy to gather the experienced group of instructors that we have at OPC today, but it is almost too easy to see why they were hard to find before. Maybe an institution like the centre must mature before it deserves mature staff?

Sensitive people who are also top performers and are prepared to give their time to youngsters are rare indeed. Performers often find it impossible to understand why a novice can't master fundamental tasks which to them are second nature.

Personally I have no interest in forcing people to do things they don't want to. It is a fruitless exercise, and in this aspect we are fortunate at OPC because almost all those who come here do so of their own free will — the fee ensures that. Once they are here an activity may frighten them and they might baulk and make a fuss, but situations like this help measure the worth of an instructor — he or she must decide whether the course members really want to do an activity. If they don't and are forced to do so it will be a negative activity.

Here I come head on with Kurt Hahn's philosophy of Outward Bound. He wrote "It is culpable neglect not to *impel* youth into adventure." I believe that to force anyone, particularly youngsters, into adventure is wrong. The effect of a frightening experience could psychologically damage a youngster for life — at best it may turn him or her against the medium that was meant to promote adventure, be it forest, mountain, sea or river.

Many of the good instructors we have at OPC are ex-Outward Bound instructors. They include Ray Button (Devon and Moray Outward Bounds), Graham Westerby (Anakiwa), John Davidson (Anakiwa), John Watson (Kenya and Anakiwa) and Jo Straker (Rhownia and Keremeos). The influence of both philosophies must therefore be present, but I believe the philosophies of these two organisations in New Zealand are coming closer together. I do not want to discredit Kurt Hahn, who was a great man, but I do want to refute his idea of impelling youth into adventure.

K. G. Ogilvie, an outdoor educationalist, writes some very wise words on the subject. These are very close to my own ideas on philosophy of leadership and instruction, so I now quote them at length.

"You need to have examined within yourself your own reasons and motives for wanting to take groups into the hills. You need to have clarified for yourself why you are wanting to do it at all and to what end. There needs to be a clear realisation that the responsibilities of leadership impose a discipline that allows no room for your own wishes, ambitions or aspirations. Leadership in this context is a state of mind that is largely selfless. [I wonder how many politicians will read this!]

"Leadership used for selfish ends is both empty (i.e. non-creative) and sterile. Leadership used to inflate your ego, such as needing to demonstrate your own superiority or prowess to the group, is a destructive exercise without value to your group. The group should be approached with humility rather than arrogance. Do not assume you will always know what is best for them. Do not think you understand their needs so well that you do not need ever to consult them or ask for opinions. How could you otherwise ever hope to pitch things at their level of expectation, motivation, interest and capabilities?

"A leader should be concerned that his interest in mountains (or other activities) does not overshadow his interest in the group. If getting into the hills means more to you than having a group with you, you should think twice before taking it. By this I mean that if your satisfactions derive primarily from personal reasons (i.e., so many miles covered or peaks climbed) you are going to be a disappointed, frustrated person who is unsympathetic to the group and a rotten leader. Very rarely will the motives, ambitions, interests and capabilities of the group coincide with yours.

The Tawhitikuri artificial climbing wall was built to enable students to learn to climb in a very controlled situation. They can relax more there than in the austerity of a real cliff situation.

The wall was constructed by spraying concrete over mesh and reinforcing iron. Cracks were mainly formed by placing wood where the crack was required and removing this once the concrete had dried. Lightweight packing foam would have been more satisfactory as the wood was difficult to remove.

Climbing walls can also be made from brick, concrete blocks, timber and fibreglass.

Holds and protection bolts were mainly placed once the concrete was finished. Belay rails were also placed along the top. This wall includes about 20 climbing routes, ranging in difficulty from grades 12 to 20.

Me working on the construction of the climbing wall.

A student climbing on the artificial wall at Tawhitikuri.

"If your concept of your job consists solely in imparting as much technical know-how to your group as you can, think again! There is much more to mountains than teaching the skills and techniques of mountaincraft. These things are essential aids and tools, but such a day so spent may be too clinical, too mechanical and so without life. The essential nature of the mountain experience may be missed. Under this mass of time calculations, distances, bearings, conventional signs, contour lines, do's and don'ts, the mountains may be so obscured that they never have the chance to reveal their inherent attraction to the group. If the gathering of your own experience was a chore, you will never be able to set the atmosphere so that a love and feeling for the mountains can be transmitted to the group. Time should be given for the aesthetics and spiritual feelings to impinge on the awareness of those in the group for whom such things will have meaning and great importance. Colours, light and shade, shape and form, textures, sounds and sense are all part of the mountain scene. Sometimes they will work their own magic unassisted. At other times the leader may find he is able with benefit to heighten the group's awareness of them.

The ability to interpret the mountain scene is of enormous value, for walking can be a monotonous business for many children. They sometimes need to have been exposed to the hills a number of times before they come to appreciate that a great deal of the charm lies in their contrast and infinite variety. Any snippet of information about the flora, fauna, natural and man-made features is grist to the leader's mill. Curiosity starved often dies quickly. Feed it and the results are often very surprising and fruitful. There are some leaders who seem to feel it necessary to impose a very rigid structure on a group. Each person is given a place and number in a fixed order of march and no deviation from the line is permissible. One can only assume that such leaders either feel their responsibilities too acutely or have an underlying sense of anxiety and lack of confidence in their own ability to handle a group on mountains. How sadly at variance this is with the freedom and informality of the outdoors. How much more acceptable to see a group flowing freely and flexibly up a hillside, interchanging at the dictates of the social interaction going on within the group. The leader only needs to intervene when weather (mist) or difficult terrain require it. Often these factors will exert their own pressures on the group without the leader needing to say anything. This is how it should be. Neither is there any need to be rigid and precise about the stops for breathers. The group will not let you anyway, so why bang your head against a wall?

"Because of the serious nature of your responsibilities, however, your approach to the leadership situation must be systematic — the woolliness of the 'walk with friends' situation will no longer suffice. All the detailed factors relating to good practice and comfort (i.e., safety) must be identified and, in this context, there must be a reason for everything you do and say and you must be conscious of the reason. There will be many things you learnt in the early days by experience which you now do unconsciously without thought, (e.g., the way you walk, pick your way up a path). All these things now have to be brought as it were from the back of your head to the front and consciously stored ready for use. In these areas which relate to safety and comfort you must be able to justify in every minute detail everything you do or choose not to do. This implies a very articulate grasp of the (mountain) situation which only a process of self-analysis and self-questioning about your own experience (mountain and otherwise — both are relevant) will give.

"It is not enough to know the right thing to do. You must know why it is right and what the consequences will be if it is done incorrectly or differently."

# Accidents and incidents

Nearly 30,000 people have now attended courses at OPC (1983). Accidents have been very few, but two have been serious, resulting in one death. During 1973 our fear of an accident crippling the delicate centre existence and a good degree of luck kept us accident free, barring a few cuts and bruises. This was mainly attributable to the experience and care of that first group of instructors and a more moderate programme of activities than was the case in latter years. Despite a much less experienced group of instructors, 1974 left our record as unblemished as the previous year, except for one incident where an instructor twisted his knee while demonstrating boulder hopping. He was carried home by his group. The year 1975 produced a cracked leg bone and two broken collar bones; however, one victim was an instructor tobogganing on Ruapehu and the other a girl falling from a bunk in her sleep.

One of the bitter ironies of the centre is that despite our dedication to care for young people, things occasionally go wrong. The ways of nature are harsh: late 1976 brought tragedy. A group was descending the Mangatepopo Gorge, a trip which had always worried me as a school group activity. However, centre staff pressure led it to be treated as a normal event. The dozens of descents that had occurred without incident seemed to prove my earlier judgment wrong — I began to think I was the only one frightened by such dark and wet places. The group was doing a relatively straightforward river crossing about 400 m from the centre. There were two instructors, and one stood in the middle of the current, helping the students across. Suddenly someone shouted, and the instructor looked around to see Sally, the girl he had just helped to the bank, being bundled down the rapid below. He ran down the bank to where she was caught in a small log jam. Several members of the group tried to help the instructors drag her out, but in vain. By the time the log jam had been pulled to pieces Sally was dead. Thirty minutes of rescue

breathing was to no avail.

This accident was one of those where all the instructional expertise in the world could not have averted tragedy. It was a bitter but somehow inevitable result of circumstances.

The accident had a long-lasting depressing effect on the centre. To make matters worse, our only other serious accident happened scarcely six months later.

A group of 10 spent the night in a snow cave on the summit of Ngauruhoe. The night was cold and windy, and by morning the soft slopes the party had climbed the day before were hard and icy. The group had a preconceived idea that they would slide down the mountain, because they had seen another group do this in the previous day's soft snow.

The instructor led the group down, cutting large steps in the ice as he went, but the inevitable happened. One of the group, Ann, slipped out of the steps and shot down the long slope. The instructor told the rest of the group to stay where they were and he glissaded down to her. She had severely abraded one arm, but apart from that she was okay. Meanwhile, high above, the group decided to try to reach the gully down which they had watched the other group slide. On the way they slipped, one by one.

By the time I reached the scene it looked like a battlefield. Several youngsters were grazed and there were two serious casualties. One girl, Sandy, had a broken leg, and a lad, David, had hit his head and was unconscious. David, was unconscious for several months. It was a disaster, and there was no avoiding the fact that the group should not have spent the night on top of the mountain. But seeing that they had, the instructor should have safeguarded them down with a rope, or waited for the snow to thaw a little.

After such a horrible event there is inevitably much witch hunting, and many wildly inaccurate stories circulate. Perhaps the worst aspect is the restrictive legislation that is often introduced to avoid such incidents recurring. However, legislation is not always the best answer, although in this case I did draw up a list of outlawed activities. The OPC Trust were divided on this action and some trustees felt that truly professional people did not need such restrictions. But the list was passed when the Instructors' Association was tabled. It stated that the instructors would work only if such a list was adopted. Perhaps this is the crux of restrictive legislation — if the people who have to operate under it do not agree that it is of overall social benefit, implementation will be impossible.

Only one other incident bears mentioning. During June 1978 one of the teachers on a six-week course was taking her group on an afternoon's walk (about 2,000 m) in easy country near the centre. She had done most of the trip before, and had spent five weeks in the area being trained.

The group did not return that night, and the next morning, Tuesday, I organised fast searches of the area. These uncovered nothing, neither did an aerial search which totally covered the area on Tuesday and again on Wednesday. The search became "official" on Wednesday morning after we had thoroughly combed the area on the ground and from the air.

We had now isolated the party's likely position and drew a small circle around this. At about 3 p.m. on Wednesday a helicopter flew from Taumaranui to assist — on the way it met the missing party walking home, safe, sound and very happy.

The teacher had missed the track back towards the centre (grid reference 950048, see map on page 53). The party had then continued along a broad bulldozer track which descended to the junction of the Okupata and Mangatepopo Streams. They wrongly calculated that the Okupata was the Mangatepopo and followed this. Monday night was spent huddled together with no fire — the matches had got wet crossing the stream. Tuesday was spent trying to find their bearings, but they first descended the Okupata then climbed a hill to the west of the Okupata. Tuesday night found the party on the hill, with no more comfort than the previous night. On Wednesday the party began back toward OPC. If they had not met the helicopter they would have reached the centre an hour later. Despite their three days out in cold June rain they were well and morale was very high.

The teacher had made three crucial mistakes: navigation errors, getting the matches wet and not making an all-out effort to attract the plane. However, she had kept the group together really well, she had kept their morale high, rationed the food (there was still food left when they returned) and, above all, the group was well equipped. As far as I was concerned they had benefitted from their trip. Unfortunately, one parent, who also happened to be an eminent police officer, stirred up a lot of trouble at a high level in the Department of Education, and the teacher who had performed very well as a leader in the most trying situation was much maligned and disallowed by her school to take future groups into the outdoors.

Towards the end of 1979 I resigned my position as director of OPC and took up a new position as technical advisor to Hallmark International, manufacturers of outdoor equipment. I did this so I could achieve some mountaineering dreams before I became too old for such energetic pursuits. My last duty as director was to take the OPC staff on an expedition to the Himalayas. This was a great experience and we succeeded in climbing two high peaks and making the first descent by canoe and raft of one of the major tributaries of the Ganges River.

Stu Allan, an extremely good teacher, canoeist and mountaineer, is now the OPC director.

# A sad goodbye

The growth and development of Tawhitikuri is very closely linked to the growth and development of outdoor pursuits in New Zealand. Tawhitikuri and all it embodies (trust, staff, buildings) has been, and is, an inspiration. It has meant lightning development for me — the wide-eyed unworldly boy I was has somehow blundered out the other side, eight years later, grown up.

This period was one of the most fulfilling of my life. There have been many problems, many heartaches and much struggling, but the results are worth it. We now have a truly great outdoor pursuits centre, giving fun, knowledge and pathways to self-knowledge, contentment and environmental awareness to several thousand New Zealanders each year. It also offers a home and a place of friendship, in an environment they love, for 12–15 people (the staff and their families). I hope that Tawhitikuri is a monument to our care and love for humankind and for all life.

This is not to say the job is done. My own strength for the task is diminished and I must move on (there are many mountains still to climb), but the centre must continue to develop — to cater for the needs of New Zealand's young — and this it can do only through strong leadership, a united staff and Trust and, above all, clear objectives and a sincere approach.

The problems and growing pains seem a thing of the past, and we need now to stabilise our position and consolidate; but we must not become entrenched in our approach to running courses. We live in a fast-changing world; to survive we must adapt to current trends and needs.

I have realised one of my ambitions, but only with the help of many friends. To all the OPC staff, past and present; to the trustees; to Ed Hillary and Arthur Porritt; to Roy Turner; to the hitch-hikers who stayed a day or two to dig holes; to the Jaycees and other service clubs that assisted; to Rex Giles and, particularly, to the kids and teachers who made Tawhitikuri a reality, I offer my deep and unending gratitude.

# Typical schedule of courses

### Five-day secondary school course
These courses are the most numerous at the centre, each year catering for about 1,500 people between the ages of 14 and 18. A summer programme (October-May) normally includes bushcraft, canoeing, rock climbing and an outcamp in the mountains or in the bush. There are also evening lectures. Other inclusions in the programme may be caving, confidence courses, orienteering, environmental studies, and so on. During winter this course is adapted to the season, and snow climbing is substituted for rock climbing, skiing for canoeing; usually the outcamp is in a snow cave or igloo.

### Mobile expeditions
These vary from 5 to 10 days, and are in the form of either transalpine trips or extended canoe trips down rivers such as the Wanganui.

### Hallmark retailers' course
A six day course (Sunday evening to Saturday evening) designed to help retailers become more familiar with the equipment they sell. The course is sponsored by Hallmark International of Hamilton.

### Teachers' course
This is a six-week course in outdoor pursuits designed to equip teachers with the knowledge and skills required to conduct outdoor education programmes in their own schools. The course is funded by the Department of Education.

**Physically disabled course**
These courses are organised by the Crippled Children's Society and cater for physically disabled people from all over New Zealand.

*Winter course*: Activities include skiing, tobogganing and outcamps in the snow.

*Summer course*: Activities include canoeing, climbing, a confidence course and sailing.

**Mountaineering course**
A five-day course (Sunday night to Friday night) designed as a specialist course for people with some experience. Activities include all aspects of snow and ice climbing, as well as living out in igloos and snow caves.

**Lions International course**
A 15-day course sponsored by the Lions organisation and designed to bring together potential young leaders from all nations.

**Service club course**
A 10-day course. Students are sponsored either in small groups or individually by service clubs from all over New Zealand. The course is designed to promote outdoor opportunities, self and social knowledge and leadership among young people.

Other courses are conducted by arrangement and include the wildlife trainees' course, the national park rangers' course and courses in leadership, rescue, bushcraft, skiing and so on.

# Last words — kiwis

When I was trying to establish the centre some people told me not to bother because "all New Zealanders go into the outdoors, camping and so forth". I have subsequently found this to be untrue. The majority of New Zealanders live in large cities and never get closer to the wilds than the beach or rugby field. A lot of water has gone under the bridge since King Dick Seddon encouraged national pride in New Zealanders by calling this "God's own country". We have cut down most of our natural forests, polluted our streams and threatened more species of wildlife than any other country in the world. We have moved away from the land and now the previously prized Kiwi ingenuity, a product of our past rural existence, is almost only a memory. In the long run, however, perhaps this trend will be our protection

# and the outdoors

and the protection of our land as we may cease to leave long-lasting scars on the countryside.

We do occasionally throw up exceptional performers like the Ed Hillarys, Peter Snells and John Walkers, but today in competitive outdoor areas like canoeing, skiing, rock climbing and mountaineering, we scarcely rank. This seems largely due to our isolation, as we certainly have the natural facilities.

As a nation we are inflicted with a smothering "isolation complex". Too often we seem to accept that things from other countries must be

Trespasser's grave near Ruatoria! Always ask permission to cross land. It is very important to have good relationships with farmers and landowners.
*Graeme Dingle*

better and this frequently extends to our judgment of ourselves as people and of our land.

In 1968, when Murray Jones and I set off to try to climb all the classic European north faces in one season, most climbers considered us to be suicidal maniacs — one alpine club member wrote to me saying, "Walter Mitty has nothing on you guys — you would make more of a name for yourselves by walking up Mont Blanc backwards. Even if successful, the dangers on Eiger and Matterhorn faces would render the feat unpraiseworthy". When we returned successful, New Zealand mountaineering, strangely enough, took a surge forward.

This is not to say that I believe New Zealanders should always be pushing standards and the level of technology, as this is one of humanity's major problems. All we need to do is to start thinking for ourselves. (We scarcely even react when our personal freedoms are threatened by political megalomaniacs.)

New Zealand is blessed with hundreds of outdoor clubs: tramping clubs, canoe clubs, ski clubs, sub-aqua clubs, yachting clubs, hang-gliding clubs — the list could fill an entire chapter. For example, we have over 100 hill- and mountain-oriented clubs and approximately 150 boating clubs. Probably nowhere else in the world are so many outdoor activities packed into such a small area.

Human beings are generally very protective of their own kind, and New Zealanders are no exception. We are a relatively adventurous people, and long may this last; however, there are some quasi-Government groups dedicated to safeguarding people at the expense of individuality. Unfortunately, these groups rarely attract adventurous people and we have to be continually on the lookout for restrictive legislation. (After all, most outdoor activities are inherently more dangerous than indoor activities.)

It is a strange fact that danger in the name of nationalism or money seems to be acceptable — war, for example, or danger to health from industrial pollution. It is hard for many to understand that the sanest and safest personalities often do the most apparently insane and dangerous things — one of nature's strange paradoxes, no doubt. Safety for mankind in the long term is in health (physical and mental), strength, alertness and ability to defend oneself against all threats. The most serious dangers are often the least obvious — many of us will die, not on the roads, in the bush, on the mountains or in the sea, but in a hospital bed, rotten with cancer because we polluted our beautiful land trying to provide ourselves with more comfort. This we call a higher standard of living. We have over 8 million hectares of national park, scenic reserves, forest parks and wilderness areas — this represents about 30 per cent of our land area, and tens of thousands of New Zealanders make good use of this land, not to mention many thousands of overseas visitors.

We have a great land and a great people, and we could protect these assets by turning New Zealand into a massive park that all the world would want to see. This doesn't mean building hotels in our wild places and bringing in more restrictive legislation. People are sick of these; they want natural experiences. Organised fun is becoming dreary — one only has to look at the tremendous growth of trekking-type tourism in Nepal. Tourism combined with uncompromising strength in protecting our natural facilities could be New Zealand's greatest asset and, as I have already said, long-term protection.

One of my great hopes for our land and people is the tremendous interest that young New Zealanders are showing in outdoor education. Each year thousands of school children take part in outdoor education programmes. There are presently around 200 school camps in the national directory scattered about the country — one for every two secondary schools. This trend must have far-reaching effects on our attitudes to the outdoors, particularly our performance in the outdoor fields, our spiritual and physical well being and in the protection of our land. I hope the Department of Education will recognise this potential by openly, enthusiastically and financially supporting outdoor education. New Zealand has a tremendous capacity to develop many more honest and down-to-earth individualists like Ed Hillary.

# Appendix

## Outdoor pursuits clubs in New Zealand

**Tramping and mountain clubs**

*Affiliated members of the Federated Mountain Clubs of New Zealand Inc.*

Alpine Sports Club, P.O. Box 131, Auckland
Aorangi Ski Club Inc., P.O. Box 1945, Wellington
Auckland Catholic Tramping Club, P.O. Box 3690, Auckland
Auckland Tramping Club, P.O. Box 2358, Auckland
Auckland University Tramping Club, Private Bag, Auckland 1
Bush Tramping Club, C/– R.D. 1, Pahiatua
Central Otago Tramping Club, P.O. Box 33, Alexandra
Canterbury Mountain Radio Service, P.O. Box 22342, Christchurch
Canterbury Winter Sports Club, P.O. Box 1893, Christchurch
Canterbury Catholic Tramping Club, P.O. Box 2393, Christchurch
Christchurch Ski Club Inc., P.O. Box 2493, Christchurch
Christchurch Tramping Club, P.O. Box 527, Christchurch
Christiania Ski Club, P.O. Box 367, Hamilton
Craigieburn Valley Ski Club, P.O. Box 1742, Christchurch
Desert Alpine Club, P.O. Box 3415, Auckland
Fiordland Tramping Club, P.O. Box 29, Te Anau
Gisborne Canoe & Tramping Club, P.O. Box 289, Gisborne
Golden Bay Alpine & Tramping Club, P.O. Box 90, Takaka
Headquarters & Overseas Branch N.Z. Deerstalkers Association, P.O. Box 6514, Wellington
Heretaunga Tramping Club, P.O. Box 447, Hastings
Hokonui Tramping Club, P.O. Box 334, Gore
Hutt Valley Tramping Club, P.O. Box 183, Wellington
Kahui Alpine Club, P.O. Box 20, Rahotu
Laingholm Cliff Rescue Unit, C/– Fire Station, 75 Victoria Rd, Laingholm, Auckland 7
Levin-Waiopehu Tramping Club, P.O. Box 144, Levin

Manawatu Tramping & Skiing Club, P.O. Box 245, Palmerston North
Manakau Tramping Club, P.O. Box 376, Papakura, Auckland
Matamata Ski Club, P.O. Box 126, Matamata
Marlborough Tramping Club, 11 Gilbert Street, Blenheim
Masterton Tramping Club, P.O. Box 334, Masterton
Massey University Alpine Club, Massey University, Palmerston North
Mt Egmont Alpine Club, P.O. Box 62, Hawera
Nelson Tramping Club, P.O. Box 225, Nelson
New Plymouth Tramping Club, P.O. Box 861, New Plymouth
N.Z. Alpine Club Inc., P.O. Box 41038, Eastbourne, Wellington
    Auckland Section, P.O. Box 3036, Auckland
    Canterbury/Westland Section, P.O. Box 1700, Christchurch
    Nelson/Marlborough Section, P.O. Box 533, Nelson
    North Otago Section, P.O. Box 191, Oamaru
    Otago Section, P.O. Box 409, Dunedin
    South Canterbury Section, P.O. Box 368, Timaru
    Southland Section, P.O. Box 965, Invercargill
    Taranaki Section, P.O. Box 527, New Plymouth
    Wellington Section, P.O. Box 1628, Wellington
    Australian Section, P.O. Box 41038, Eastbourne, Wellington
Napier YMCA Tramping Club, P.O. Box 992, Napier
Nga Papuwae o Taneatua Tramping Club, P.O. Box 360, Whakatane
North Canterbury Branch New Zealand Deerstalkers Association, P.O. Box 9034, Addington, Christchurch
North Shore Tramping Club, P.O. Box 33262, Takapuna, Auckland
Otago Branch New Zealand Deerstalkers Association, P.O. Box 701, Dunedin
Otago Ski Club, P.O. Box 995, Dunedin
Otago Tramping & Mountaineering Club, P.O. Box 1120, Dunedin

Otago University Tramping Club, Otago University, Dunedin

Otaihape Alpine Club, P.O. Box 180, Taihape

Palmerston North Tramping & Mountaineering Club, P.O. Box 1217, Palmerston North

Parawai Tramping Club, P.O. Box 2027, Raumati Beach

Peninsula Tramping Club, P.O. Box 13258, Christchurch

Poverty Bay Branch New Zealand Deerstalkers Association, P.O. Box 717, Gisborne

Puketoi Mountain Club, P.O. Box 617, Masterton

Rangitikei Ski & Tramping club, P.O. Box 20, Ohingaiti

Rotorua Tramping & Ski Club, P.O. Box 337, Rotorua

Royal N.Z. Navy Alpine & Ski Club, HMNZS *Philomel*, C.P.O. Auckland

Stratford Mountain Club, P.O. Box 82, Stratford

Skyline Ski Club, P.O. Box 3694, Wellington

South Canterbury Tramping Club, P.O. Box 309, Timaru

South Wairarapa Tramping Club, 75 Cologne Street, Martinborough

Southland Tramping Club, P.O. Box 41, Invercargill

Summit Skiers Inc., P.O. Box 142, Feilding

Tahurangi Ski Club, P.O. Box 1669, Wellington

Taranaki Alpine Club, P.O. Box 356, New Plymouth

Tararua Tramping Club, P.O. Box 1008, Wellington

Tasman Ski Club, P.O. Box 368, Timaru

Taumarunui Tramping Club, P.O. Box 61, Taumarunui

Taupo Ski Club, P.O. Box 67, Taupo

Taupo Tramping Club, P.O. Box 650, Taupo

Tauwira Ski Club, P.O. Box 1741, Wellington

Tauranga Ski Club, P.O. Box 476, Tauranga

Tauranga Tramping Club, P.O. Box 1162, Tauranga

Toi Toi Tramping Club, P.O. Box 23678, Hunters Corner, Auckland

Tokoroa Alpine Club, P.O. Box 290, Tokoroa

Tongariro Tramping Club, 6 Rawhiti Road, Pukerua Bay

Upper Hutt Branch New Zealand Deerstalkers Association, P.O. Box 40226, Upper Hutt

Upper Valley Tramping Club, P.O. Box 40063, Upper Hutt

Victoria University Tramping Co, Private Bag, Wellington

Waikato Tramping Club, P.O. Box 685, Hamilton

Waitaki Ski Club, P.O. Box 191, Oamaru

Wairoa Tramping Club, C/- Mrs Z. Bishop, Bishops Garden Centre, Marine Parade, Wairoa

Wanganui Tramping Club, P.O. Box 679, Wanganui

Whangarei Tramping Club, P.O. Box 436, Whangarei

Whakapapa Mountain Club, P.O. Box 128, Whakatane

Wellington Catholic Tramping Club, P.O. Box 2743, Wellington

Wellington Tramping & Mountaineering Club, P.O. Box 5068, Wellington

West Auckland District Tramping Club, P.O. Box 20058, Glen Eden, Auckland

West Coast Alpine Club, P.O. Box 136, Greymouth

West Coast Branch New Zealand Deerstalkers Association, P.O. Box 359, Greymouth

Waimea Tramping Club, 298 Nayland Road, Nelson

*Associate clubs*

Ashburton College, P.O. Box 204, Ashburton

Auckland Technical Institute Tramping Club, P.O. Box 6116, Auckland

Awatapu College, P.O. Box 1143, Palmerston North

Bohally Intermediate, McLauchlan Street, Blenheim

Boystown Police & Citizens Club, P.O. Box 39062, Auckland

Canterbury University Tramping Club, Private Bag, Christchurch

Christs College, Private Bag, Christchurch

Colenso High School, Enterprise Street, Alexandra

Elusive Trackers Club, P.O. Box 720, Tauranga

Eros Club, P.O. Box 58, Palmerston, Otago

Fraser High School, 72 Ellicott Road, Hamilton

Freyberg High School, Freyberg Street, Palmerston North

Hawera High School, Camberwell Road, Hawera

Hawera Intermediate School, South road, Hawera

Hornby High School, 49 Carmen Road, Christchurch

Kaiapoi High School C/- Box 1463, Christchurch

Kings College, P.O. Box 22012, Otahuhu, Auckland

Lincoln College Alpine Sports Club, P.O. Box 55, Lincoln College

Marlborough Boys College, P.O. Box 353, Blenheim

Nayland College, Nayland Road, Stoke, Nelson

Nelson College, P.O. Box 64, Nelson

Onslow College, Burma Road, Johnsonville, Wellington

Otamatea High School, Private Bag, Maungaturoto

Otago Boys High School, Arthur Street, Dunedin

Pakuranga College, P.O. Box 38002, Howick, Auckland

Piopio College, Private Bag, Piopio

Putaruru High School, P.O. Box 184, Putaruru, Auckland

Rangiora High School, Rangiora

Rifle, Rod & Gun Club, P.O. Box 1199, Palmerston North

Rutherford High School, Kotoku Street, Te Atau North, Auckland

Shirley Boys High School, P.O. Box 27025, Shirley, Christchurch

Southland Boys High School, Herbert Street, Invercargill

St Mary's School Tramping Club, St Mary's School, Stratford

Te Awamutu College, Te Awamutu

Waimate High School, Waimate

Wellington High School, Private Bag, Wellington

## Orienteering clubs

New Zealand Orienteering Federation, P.O. Box 358, Papakura, Auckland

Bay of Plenty Orienteering Club, P.O. Box 565, Tauranga

Central Auckland Orienteering Club, 24 Dingle Street, St Heliers, Auckland 5

Dunedin Orienteering Club, P.O. Box 159, Dunedin

Forest Fanatics Orienteering Club, 616 Park Road, Hastings

Hamilton Orienteering Club, 12 Maple Street, Hamilton

Hutt Valley Orienteering Club, P.O. Box 90, Hastings

Kapiti Havoc, 145 Wellington Road, Paekakariki

North West Auckland Orienteering Club, 8 Agathis Avenue, Mairangi Bay

Otago University Orienteering Club, C/– P.O. Box 1436, Dunedin

Peninsula and Plains Orienteering Club, 42 Waiau Street, Christchurch

Pinelands (Tokoroa Putaruru) Orienteering Club, 12 Riverview Street, Putaruru

Red Kiwis Orienteering Club, 33 Ihaka Street, Palmerston North

Rotorua Orienteering Club, 20 Rimuvale Street, Rotorua

South Auckland Orienteering Club, P.O. Box 415, Papakura, Auckland

Southland Orienteering Club, 178 Lewis Street, Invercargill

Wairarapa Orienteering Club, 17 Coronation Street, Feilding

Wellington Orienteering Club, 45 Chapman Street, Johnsonville, Wellington

## Canoeing clubs

New Zealand Canoeing Association (Inc.), P.O. Box 5125, Auckland

*Clubs affiliated to the New Zealand Canoeing Association (Inc.)*

Arawa Canoe Club, P.O. Box 13177, Armagh, Christchurch

Auckland Canoe Club, P.O. Box 3253, Auckland

Christchurch Canoe Club, P.O. Box 13176, Armagh, Christchurch

Dunedin Canoe Club, p.O. Box 5404, Dunedin

Garden City Kayak Club, 36 Linwood Ave, Christchurch

Gisborne Canoe & Tramping Club, P.O. Box 289, Gisborne

Hamilton Canoe Club, P.O. Box 9497, Hamilton

Hauraki Kayak Group, P.O. Box 3580, Auckland

Hawke's Bay Canoe Club, P.O. Box 883, Napier

Kaimai Canoe Club, P.O. Box 2354, Tauranga

Kupe Canoe Club, P.O. Box 3768, Wellington

Nelson Canoe Club, P.O. Box 793, Nelson

New Plymouth Kayak Club, 29A Clawton Street, New Plymouth

Northland Canoe Club, 130 Beach Road, Onerahi, Whangarei

North Shore Canoe & Youth Club, 35A Taharoto Road, Takapuna, Auckland

Palmerston North Canoe Club, P.O. Box 1126, Palmerston North

River City Canoe Club, P.O. Box 129, Wanganui

Rotorua Canoe Club, P.O. Box 1484, Rotorua

Ruahine White Water Club, 71 Salisbury Street, Ashhurst

Secondary Schools Canoe Association, P.O. Box 923, Hamilton

South Auckland Canoeists, C/– 31 Sayegh Street, St. Heliers, Auckland

Southland Canoe Club, P.O. Box 1379, Invercargill

South Taranaki Canoe Club, C/– Dennis Bourke Te Roti RD 13, Hawera

Tarawera Canoe Club, 49 Porritt Drive, Kawerau

Taumaranui Canoe Club, P.O. Box 77, Taumaranui

Te Marua Canoe Club, 27 Argyle Grove, Upper Hutt

Timaru Canoe Club, C/– 79 Hassall Street, Timaru

Tokoroa Canoe Club, 29 Edinburgh Street, Tokoroa

(Other clubs associated with the association)

University of Canterbury Canoe Club, 56 Dudley Street, Christchurch

Motueka Canoe Club, 63 Pah Street, Motueka

Pakuranga Canoe Club, 5 Dolphin Street, Pakuranga, Auckland

Westland Canoe Club, 4 Walker Street, Ranunga

Kapiti Coast Paddlers, Recreation Officer, Paraparaumu

# Glossary

**abseil** (or **rappell**) a descent technique using the rope

**aid** the use of climbing gear rather than the rock itself to make progress

**arête** a narrow ridge

**argillite** a type of sedimentary rock

**arrest** to stop a fall or slide

**ascender** a piece of equipment used to climb ropes

**ascentionist** person who makes an ascent

**Bachmann knot** a knot often used when ascending ropes

**belay** to secure the rope

**bergschrund** a crevasse where ice meets rock on a mountain

**bight** loop, or doubled rope

**bollard** a large lump sometimes used as a belay

**bomb-proof** extra-strong

**buttress** a very steep ridge, usually rock

**carpus** bone of the wrist

**cataract** a steep section of water in a stream or river

**chimney** a wide, vertical fissure in rock or ice

**chimneying** ascending a chimney

**chock stone** a stone jammed in a crack and used as a climbing aid

**cirque** a semi-circular rock wall, often at a valley head

**clavical** collar-bone

**coaming** edge of canoe cockpit

**coccyx** tailbone

**col** depression in a mountain chain

**cornice** snow overhang

**couloir** a steep, deep and often narrow valley

**crampons** spikes strapped to boots when climbing ice

**cushion wave** heaped-up water upstream of a rock in a river

**descender** device to aid descent — for example, in abseiling

**Eskimo roll** method of righting an upturned canoe

**etrier** rope ladder

**exposure** medical condition brought on by exposure to cold

**fibula** outer lower leg bone

**Föhn** a warm, dry wind on the lee side of mountains

**gaiters** coverings for the tops of boots to keep out stones, grit, etc.

**gear sling** a sling used around the shoulders to hold climbing equipment

**glissade** to slide down snow on one's boots

**Goretex** *see* Klimate

**hawser-laid rope** rope made up of strands twisted together

**humerus** upper arm bone

**hypothermia** lowering of body temperature

**ice axe** hand implement used when climbing ice

**ice screw** metal peg which screws into ice for the protection of the climber

**ice hammer** similar to an ice axe, but with a hammer head instead of an adze

**Innominate bone** pelvis

**Jumar** *see* ascender

**karabiner** a snap link of metal

**Kernmantel rope** a rope with the inner core covered by a sheath of nylon

**Klimate** waterproof, breathable fabric used in tents and outdoor clothing

**lateral moraine** rock-debris left at the sides of a glacier

**layback** climbing move

**layer sample** section of snow to determine avalanche danger

**leader** (climbing) the one who leads or goes first

**line** (mountain) a climbing possibility

**medial moraine** secondary mass of glacier debris

**metacarpus** bones of the hand

**metatarsus** bones of the foot

**névé** snow on the head of a glacier that is turning into ice

**nut** an artificial chock stone

**orienteering** a race with map and compass

**overhang** rock jutting out over a vertical face

**patella** kneecap

**pendulum** to swing horizontally on the rope

**phalanges** finger and toe bones

**piolet traction** climbing ice with front points and curved-pick ice tools

**pitch** the distance between belays

**piton** a metal spike which is hammered into cracks

**protection** equipment or methods used to limit a climber's fall

**Prusik knot** knot used as an ascender

**putties** *see* gaiters

**radius** thicker bone of forearm

**roof** the underside of an overhang

**runner** running belay

**sacrum** back of pelvis

**scapula** shoulder blade

**schist** type of rock

**schrund** a crevasse

**scroggin** a mixture of nuts, raisins and so on

**second** person(s) who follow(s) the leader in climbing

**sérac** a pinnacle of ice, usually on a glacier

**sling** a loop of rope or tape

**spray skirt** worn by the canoeist to keep water out of the canoe

**sternum** breast bone

**tarsus** ankle bone

**terminal moraine** rock and boulder debris at the end of a glacier

**Terrodactyl** a type of ice-climbing tool

**thread belay** a natural hole in a rock through which a tape or rope may be threaded

**tibia** lower leg (shin) bone

**trade route** a route that has become commonplace

**traverse** move horizontally across a face, slope, or mountain(s)

**ulna** thinner bone of forearm

**wart hog** a type of ice piton

**wind slab** a hard crust of snow blown by the wind on top of old snow

# Index

# Other Reed Books

**To the Untouched Mountain: The New Zealand Conquest of Molamenqing, Tibet** Warwick Anderson

For more than a generation the giant peaks of Tibet remained isolated from the western world. But in 1981 the Chinese Government granted access to a New Zealand expedition and the long journey to the peak of Mount Molamenqing, the world's third-highest unclimbed mountain, was under way.

The New Zealanders gained only modest financial backing and made the ascent without the aid of high-altitude porters or proper reconnaissance. They suffered an exhausting journey even to get to the mountain, they found it almost impossible to discover an accessible route to the summit and they were subject to the full rigours of frostbite, debilitating altitude and terrifying blizzards. Warwick Anderson, the climber chosen by the expedition as writer and photographer, was also chosen by the mountain as a victim of a savage case of frostbite which led to the amputation of eight of his toes. His story is a vivid evocation of hardship and pain, but above all, of tremendous achievement.

**Beyond the Snowline** Aat Vervoon

This book follows the experience of a group of climbing friends in New Zealand and around the world, at the same time describing the relationships they form and the types of lives they lead on the fringe of "normal" society. Apart from allowing the reader to share in the intensity of climbing experiences, it offers fascinating insights into why people climb and the new world of creative freedom that can be found high up beyond the snowline.

**A Guide to the Ski Fields of New Zealand** Rodney Smith

A comprehensive guide to the conditions and facilities at each of New Zealand's commercial and club ski fields. Maps, photographs and diagrams portray locations, terrain and facilities, making planning a skiing holiday easy. There are also detailed listings of accommodation, ski hire facilities, restaurants and entertainment on or adjacent to each field.

**The Mobil New Zealand Camping and Caravanning Guide** Brian Joyce and Eric Turner

No New Zealand camper or caravanner will want to be without this totally comprehensive guide to enjoying a holiday in the outdoors. This book presents for the first time everything the novice or experienced camper needs to know about buying or hiring equipment and setting up camp.

An outstanding feature of the book is the complete detailed listing of camp sites and camping grounds available throughout New Zealand.